FIVE
O'CLOCK
LIGHTNING

HARVEY FROMMER

FIVE O'CLOCK LIGHTNING

BABE RUTH, LOU GEHRIG, AND THE GREATEST BASEBALL TEAM IN HISTORY, THE 1927 NEW YORK YANKEES

TAYLOR TRADE PUBLISHING
Lanham • Boulder • New York • London

Published by Taylor Trade Publishing
An imprint of The Rowman & Littlefield Publishing Group, Inc.
4501 Forbes Boulevard, Suite 200, Lanham, Maryland 20706
www.rowman.com

Unit A, Whitacre Mews, 26-34 Stannary Street, London SE11 4AB, United Kingdom

Distributed by NATIONAL BOOK NETWORK

Photo credits: Pages 10, 30, 40, 48, 65, and 99 courtesy of Photofest/Icon Archives; pages 15, 23, 53, and 90 from the Seth Swirsky Collection/SETH.com; pages 120, 131, 143, 190, and 205 courtesy of the National Baseball Hall of Fame Library.

British Library Cataloguing in Publication Information Available

A previous edition of this book was previously catalogued by the Library of Congress as follows:

Frommer, Harvey.
    Five o'clock lightning : Babe Ruth, Lou Gehrig and the greatest team in baseball, the 1927 New York Yankees / Harvey Frommer.
        p. cm.
    Includes bibliographical data and index.
    1. New York Yankees (Baseball team)—History. 2. Baseball—New York (State)—New York—History—Miscellanea. 3. Baseball players—United States—Biography—Miscellanea. I. Title.
    GV875.N4F757 2007
    796.357'64097471—dc22

                                                                    2007006007

ISBN 978-1-63076-004-5 (pbk. : alk. paper) — ISBN 978-1-63076-005-2 (electronic)

♾™ The paper used in this publication meets the minimum requirements of American National Standard for Information Sciences—Permanence of Paper for Printed Library Materials, ANSI/NISO Z39.48-1992.

Printed in the United States of America

For the newest Frommers,
Arielle Cecelia, Gabriel Eli, and Alexander Melendez
with all my love

CONTENTS

ACKNOWLEDGMENTS

Myrna Katz Frommer, Number One, As Always.

Jennifer Frommer and Jeff Schock.

Fred Frommer and Michele Melendez.

Ian Frommer and Laura Frommer.

Seth Swirsky for his magical website, http://www.seth.com.

The readers of FrommerSportsNet for their suggestions.

Search engine ProQuest, an invaluable tool that enabled me to be transported back in time to the pages of the *Boston Globe*, the *New York Times*, the *Atlanta Constitution*, the *Hartford Courant*, the *Chicago Tribune*, and the *Chicago Defender*.

Ron and Howard Mandelbaum of Photofest, New York.

Pat Kelly, photo archivist at the National Baseball Hall of Fame in Cooperstown, New York, and Jeff Idelson, vice president, communications and education, for their special help at deadline time.

Sean Holtz, *Baseball Almanac* http://www.baseball-almanac.com, "Where what happened yesterday is being preserved today." And Michael Aubrecht, http://www.pinstripepress.net.

Bradford H. Turnow, http://www.ultimateyankees.com

Aron Wallad, http://www.baseballsprideandjoy.com.

Herb Rogoff—"One More Inning."

Finally, special thanks to Rick Rinehart, who has the good sense to bring some of our favorite "Frommer Books" back to life. It is a pleasure working with him. Also to Karie Simpson and Kalen Landow of Taylor Trade Publishing, who stepped up to the plate to make this book come alive one more time.

THE BEST OF TIMES

With vim and verve he walloped the curve
From Texas to Duluth;
Which is no small task, and I rise to ask;
Was there ever a guy like Ruth?

—John Kieran, *New York Times*

The Roaring Twenties was a decade of ballyhoo, silly crazes, and out-rageous stunts; of flagpole sitters and marathon dancers; of new games such as mah-jongg. It was a boom, boom time in America when even the impossible seemed possible. It was a time of new beginnings.

Stock market prices were zooming. Wall Street fortunes were made and made again. People became millionaires overnight, it seemed. By the end of the decade Americans were shelling out $5 billion annually on recreation and entertainment and were spending money like never before.

Industrial production doubled in the 1920s. Hyperbole was on parade. *More* was the operative word of the times. There were more and more products, more and more cars, and more and more highways, giving people more freedom to go more places and do more things. More and more heroes.

Twenty-three million cars were sold in the United States in 1927, one car to every 5 persons, compared to one car to every 43 persons in Britain, one to 325 in Italy, and one to 7,000 in Russia. Massachusetts became the first state to require auto insurance. Some families who lacked indoor toilets and baths owned automobiles. The Ford Model T was giving way to the Ford Model A. Construction of roads became a national priority in the United States, where one could drive on paved highways only from New York to St. Mary's, Kansas. Beyond that, until one reached the West Coast, were dirt roads often made soft by rain, where cars got stuck in the mud. Gasoline stations and rest stops were few and spread out.

Women smoked cigarettes, danced, flapped, bobbed their hair, wore skirts just above their knees, consumed bootleg whiskey in public, and had the right to vote. Gertrude Ederle swam the English Channel. Dorothy Gerber invented commercial baby food after tiring of straining the stuff at home.

It was a consumer's paradise, a time of Wonder Bread, introduced in a balloon-image wrapper, Band-Aids, Kleenex, the pop-up toaster, and the recliner. Sears launched its Craftsman and Kenmore brands.

Bloomingdale's opened in Manhattan, taking up an entire city block from East 59th to East 60th streets, from Lexington Avenue to Third Avenue. The Sherry-Netherland was the world's largest apartment building. In Coney Island, the Cyclone made its debut. The book publisher Random House was founded. In 1927 the New York–New Jersey Holland Tunnel, the first twin-tube underwater auto tunnel, began operation. Pan American World Airways launched the first scheduled international flight. The first iron lung, to help polio victims breathe, was installed at Bellevue Hospital in Manhattan. The Brooklyn Museum opened, and the first automatic record changer was introduced.

In Manhattan, on hot summer nights, hundreds of East Siders slept alfresco on their fire escapes, laughing and gossiping and enjoying a breeze when it happened to come by.

An automobile tunnel was constructed stretching seven miles through the Rocky Mountains. The St. Lawrence Seaway was in the planning stage. Gutzom Borglum began drilling into the 6,200-foot mountain that would become Mount Rushmore.

Eleven-year-old Yehudi Menuhin made his Carnegie Hall debut, playing Beethoven's Violin Concerto. Calvin Coolidge Jr. was president of the United States. Italian-born anarchist immigrants Nicola Sacco and Bartolomeo Vanzetti, convicted of murder in 1921, were executed in Boston in 1927 despite worldwide protests.

New York City was the commercial and media capital of the world. At Bell Labs on West Street, television was introduced, and its pictures were sent over phone lines from Washington, D.C., to New York City. Radio brought the world into the living room. The Grand Ole Opry made its first broadcast in Nashville. Al Jolson starred in *The Jazz Singer*, the first talking film. Fox Movietone News was first with sound news film in New York City. Theaters projected moving pictures, then talking pictures into towns and boroughs across the country. Steel Victrola needles traced discs, producing simulated sound. The Academy of Motion Picture Arts and Sciences was founded. The first transatlantic commercial telephone service offered connection between New York and London. For $75 a New Yorker was able to speak to a Londoner for three minutes on a transatlantic phone.

Newness, new starts, echoed the time. Duke Ellington first played the Cotton Club. The first snowmobile patent was granted. The Roxy, Royale, and Ziegfeld theaters opened in Manhattan. In 1927 "Ain't She Sweet?" was number one on the pop singles chart. Other hit songs included "Blue Skies" and "Ol' Man River." A record 270 shows opened on Broadway, including 53 musicals, such as *A Connecticut Yankee, Hit the Deck, Rio Rita, The Royal Family, Show Boat, Funny Face,* and *Porgy.*

A dozen shows were padlocked for being immoral or obscene. Comedienne Mae West was found guilty of obscenity for off-color material and suggestive ad libs in her Broadway show *Sex.* She was sentenced to 10 days in jail by a New York City court. The Ziegfeld Follies and George White's Scandals showcased what newspapers called "bare-chested women." New York City police looked the other way. When these shows toured, more clothing was supplied for the performers to cover up. Newspapers featured scantily clad favorites such as "Flapper Fanny" and "Syncopation Sue."

Despite a failure rate of about 50 percent, the rubber condom grew in popularity. It was reported that about 2 million were put to use daily.

Babies born that memorable year of 1927 included Clive Barnes, Harry Belafonte, Geoffrey Beene, Erma Bombeck, Rosalynn Carter, Cesar Chavez, Roy Cohn, Barbara Cook, David Dinkins, Isadora Duncan, Bob Fosse, Stan Getz, Althea Gibson, Hubert de Givenchy, Günter Grass, Alan King, Coretta Scott King, Eartha Kitt, Tommy Lasorda, Janet Leigh, Robert Ludlum, Sidney Poitier, Leontyne Price, Vin Scully, Neil Simon, Jerry Stiller, Kenneth Tynan, and Andy Warhol.

Americans ate hundreds of thousands of Eskimo Pies. More than $1.5 billion were spent on advertising, much of it designed to arouse feelings of guilt and anxiety over body odor and bad breath. The beautician became a recognized professional. In 1927, 18,000 income-tax payers listed themselves as beauticians.

Josef Stalin became the undisputed ruler of the Soviet Union. Adolf Hitler held the first Nazi meeting in Berlin. In New York City and in grim small towns across America, workers labored long and hard under horrible conditions in sweatshops.

Despite Prohibition, which forbade Americans to engage in commerce in hard liquor, beer, or wine, all were readily available in ample supply. It was said that Prohibition doubled the amount of drinking outlets in New York City and that there were tens of thousands of speakeasies. "Scarface" Al Capone became the country's biggest bootlegger, making many millions from illegal liquor sales, the protection racket, gambling, and prostitution.

Charles Lindbergh was given a grand ticker tape parade on his return from Paris after his solo, nonstop transatlantic flight that began on Long Island, New York. In Harlem, dancer Shorty Snowden—inspired by the headline "Lindy Hops the Atlantic"—named his dance step the Lindy Hop.

William Randolph Hearst's twenty-two newspapers, published in fifteen cities, had a daily circulation of 3.5 million, reaching 4 million on Sundays. New York City had 18 daily newspapers in the 1920s. The *New York Daily Mirror* was a morning tabloid first published in 1924 by the Hearst organization to compete with the *New York Daily News*, the most widely circulated newspaper in the United States. The *News* had begun in 1919 as the first picture newspaper, one that sports fans loved. In 1923, the year Yankee Stadium opened, the circulation of the *News* moved past 600,000, making it the best-selling newspaper in the United States. In that year 17 percent of newsprint was devoted to sports; in 1890 it was 4 percent. Widespread coverage of baseball was already in place in specialized publications such as the *Sporting News* and *Baseball Magazine*.

By 1927, newspapers in New York had 10 columns of sports. The news tabloids often led their front pages with sports news and pictures. Even the *New York Times* and the *New York Herald Tribune* were giving over more and more column space to sports.

It was a time when most people received virtually all of their current information from newspapers. Afternoon newspapers cost 3 cents; morning papers were 2 cents. The half dozen or so afternoon papers such as the *Sun*, the *Telegram*, and the *Journal*, featured baseball results on page one. Papers were positioned face up on newsstands, and fans could see the score without buying the paper.

Arguably, the most talented bunch of newspaper sports journalists in action at one time worked back then. They called themselves "the Gee-Whizzers," and their zeal and love for sports and games at times surpassed that of the people they wrote about and for. They told the stories, provided the game accounts, and wrote the poems. There was no television coverage and little radio, and photographs were somewhat limited. What images, views, and information on sports there was came in the main from these sportswriters.

The sports pages had the facts but were also sources of entertainment—soft news. Educated and eloquent, dedicated and opinionated, lyrical and knowledgeable, the sportswriters of that time plied their trade in an era when players were their drinking buddies, not their antagonists. Yet the writers competed among themselves to tell the stories, break the scoops, and come up with new angles.

Those who plied their trade on the New York City newspapers were a who's who of sportswriters. The *New York Times* boasted sports editor and columnist John Kieran and Yankee writers Richards Vidmer and James Harrison. W. B. Hanna, Rud Rennie, and sports editor W. O. McGeehan worked for the *Herald Tribune*. *New York Daily News* writers included Paul Gallico, Marshall Hunt, and Roscoe McGowen. Ford C. Frick wrote for the *Evening Journal*. Frank Graham, Joe Villa, and Will Wedge did their stuff for the *New York Sun*. The *New York Telegram* featured Fred Lieb, Dan Daniel, and Joe Williams. Lieb later wrote for the *New York Post*. The *Monitor* had George Bailey. Dan Parker and Charles Segar were on the *New York Mirror*, Edward Luster and Bill Slocum wrote for the *New York American*, and Arthur Mann was on the *New York Evening World*. Still doing their thing on the newspaper scene were icons Ring Lardner and Damon Runyon.

Jack Dempsey held the heavyweight boxing title from 1919 through 1926. Then in 1927, in an epic grudge match seen by more than 150,000 fans who had paid $2.5 million at Soldier Field in Chicago, Gene Tunney won a controversial decision over Dempsey for the title. "Big Bill" Tilden dominated a lot of the tennis news in a sport that was the most rapidly growing one in America. Golf was also expanding bigtime. The great golfers Bobby Jones, Walter Hagen, and Gene Sarazen dominated not only American courses but the venerable British greens as well. Red Grange at Illinois was a three-time football All-American. At Notre Dame, Knute Rockne coached the "Fighting Irish" to three national championships. The Harlem Globetrotters played their first basketball game in 1927. The New York Giants won the National Football League title game, and Johnny Weissmuller set several swimming records. Henry G. Steinbrenner (the father of George) won the 1927 NCAA low-hurdles championship.

In that golden age of sports there were those who towered above the rest: Red Grange in football, Jack Dempsey in boxing, Bobby Jones in golf, Big Bill Tilden in tennis, and the poster boy for excess, George Herman "Babe" Ruth in baseball.

The 1920s, the age of Ruth, witnessed the largest increase in a decade for recreation and entertainment. In the previous decade those who attended baseball games were mainly affluent, white-collar workers. In the twenties a better standard of living and the introduction of Sunday baseball widened the audience, attracting all classes, including recent immigrants. Like the cities baseball was played in, urban stadiums were now becoming meeting and melting grounds for Americans of all classes and backgrounds.

Major league baseball, played in the daytime and concluding before darkness fell, saw its average annual attendance rise 50 percent in the Roaring Twenties, reaching 93 million—nearly 3,000 a game more than it had been in the previous 10 years.

In New York City all sports were pretenders to the throne that baseball sat on. In the 1920s, at least one Big Apple baseball team played in the World Series in eight of the ten World Series. From 1921 to 1923 the Yankees and the Giants played in the Subway Series.

According to one 1927 estimate, 107 men from 79 colleges made up nearly one-third of big league regulars. The farm system belonged to the future.

Players spent a lot of time on long train trips. It was time to bond, rest, eat and sleep, play cards, or read books and newspapers. Liquor and beer were the refreshments of choice, both available in abundance. Baseball was the national pastime; all the best athletes gravitated to it. So many with a very strong work ethic and competitive fire were drawn to the game.

The game was very different from baseball in the twenty-first century. Pitchers didn't throw nearly as hard. Strikeouts were way down because batters focused more on putting the ball in play by making contact. Pitchers threw far fewer pitches. Conserving strength and going the distance were the goals.

In 1927 batted balls bouncing into the grandstand were counted as home runs instead of ground-rule doubles as they are today. But each of Babe Ruth's home runs hit that year has been examined by historians, and they are convinced that none bounced into the seats. But there were four-baggers smacked by others that got where they got on the bounce.

The time it took for games to be played was much less than today. There was no need to build advertising into the structure of the contests. A batter rarely got in and out of the batter's box during his at-bat. When he did, the home plate umpire would call for a pitch. And if it was anywhere near the plate, it was deemed a strike.

Babe Ruth totally dominated the game. In that glorious decade he finished number one in home runs (467), RBIs (1,328), walks (1,240), strikeouts (795), and slugging percentage (.740). Ruth was a self-made man, the American dream come true, a free swinger in a free-swinging time.

"Once my swing starts," he said, "I can't change it or pull up on it. It's all or nothing."

Babe Ruth was the king. The 1927 New York Yankees were royalty.

Historian A. D. Suehsdorf said: "If you didn't like the Yankees, it was a tough time to be alive."

But if you loved the Yanks, it was the best of times.

PRESEASON

Again that joyous, thrilling shout.
The happiest cry of all.
The hardened umpire's gruff command.
"Come on you gents. PLAY BALL!"

—Marshall Hunt, *New York Daily News*

The press release on December 30, 1926, out of the offices of the New York Yankees in Manhattan on 42nd Street overlooking Bryant Park and the old Sixth Avenue el began, "Yankees Will Play 21 Spring Battles."

There would be a dozen games in Florida, seven heading north with the Cardinals, and two against the Brooklyn Robins at Ebbets Field. The Yankee schedule was of interest to a multitude of fans and to the players themselves, but to no one more than 23-year-old Tony Lazzeri.

For on a gloomy and overcast October 10, 1926, at Yankee Stadium, he came to bat for the Yankees, who had loaded the bases in the seventh inning of the seventh game of the World Series with the St. Louis Cardinals clinging to a 3–2 lead. There were two outs.

"The bullpen in Yankee Stadium was under the bleachers then," Redbird pitcher Grover Cleveland Alexander recalled, "and when you're down there you can't tell what's going on out in the field only for the yells of the fans overhead. There was a telephone in the only real fancy, modern bullpen in baseball. Well, I was sitting around down there not doing much throwing. The phone rang and an excited voice said 'Send in Alexander.'"

Having already pitched complete-game victories in games two and six, it was said that the grizzled veteran was recuperating from too much celebrating of his victory the previous day.

"So I come out from under the bleachers," Alexander continued. "I see the bases full and two out and Lazzeri standing at the box. Tony is up there all alone with everyone in that Sunday crowd watching him.

The House that Ruth Built

So I just said to myself, 'Take your time, Lazzeri isn't feeling any too good up there and let him stew.'"

The crowd chanted: "Poosh-em-up Tony! Poosh-em-up Tony!" In four at-bats the day before against the 39-year-old right-hander Alexander, Lazzeri had gone hitless.

The first pitch, a curve, got a swinging strike.

The next pitch lined into the left-field seats. Foul ball.

"Lazzeri swung," said Alexander, "where that curve started but not where it finished. The ball got a hunk of the corner and then finished outside. If that line drive Lazzeri hit had been fair, Tony would be the hero, and I'd just be an old bum."

Then an overanxious Lazzeri swung and missed and struck out.

Alexander breezed through the eighth inning. In the ninth, he pitched around "the big son of a bitch" Babe Ruth and walked him with two outs. The very dangerous Bob Meusel was next.

"If Meusel got hold of one, it could be two runs and the Series," Alexander later said. "So I forgot all about Ruth and got ready to work on Meusel. On my first pitch, the Babe broke for second. I caught the blur of Ruth starting for second as I pitched and then came the whistle of the ball as catcher O'Farrell rifled it to second. I wheeled around and there was one of the grandest sights of my life. Hornsby, his foot anchored on the bag and his gloved hand outstretched, waiting for Ruth to come in."

Incredibly, the Babe had attempted to steal second base and was thrown out. The Cardinals had their first world championship. The Yankees had a long winter talking about what might have been.

Somehow, Babe Ruth got off the hook. The story that made the rounds was that the "Big Bam" had not attempted to steal a base but was cut down in a botched hit-and-run. The man on the hook was young Tony Lazzeri, who spent a lot of his winter suffering the slings of "what happened?" and the pain of boils.

And that is why when he received the news that the Yankees and the Cardinals would play a series of exhibition games barnstorming north after spring training, the San Franciscan reportedly shouted, raising his fists into the air, "Vendetta! "I shall have revenge!"

There was no doubt that the 1926 loss to the Cardinals stung Babe Ruth. But he did not suffer from boils. He also did not lust for any revenge. An incredible force of nature, he just kept rolling along, engaging in a tsunami of activities after making the final out of the World Series.

Hither and yon, the great Ruth went, barnstorming vigorously for two weeks. On October 17, in Montreal, the Yankee slugger slammed so many shots into a nearby river, according to a report in the *South Bend Tribune*, that the game was called for lack of baseballs. In South Bend, Indiana, on October 23, they were ready to handle that little problem.

The local team stocked up on baseballs, which cost $1.23 each. The game was called after six innings in large part because the Babe Ruth All-Stars arrived two hours late. The South Bend Indians were beaten, 7–3, and the "Bammer" Ruth was 3 for 4 with a home run estimated to have traveled 600 feet.

Barnstorming completed, the Babe switched gears, embarking on a 12-week Pantages circuit single-act vaudeville tour. It kicked off in October 1926 in Minneapolis and concluded in January 1927, in Southern California. The gig netted Babe Ruth $8,333 weekly. No performer had ever made that kind of money, not Al Jolson, not Fanny Brice, not even W. C. Fields. There were those who said the Yankee slugger had to be doing something right to be earning all that money. But one of many who were not impressed was Mark Koenig, teammate and buddy and sometime entertainment critic. He called Ruth's performance "boring as hell."

Part of the performance involved children coming up onstage, talking to the Babe and receiving baseballs. Amazingly, the man who loved children so much was charged and arrested for violation of child labor laws in San Diego. It was a silly nuisance charge. But it took time and some cash expended on attorney's fees before the Yankee icon was cleared.

In 1927 George Herman Ruth was everywhere doing everything leading up to spring training. He was a one-man endorsement machine—for pure milk, home appliances, housing developments, and cars, including Reos, Auburns, Packards, and Studebakers—models that no longer exist.

All told, it was estimated that the Sultan of Swat earned $250,000 in 1926 from baseball, acting, barnstorming, endorsements, and syndicated ghost-written pieces.

And the Babe, who claimed to need little sleep, even had spare time for golf, women, fishing, and mingling with celebrities and common folk.

On January 13, 1927, the Yankees announced they had acquired Ray Morehart and Johnny Grabowski from the White Sox for Aaron Ward. It seemed like a minor transaction then, getting backup catcher Grabowski and the smallish left-handed-hitting utility player Morehart, who had begun his major league career with the White Sox as a 25-year-old in 1924. But Morehart and especially Grabowski would be two useful supplementary pieces of the 1927 team. Regular Yankee catcher Benny Bengough had injured his arm in 1926, and the 27-year-old Grabowski was looked upon as insurance.

Tweaking the team once again on February 8, the Yankees shipped veteran hurler Sad Sam Jones to St. Louis for pitcher Joe Giard and outfielder Cedric Durst. It was another example of the attention to detail that Yankee general manager Ed Barrow, manager Miller Huggins, and the owner, Colonel Jacob Ruppert, were adept at—acquiring the spare parts to keep the mighty Yankee engine operating at full bore.

The pieces were falling into place for the 1927 Yankees. But the biggest piece, Babe Ruth, had not signed a new contract and seemed not likely to do so anytime soon. Hands down, he had rejected the $52,000 salary he earned in 1926. That was out of the question.

In early February, Jake Ruppert sent another in what would be a series of contract offers to Ruth. This one was for $55,000. The offer annoyed the competitive Babe, who said he had it on good authority that Ty Cobb, now with the Philadelphia Athletics, was slated to get $75,000.

The peripatetic Yankee outfielder moved on to "Hooray for Hollywood" time. He was now a star on the East Coast and the West Coast, now making his first movie, *The Babe Comes Home*, for First National Pictures.

In a break during shooting he said: "Reading, like picture shows, is almost taboo. I've got to watch the old optics closer than anything else."

Under strict orders from his trainer, Artie McGovern, the Bambino also got his beauty sleep. He was early to bed by nine o'clock (alone or with company) and early to rise, arriving at the movie set no later than six.

On Hollywood Boulevard, running three to five miles a day, George Herman winked and smiled at folks all along the way, truly a sight for all. After circulating the streets, Ruth was rewarded back at his Hollywood Plaza Hotel with a comforting and stimulating rubdown by McGovern, who had taken leave of his gymnasium on 42nd Street and Madison Avenue to press the flesh of his most illustrious client— still unsigned to a 1927 Yankee contract. McGovern, praising himself and the wondrous work he was accomplishing, remarked about his beginnings with Ruth: "He was as near to being a total loss as anyone I ever had under my care."

On February 22, six days before the first Yankees were scheduled to arrive in St. Petersburg, Florida, for spring training, Babe Ruth mailed to Colonel Ruppert from Hollywood an outline of what he thought he should be paid for 1927, just another salvo in their continuing public contract wrangling. The Babe was adamant as he spoke to reporters. He pressed the point that he would retire from baseball and organize a string of gymnasiums with Artie McGovern if his salary needs were not met.

On February 25, the day before the big man left California for New York, his salary demands were published in the *New York Daily News*. Two days later a letter he wrote to Colonel Ruppert appeared in the *New York Times*. The letter's tone was conciliatory. It was also forceful.

You will find enclosed contract for 1927 which I am returning unsigned because of the $52,000 salary figure. I am leaving Los Angeles February 26 to see you in New York and will be prepared to report at St. Petersburg but only on the basis of

Jake Ruppert and Babe Ruth when Ruth signed a contract with the Yankees

$100,000 a year for two years, plus $7,700 held out of my salary in the past. . . .

In fine physical condition today I hope to play as good as last year or better. I have exercised all winter and for the past twelve weeks have been working out of doors. At my own expense I have brought Arthur McGovern from New York to condition me.

The New York club has profited from five of the best years of my baseball life. During that period my earning power to the club has greatly increased while my salary has remained unchanged. . . .

During the winter season I booked my own exhibition games and without support from other players I have received more in three weeks than the New York club pays me in three months. . . .

I have refused to discuss my new contract or salary during the Winter but now that I have returned my contract unsigned an explanation will be expected, and I wish you would show this letter to any newspaper writer who wishes to see it.

With best personal wishes, I am

Yours truly, BABE RUTH

After the long trip from California, Babe Ruth arrived on the morning of March 2 at Grand Central Station on the Twentieth Century Limited. Half a dozen gate tenders, a squad of private police, and railroad security were powerless to hold back more than a hundred of the more ardent and adoring fans who had broken through and gained access to the train platform. They roared at their idol, easy to spot in his brown cap and tan overcoat, as he got off the train. Outside the entrance to the station, more than two thousand excited fans waited, cheering as their hero came through, a wide smile on his face.

The smile remained as the Babe wended his way through the crowd like a big fullback and then rushed half a block to Arthur McGovern's gymnasium. There Ruth primped and posed for almost an hour for dozens of photographers, then phoned St. Vincent's Hospital to ascertain the condition of his wife, Helen. They had been married in 1914 when she was 17 and he was 19. Now she was ill, a victim of what was called "nervous exhaustion." The other call was to Colonel Ruppert's office, to lock in a time for a contract conference. A limo took him to St. Vincent's for a 45-minute visit.

The Ruppert Brewery, in Yorkville, then a heavily German neighborhood, occupied four city blocks—East 90th to East 94th between Second and Third avenues. It was a complex of 35 fortresslike brick buildings whose chimneys spewed smoke carrying the sulfurous smell of malt from the boiling vats into the air. On windy days the smell was especially foul and noxious. Even in summer, maids in the area closed windows, pulled down drapes, and did what they could to keep the stench out of their employers' dwellings.

At twenty minutes past noon, George Herman Ruth, dressed in a full-length raccoon coat, arrived at the brewery. The busy offices revealed carefully thought-out organization, reflecting the brewery's owner. Expensive rugs on the floors and hunting trophies on the white marble walls set the tone. The Babe mugged that famous moon-face smile for photographers for more than half an hour as they snapped away, capturing him in many poses. Promptly at one, contract talks got under way in the 59-year-old Ruppert's spacious private office. Just fifty-five minutes later, stolid Edward Grant Barrow invited twenty writers to come in.

"Babe has accepted a three-year contract calling for $210,000," Ruppert announced. "Babe Ruth now is the highest paid man in baseball. We came to terms without any trouble. Babe will go to camp on Saturday and everything is fine."

A smiling Ruth added, "And I'm glad that's off my mind."

The Prince of Beer and the King of Clout were known for their public disagreements about contracts. Nevertheless, they were personal friends and liked each other. Once the contract parameters had been decided, there was a lot of good-natured banter between the two men and the gathered reporters in a kind of extended press conference.

Colonel Ruppert told reporters that his time and talk with Ruth were "cordial, businesslike, and, as you can see, very much to the point and successful for both of us. It's a big gamble with me, but I am convinced that Ruth, a remarkable fellow physically, won't make me sorry. He thinks he has five more years of baseball in him and I believe he is right. I am sure he will take better care of himself now than he ever has. He isn't growing any younger, and he realizes it."

"Jake did the right thing as I knew he would," said Ruth, who had just turned 32 and had been in baseball since 1914. "Of course I had no intention of quitting baseball. I knew that everything would be all right. The Yankees have always treated me right and I knew they would this time. You can say for me that I'll earn every cent of my salary," the Babe bragged to reporters. "There'll be no more monkey business for me."

In a time when Barrow, also referred to as "Cousin Ed" and "Cousin Egbert," made $25,000, when Commissioner of Baseball Kenesaw

Mountain Landis made $65,000, when the average American League player made about $10,000, when girls laboring in sweatshops on the Lower East Side of Manhattan sewed for $10 a week, Ruth's salary was quite a princely sum. The only sports figures who made more money than the Sultan of Swat in 1927 were Jack Dempsey and golfer Walter Hagen.

The most celebrated sports figure of his time, perhaps of all time, Babe Ruth was now the highest-paid player in baseball history. His salary would top that of the rest of the Yankee starting lineup combined: $454.54 per game, $56.67 per inning. On the basis of the 47 home runs he hit in 1926, the Babe would get $1,489.34 for each homer he recorded in 1927. Biweekly checks would be issued to George Herman Ruth by Manufacturers Trust Company, Yorkville Branch Office, 1511 Third Avenue, New York, New York, in the amount of $6,595.38.

As the story goes, the Babe was asked later on how he felt making more money than the president of the United States. "I had a better year than he did," was his reported response, though it was widely known that Babe Ruth was not that well informed on national affairs.

The $70,000 salary paid to George Herman Ruth in 1927 would today be about $714,000—truly a bargain when one realizes that major leaguers in 2007 earned an average of more than $3 million per year.

Weighing 221 pounds when he left Los Angeles, Ruth had gained 4 pounds en route to New York. He said his waistline was 39 inches. "I have worked harder in the past four weeks than I ever did in my life," Ruth told Ruppert. "This making a moving picture is no joke. Maybe you think it's all play, but take it from me, it is nothing but twelve to fifteen hours hard work every day. I never had an hour to myself from the minute I started until I left town. I'm mighty glad the picture is finished and I am anxious to see it. I think I will make a hit as an actor."

Ruppert responded: "You will make a bigger hit as a ballplayer. I pointed out that his loss would be as great as ours if he ever quit baseball and that movie contracts wouldn't be so freely offered in such a contingency. The Babe is a sensible fellow."

Babe Ruth said, "I like the movies, but I would rather play baseball than anything else I know of. I know I have a lot of good baseball still left in my system. You fellows won't be able to play taps over Babe Ruth for five or six years yet. That I am willing to bet on. I figure I will have a mighty fine season. Gee whiz, everything points that way. My mind is at ease and I feel fine. I guess Huggins won't know me when I get into camp. I will get off the rest of this excess weight and by the time the exhibition games start I will be in prime shape."

On Saturday night, March 5, Babe Ruth arrived at Penn Station ready to board the sleeper Seaboard Airline train for the trip to St. Petersburg. Swarming all over him were a battalion of reporters and photographers and more than 50 excited youngsters. He obliged everyone—posing, talking, giving autographed baseballs to the kids. It was just amazing how the affable Ruth—unlike many sports icons who would follow him—basked in his celebrity status, enjoying the give-and-take with fans and the banter with sportswriters.

"I am glad to get going," he told reporters. "These last three days have been the busiest I ever remember. However, I feel fine. Everything has turned out great. I will be out hittin' 'em on the nose Monday morning and glad I can do it."

The Big Bam arrived in St. Petersburg for another spring training. His first time there had been two years earlier. With his marriage failing at that time, he had been chasing and bedding women, eating, and drinking—in that order and in the Ruthian manner, over the top.

When that spring training ended and the Yankees headed north, the Babe appeared deathly ill in North Carolina. He was hospitalized for weeks. It was called "the bellyache heard around the world." "Too many hot dogs" was the word on the street. But insiders said that the big man had contracted a severe case of the clap.

His sex life was high-wire, full-bore, no regrets, and reckless. "I only have two superstitions," Ruth said. "Make sure to touch all the bases when you hit a home run, and don't call your girlfriend 'Tina' if her name is 'Susan.'"

A legendary story from his spring training escapades involves the time he brought a woman into the hotel suite he shared with outfielder Bob Meusel. Half-asleep in his own room, "Long Bob" tried to ignore the commotion coming from Babe's room. Finally things quieted down. Then Meusel smelled cigar smoke. Minutes later, the yells and cries returned. Then, more quiet. Cigar smoke and noise alternated, giving Meusel a fitful night of sleep.

In the morning, as the story goes, the woman was nowhere to be found. Meusel asked Ruth how many times he had gotten laid.

"Count the cigars," Ruth said.

Seven butts were in the ashtray.

This 1927 spring was a different spring with a different Babe, one more circumspect and more intent on taking care of his body. It began after the 1925 season, during which he weighed more than 250 pounds and played abysmally. For the first time he started to watch somewhat what he ate and drank.

His first appearance in 1927 was filled with hype, hullabaloo, and hoopla as befitted the King of Clout. Reporters swarmed about, crowded around him. They looked him over. All the stories about the terrific shape he was in seemed true. The great Ruth announced in that deep voice that had just a hint of a southern accent, "I never felt better in my life. I weigh 223 pounds and will lose only 3 pounds while here."

Showing off his expanded 47-inch chest, he bragged about the hardened belly. "Hit me," he said with a smile. "Hit me as hard as you can." One of the more intrepid scribes, James R. Harrison of the *Times*, went for the suggestion. Ruth took the poke, feigned some pain, and kept on smiling.

"Twenty-four gaping rookies stood at attention as he sauntered through the lobby of the hotel," Ford C. Frick wrote in the *New York Evening Journal*, "and flocks of femininity dogged his footsteps to the very portals of the elevator where a flunkey in uniform barred the way. . . . The Babe was friendly to all, smiling, bowing, yelling in a hoarse voice to teammates."

That morning he played golf, a round of 92, violating the training rule set by Miller Huggins that banned participation in the sport by players except on Sundays. "Special permission," Huggins explained to reporters, was given to Ruth. "The Big Bam," the *New York Evening*

World's Arthur Mann wrote, "shags flies to begin the day's work, fields bunts, and then warms up with a catcher. By this time he is ready to go into the box, and there he remains, pitching for about 25 minutes. His batting practice consists of about 12 good wallops."

Billy Sunday visited the Yankee training camp. Ex-major leaguer, ex-drunk, celebrated revivalist, umpire, and scribe, he hit some balls—one was a shot he got good wood on that according to one scribe "was still smoking."

Smoking characterized the way many Yankees reacted to this Billy Sunday comment: "Of all the ball clubs I have looked at this spring the Athletics are by far the most impressive. The club doesn't appear to have a single weakness."

But Sunday was not the only one with the pro-Philly point of view. The New York Betting Commission had installed the Philadelphia Athletics favorites to win the pennant because of their addition of veterans such as Ty Cobb, Eddie Collins, and Zach Wheat. Only 9 of 42 writers polled gave the Yanks any chance to repeat as pennant winners. American Leaguer Ban Johnson predicted a historic-five team pennant race. An AP poll of 100 players and "baseball experts" tabbed the Athletics to win it all.

Grantland Rice wrote in the *New York Herald Tribune*, "From present indications, the American League race figures as follows: Philadelphia, New York, Washington, Cleveland, Detroit, Chicago, St. Louis, Boston." Professional oddsmakers set the Athletics at 2–1, the Yankees at 3–1, and the Senators at 7–2.

The relative youth of New York's pitching was considered suspect by some. But Miller Huggins said: "If any of the young pitchers show me anything they will get a chance. I'll admit that in the past I've been cautious about using rookies, but that was the past. This year experience isn't going to cut so much of a figure; a young arm is sometimes better than an old head."

Pitching was also key in the views of *New York Times* reporter Richards Vidmer and columnist John Kieran. The former wrote on March 31: "The Yankees aren't any stronger than they were a year ago and they will have stronger opposition."

Crescent Lake Park in St. Petersburg had a gem of a playing field at its south end, built especially for the Yankees to perform on under the Florida sun. Phil Schenk, groundskeeper at Yankee Stadium, supervised the laying out, the filling in, and the sodding of the Florida field, especially concentrating on creating a deep right field, at 390 feet.

The thinking was that more baseballs would be lost than the manufacturers could ship into the Sunshine State if there was a short right field with the foreboding swamp behind it. The retail price of a new baseball was $2, and though they were cheaper wholesale, they still cost money. Ruth, it was said, might easily lose $50 worth of baseballs each day he practiced.

The Babe's first spring training home run wound up in the general direction of Tampa, with the ball allegedly landing at the feet of a farmer who told his son, "Well, I see Babe Ruth is in town again."

When it came to the Babe, it was always no-holds-barred hyperbole.

As the story goes, some New York sportswriters used a surveyor's glass to measure the clout, which they claimed went 630 feet. William McGeehan was unsure how far the ball went, but he did write, "When it came down it was covered in ice."

Comfortable among the high and the mighty or the ordinary, friendly with the press, and traveling without bodyguards, Babe Ruth basked in his superstar status. Getting a close shave in a downtown barber shop, telling a few jokes each morning, visiting hospitals to cheer up the sick (especially children), patiently signing autographs at the dog track, posing for photos, followed by fans on the St. Petersburg streets, wending his way from bar to bar, boating and fishing for king mackerel or grouper in the Gulf of Mexico, then prevailing upon a hotel cook to prepare the fish for supper, the Babe was having the time of his life. A Yankee bridge game began in spring training. And the Babe plunged into that, too. The extroverted Ruth and the shy Gehrig were pitted against reserve infielder Mike Gazella and Don Miller, a young hurler from the University of Michigan.

The Yankees were quartered at the Beaux Arts–style Princess Martha Hotel, built in 1923. Babe Ruth was registered there, too, but no one saw much of him. The word was that he had his meals in his rooms and left when he wanted to through a side door.

Rising early before baseball practice, he would play golf at the two-year-old Renaissance Vinoy Resort and Golf Club in downtown St. Petersburg. Catcher Benny Bengough and pitchers Waite Hoyt and Bob Shawkey were also good golfers and would play there, too. Ruth could drive the ball farther than many pros and had scores in the

Waite Hoyt

mid-70s. However, the short game was not his forte. A lousy putter, the Babe would disgustedly toss his club after he hit the ball too hard, causing it to roll past the cup.

Much was made of the time a man came around that spring of 1927 and said he was Johnny Sylvester's uncle. He made a big deal about telling all about how well Johnny Sylvester was doing. The Bam graciously made a big deal out of sending regards.

But moments after the uncle departed, Ruth bellowed, "Who the hell is Johnny Sylvester?"

Johnny Sylvester had been the subject of much newspaper attention. He was a sick kid who the Yankee slugger had promised to hit a home run for during the 1926 World Series. Babe Ruth just could not remember names, not even the names of teammates. He called most people "kid." Others got variations like "sister" for young women and "mom" or "pop" for those with seniority.

Others were given nicknames—some logical, others not. The Babe called Waite Hoyt "Walter," but no one could explain why. Pitcher Urban Shocker was dubbed "Rubber Belly," and no one—not even the Babe—could explain why. Those who claimed to know said it had something to do with the flabbiness of Shocker's midsection, but they wouldn't swear to it. Catcher Benny Bengough, who coined the name "Jidge" (German for "George") for Ruth, was called "Googles," a kind of affectionate corruption of part of his surname. Catcher Pat Collins was "Horse Nose," a derogatory reference to his most prominent facial feature. Railroad station redcaps were "Stinkweed."

Beer baron Jake Ruppert could remember names but never addressed anyone by a first name. The Yankee owner was characterized in Ed Barrow's memoirs as an "imperious" man, one who "in all the years I knew him, always calling me 'Barrows,' adding an 's' where none belonged."

Ruppert "was a fastidious dresser," Barrow remembered, "who had his shoes made to order, changed his clothes several times a day, and had a valet." Arriving in style with his secretary Al Brennan for spring training in his own private railroad car, it was said that the honorary colonel savored the comforts of his own drawing room and slept in a silk brocade nightshirt. Ruppert was particularly interested in and impressed with the man he had sunk all that money into.

"Ruth looks great," he announced. "Watch that boy. In fact, he may set another home run record. The team as a whole is in fine shape, shows real fighting spirit, and looks like a winner, although I admit I'm not much of a prophet."

Despite the sunny-side-up outlook of their owner, there was an undercoating of gloominess that pervaded spring training for the Yankees, whose wrenching loss to the St. Louis Cardinals in the 1926 World Series was still close to the surface, especially for the frail Miller Huggins, who stayed during spring training with his sister Myrtle in a home he owned in St. Petersburg. A bachelor, he also lived with her in Manhattan.

There were times in his early years with the Yankees when he would come home dejected: "Ah, it's just too frustrating. Life is too short for this kind of rotten stuff and rowdy players I have to put up with. I think I'll chuck the whole thing."

"Stick it out," Myrtle would say to prop him up. "Don't let them be able to say that you quit when you were under fire."

Dubbed "the unhappy little man," Huggins was always with a short-stemmed pipe in hand or mouth. He had a gray visage and was a worrier, anguishing over his stock market investments although he played that game with great skill and enthusiasm and at times invested for players and turned a profit for them. He anguished over his real estate holdings, his players, his appetite, and his real and imagined medical problems. One could never tell by the way he dressed or by the little well-worn traveling bag he carried on the road that the mite manager's salary for 1927 was $37,500.

He was fond of repeating certain expressions:

"Baseball is my life. Maybe it will get me someday. But as long as I die in harness, I will be happy."

"A manager has his cards dealt to him and he must play them."

"Great players make great managers."

When Colonel Ruppert and Miller Huggins first met, the patrician owner was not at all enamored of what he called "the worker's clothes, the cap perched oddly on Huggins's head, the smallness of the man."

Truth be told, Miller Huggins was the most unlikely Yankee. The Cincinnati native stood 5'4", weighed 140 pounds, and was aloof and superstitious. He had a law degree from the University of Cincinnati, but he never practiced.

Initially, Ruppert balked at employing Huggins as Yankee manager. Huggins, for his part, viewed managing an American League team as a step down from his time as skipper, from 1913 to 1917, of St. Louis in the National League. Yet the little man, at age 39, became the eighth manager in the franchise's 16-year history in 1918.

"Huggins Is Ready To Mold Yankees" was the headline in the February 2, 1918, edition of the *New York Times*.

Dwarfed by Babe Ruth and other Yankees in size, reputation, and image, Miller Huggins bitched: "New York is a hell of a town. Everywhere I go in St. Louis or Cincinnati, it's always 'Hiya Hug.' But here in New York I can walk the length of 42nd Street and not a soul knows me."

As pilot of the Yankees it took him a while to make things happen. There was a 1918 fourth-place finish in his first year, followed by two third-place finishes. There was a pennant in 1921, the first for the Yankees. Then another in 1922. A third followed in 1923, which led, finally, to a World Series victory over the New York Giants. After a second-place finish in 1924 and a seventh place finish in 1925, the roster was reshaped for 1926, resulting in yet another pennant. But that was the year of the wrenching loss to his old St. Louis team in the World Series.

Now in spring training of 1927, Huggins, shuffling, scuffling, searching for any edge, was more intense than ever, looking for ways to improve his Yankees. In 1926, shortstop Mark Koenig had batted lead-off. Center fielder Earle Combs, "The Kentucky Colonel," had batted second. In June Huggins flip-flopped them in the lineup; they stayed that way for the remainder of the season. That would be the way it would be in 1927, too, Huggins decided.

Now in spring training, Huggins made a far more crucial, far more dramatic lineup switch. Lou Gehrig would now bat cleanup, sandwiched between the outgoing and energetic Ruth, moved to the third slot, and the taciturn and unpleasant Bob Meusel, in the fifth hole.

Huggins also added a new coach, Arthur Fletcher. The Phillies' manager in 1926, he would now be a fixture for the Yankees at third base and a heckler without equal. A former shortstop, a clone of John McGraw, whose Giant teams he had played on for more than a decade, "Fletch" was the leader and sparkplug of one of the deadball era's top infields, which featured Fred Merkle at first, "Laughing Larry" Doyle at second, and Buck Herzog at third. Fletcher was the shortstop.

"If there be one among the gamesters of baseball who is gamer than the rest, that man be Fletcher," wrote sportswriter Frank Graham. Everywhere the Giants went, Graham wrote, "There was fighting and Fletcher always was in the thick of it. He fought enemy players, umpires, and fans. He was fined and suspended frequently." A friend of Huggins from their National League days, and reluctant at first to take the job, Fletcher loved being a Yankee coach and leading a winning team.

Charley O'Leary, a buddy of Huggins, had been the Yankees' first-base coach since 1921. Skilled at and fond of getting on umpires and players, O'Leary exhibited a rowdiness sharply contrasted with the muted personality of the cerebral Huggins. The slightly built O'Leary, one of eleven boys in a family of sixteen children, was, like Fletcher, a former shortstop and had starred for Detroit's pennant winners in 1907 and 1908. Huggins would later give O'Leary credit for the development of the kid infielders Tony Lazzeri and Mark Koenig.

March 4 was the reporting date for rookies and batterymen, with the balance of the team required to be in camp by March 11. New players lusting to get a spot on the talented and virtually set roster included Henry Johnson, Baxter Williams, and Roy Chesterfield, who had been in camp the year before and then spent the 1926 season with the Newark Bears of the Class AAA International League. There was George W. Davis, a 1926 graduate of New York University, where he had starred as an outfielder. He also had played for Newark in 1926. Now where would he play?

Elias Funk, out of the Oklahoma City Indians in the Class A Western League, had hit .339 in 1926 and stolen 51 bases. Huggins liked him: "He stands well at the plate, fields beautifully and is as fast as a ray of light." There was Brooklyn's Joe Bruno, 20, a pitcher who dipped into his own funds to travel to spring training. He got a bit of publicity but could not make the team.

Seven new players would make the Yankee roster. George Pipgras, who had spent two years in the minors; rookies Wilcy Moore and Julie Wera, and Cedric Durst, Joe Giard, Johnny Grabowski, and Ray Morehart, picked up in off-season moves. Pipgras and the freckle-faced Moore were the most interesting of the bunch.

"I guess it is more sensible to take a pessimistic view of Moore because of his age," Huggins said. "He is one of those old youngsters. He is breaking into the majors at thirty, old for a pitcher."

"I didn't know anybody from the Yankees had looked at me," Moore told reporters in spring training. "I didn't know they'd ever heard of me. And nobody in our front office ever had said anything to me about me being sold. . . . Anyway, I thought I'd come up and see what it was like up here."

"The newspaper fellows used to say that I got him out of a Sears Roebuck catalogue," Ed Barrow wrote in his autobiography. "It wasn't as bad as that but I did discover him while reading the *Sporting News*."

What Barrow "discovered" was that in 1926, with the Greenville Spinners of the Class A South Atlantic League, Moore was 30–4. What he didn't know then was that a broken right wrist the Oklahoma cotton farmer sustained from a batted ball in 1925 was a gift from the baseball heavens. When Moore returned later in the season, he had a problem continuing with his overhand delivery, so he switched to sidearming the ball, which made him a pitching force. He always had excellent control. His sinker was now down, sharp and nasty. The pitch augmented his already good fastball and adequate curve. In 1926 it helped him notch 17 straight wins.

"I sent scout Bob Gilks to find out about him," Barrow wrote. "Gilks turned thumbs down on him. 'He can't pitch,' Bob said, 'and anyway, he says he's thirty but he must be forty.'

"I don't care," Barrow continued in his autobiography. "Anybody who could win that many games even in Epworth League is worth what they're asking for him."

Wilcy Moore would be the Yankees' top pitcher in spring training, working 25 innings and allowing less than a dozen hits. But there was no way for him to crack the veteran but powerful pitching rotation. Relief was now his forte, and he would become the first great relief pitcher. Moore basked in the role: "I ain't a pitcher, I'm a day laborer," he was fond of saying.

Pitching was on everyone's mind in spring training. Huggins was publicly confident about Waite Hoyt: "He has stuff and he knows how to use it. That fellow should win 20 or more games for me every season. He should be as good a pitcher as there is in the league."

Hoyt, the emerging ace of the staff, was in his tenth major league season, but still only 27 years old. The son of a professional minstrel, Waite Charles Hoyt threw three no-hitters at Brooklyn's Erasmus Hall High School, fanning 24 in one game. That's how he got the nickname "Schoolboy."

He was signed by John McGraw after pitching batting practice for the New York Giants at age 15. There were a couple of minor league seasons, and a game he got into for one inning with the Giants—striking out two against the Cardinals in 1918. And then banishment to the minors again. Furious, tempestuous, self confident, Hoyt quit.

It was Ed Barrow, then the Red Sox manager, who signed the 19-year-old Hoyt in 1919 for Boston. There, Hoyt developed a friendship with Babe Ruth. Just before the 1921 season, Barrow, now the Yankee general manager, plucked the handsome hurler from the Red Sox in an eight-player trade. One of the most sophisticated players of his era, and a skilled storyteller, the broad-shouldered right-hander became a constant winner on the Yankee pitching staff.

"Huggins took an interest in me," wrote Waite Hoyt in his unpublished autobiography, "and helped me to the best season I ever recorded. In 1927, at St. Petersburg he gave me a long fatherly lecture on concentration. I could, he told me, lead the league in pitching year after

Miller Huggins

year if I would devote myself more seriously to the job. . . . I knew that
Hug was not merely trying to con me into winning a few more ball
games. . . . And for the first time in my life the words were beginning
to sink in."

Miller Huggins was very positive about Waite Hoyt but was not as
positive about some of the others. "The pitching staff has reached a
stage where I must gamble," he said. "If any of the young pitchers show

me anything, they will get a chance. I'll admit that in the past I've been cautious about using rookies, but that was the past. This year experience isn't going to cut so much of a figure; a young arm is sometimes better than an old head."

Yankee starting pitching was a bit long in the tooth. Urban Shocker was 34 years old, Bob Shawkey, 36. Dutch Ruether and Herb Pennock, both 33, had each pitched at least a decade in the big leagues.

On March 8, the Yankee "Regulars" played the "Rookies." One of the hopefuls, Elias Funk, played center field and showed a lot, getting two hits, scoring two runs, and cutting Gehrig down at third with a powerful throw. Despite the good showing, Funk would not make the Yankee roster. There was just no room for him in the crowded outfield.

Ford C. Frick out of Fort Wayne, Indiana, joined the sports staff of the *New York American*, covering the Giants in 1922. The following year, he was with the *New York Evening Journal*, covering the Yankees. He eventually became a ghostwriter for Babe Ruth. His fellow scribes thought him "likable" and "well read." Those traits helped him to become commissioner of baseball many years later.

Writing in the *Evening Journal* that spring, Frick made this point: "Tony Lazzeri is the key man of the Yankee infield—and a good one. No man in camp is hitting the ball harder than Tony—or holding up in the field with quite the same brilliance. A budding star last season, this year Lazzeri gives promise of full bloom to stardom."

In camp, shortstop Mark Koenig and second baseman Lazzeri were inseparable. But the popular Lazzeri, whose 1927 salary was $8,000, was having a terrific spring. Mark Koenig was not. The bad memories of his bummer of a 1926 World Series were still with him, a downtime when he made three errors, hit into three double plays, and struck out six times.

"I was ordinary, very ordinary," the self-effacing Koenig said. "I had small hands and made too many errors. The only thing I had was a powerful arm. I don't think I could have stayed up on any other club. The Yankees could have carried a midget at shortstop. That's how good a club it was."

Despite Koenig's troubles that spring and his self-deprecating commentary, Huggins insisted, "My shortstop is Mark Koenig."

Grantland Rice had a rosy view of Koenig, Gehrig, and Lazzeri:

"They are still only a trifle more than baseball kids. Two of them have less than two years experience under the big top. So here is three quarters of an infield with ten or twelve more years to go. And there is no other combination so valuable to baseball in spite of their brief experience."

On March 15, Artie Fletcher was tossed out of an exhibition game that the Yanks won, 6–5 over the Boston Braves. It was reported that some of the players kidded him with the line "What took you so long?" For the Yankees, the booting of Fletcher was a good sign, showing that "Fletch" had not lost his famed heckling touch.

Babe Ruth also had not lost his mighty swing in that game. In hyperbolic and entertaining prose in the *Times*, James R. Harrison brought back that moment of the mighty man at bat: "accompanied by such agitating of the air that persons living near the ballpark bolted their shutters, fearing that another hurricane was coming. As a pinch hitter the Babe took three violent swings and a man in the front row was heard to complain of the draught."

On March 21, the Yankees nipped the Reds, 2–1. Bob Meusel, playing his first game of spring training after having reported just four days before and holding out for and receiving a two-year contract, homered in the sixth. Dutch Ruether and Waite Hoyt held Cincinnati to nine hits and the one run. But most instrumental in the New York win were bench players, especially Cedric Durst, who hit a sac fly driving in the Yankee winning run.

Two days later, behind two home runs and a double by the Bambino, the Yankees thrashed the Braves, who also trained in St. Pete, 16–7. Ruth was on base in five of his six at-bats. The Yankee romp showcased the extra-base batting force of the potent 1927 lineup. The 16 runs came off 16 hits. Meusel homered and doubled. Gehrig tripled. Koenig and Lazzeri doubled. In all, Murderers' Row recorded 30 total bases.

Fine-tuning themselves into shape that spring, the Yankees experienced good days and bad days. March 24 was not a good day for Miller

Huggins and his team. New York was embarrassed by the Braves and also by home plate umpire Frank Wilson, dubbed "the ousting arbiter of the National League" by Richards Vidmer. The Boston team romped, 10–9 and 18–0. Wilson ousted a total of 19 players from both teams.

For a few Yankees, the next day also was not so sunny. Tony Lazzeri was in a rage and full of pain. The first spring training game with the Cardinals loomed, and unfortunately an agitated Tony was told that the painful boil on his knee would keep him out of action. The pending matchup, one he had looked forward to since the 1926 Word Series defeat and his strikeout against Grover Cleveland Alexander, was almost an obsession with the young second baseman. But there would be other times for Lazzeri, whose Yankee future was so bright.

The same could not be said for three others who had been with the club all spring. That day the trio, cut from the Yankee roster, were given train tickets to other locations: Catcher Virgil "Spud" Davis and infielder Hugh Ferrell were on their way to the Reading Keystones of the Class AAA International League. James Wiltze, a pitcher, was off to the Buffalo Bisons of that league. Davis never returned to the Yankees but did manage a 16-year-career with several National League teams. Ferrell and Wiltze never graced a major league roster. The Yankee roster was now down to 29 players, with four more cuts still in the offing. Herb Pennock, who had come to camp late, would be left behind in Florida to work himself into shape, along with Benny Bengough.

At Avon Park in St. Petersburg, Florida, on March 27, it was the Yankees versus the Cardinals. Tony Lazzeri watched but did not like what he saw. The Redbirds ran wild against his teammates, 13–2. A Babe Ruth triple was one of the very few bright New York moments. St. Louis played like world champs. New York played badly and heard it from the Redbird rooters in the stands: "Get the grammar school team." "Get a new chucker."

Back in St. Petersburg the next day, the Cardinals and the Yankees, using their regular lineups, were in midseason form. New York scored four times in the first off Grover Cleveland Alexander, the only runs the

40-year-old had given up in 15 innings of spring work. Although he was on the ropes, the Yankees could not finish him off. The old-timer found his rhythm, shutting the Yankees down before exiting the game in the eighth. And the Redbirds scored two runs in the ninth to win the game, 6–4.

Six weeks in the South's sunshine had passed too quickly for the Yankees. On March 30, on one of those warm and languid evenings that St. Petersburg is so famous for, their time in camp ended. The Yankees boarded a slow-moving train for the nine-day circuitous journey back to New York. Jake Ruppert also departed the Southland that day. But his travel was in his private railroad car heading directly back to New York City.

Breaking camp and barnstorming north back then was an event for the players, but even more so for the people in the towns and cities along the way. It was a sure sign of spring, a renewal of ritual and a chance most of all to see the mighty "Murderers' Row" of New York, the most glamorous, most powerful, most famous baseball team of the time.

The training season," Frank Graham wrote in *The New York Yankees*, "was uneventful, because there was little for Huggins to do. Born of their eagerness to redeem themselves for the loss of the series (1926 against the Cardinals), a new spirit burned brightly in the players. New bonds had been forged in the crises they had met. Huggins had no need to demand their loyalty. It was his completely."

Tanned, well conditioned, fit, in good spirits, the players were eager for the season to start. Only Miller Huggins appeared as if he could still use a few weeks in the Florida sunshine. He was gaunt, pale, a gray presence accentuated by deep bags under his eyes. He had the loyalty of the players, but he fretted about some of them.

"When they pick up a newspaper now," the minimanager said, " the first thing they turn to is the financial pages and the sports section later. Those things are not good for a ball club that is trying to beat a ball club like the one Mr. Mack has." Connie Mack was the owner and manager of the Philadelphia Athletics.

He issued a set of simple rules as the Yankees headed northward:

- No smoking in uniform.
- No staying out after midnight.
- No golf to be played except on off days and Sundays.
- A limit of 25 cents betting in all card games.

The first stop out of spring training was Palm Beach, for an exhibition game, against the Reds, then on to Jacksonville to play the Cardinals.

The Jacksonville Chamber of Commerce bragged that anyone coming into or out of Florida had to pass through its lovely city. On April 1, it was Yankees versus Cardinals once again. There was a new grandstand in the Jacksonville park. Richards Vidmer reported in the *Times* that some of the 10,000 fans spilled out of it, taking up positions along the foul lines, on the roof of the bleachers, in the far reaches of the outfield. Ruth was held tightly in check for six innings by Grover Cleveland Alexander. He was twice retired on grounders, and another time he struck out. But when the mighty Alexander was taken out of the game, the Babe delivered the game's decisive blow in the eighth inning off southpaw Arthur Reinhart, locking in the 3–2 Yankee triumph.

The train wended its way north, players living on it, sleeping on it, having meals and playing cards, talking about baseball and about their lives.

"We're all one big gang together," Ruth would later write. "We know each other, trust each other, like each other. Baseball has its share of wonderful friendships and most of them have started aboard rattling old Pullman cars when the boys get a few hours to be themselves and have a chance to act natural."

The word always somehow got out that the Yankees were on the move, that the Yankees were coming, that their train was coming through. At every stop at any hour of the night there would be a cluster of men on the platform, sometimes the stationmaster, telegrapher, the baggage agent, all watching, studying the dark sleeping cars, yearning for a glimpse of a Yankee, especially Ruth.

"He was one of a kind," said Waite Hoyt. "If he had never played ball, if you had never heard of him and passed him on Broadway, you'd turn around and look."

Everywhere, Babe Ruth was comfortable and happy moving among crowds. Wherever the Yankees went, parks virtually filled to capacity with cheering throngs greeted them. It was strange, but in a town with a population of 5,000, perhaps 7,500 would turn out for the game.

A highlight of the Yankee trip north was a series of eight exhibition games—the "little World Series" against the Cardinals, in a kind of replay of the 1926 Series with their conquerors. Young and old, fans and just the curious lined up to get a glimpse of the world champions and their powerful Yankee adversaries.

On April 2, the traveling baseball show was in Savannah, Georgia, before a very interested assemblage of almost 15,000. St. Louis pounded the Yankees, 20–10. But Babe Ruth had a game of it— homering, tripling, singling, and signing anything thrust at him even while he was on the field. Pleasing the fans, getting mobbed by them, was more delight than danger for the Big Bam. A surging crowd, mostly kids, charged onto the field, their main target George Herman Ruth. Moving through the mass, struggling a bit to get to his seat on the bench, the Babe loved it. "I wish," the Babe said, "they were all mine."

On April 4, the Yankees defeated St. Louis, 4–2, and Ruth was once again the big wheel in the win. In a heavy rain the next day, the train carrying the Yankees and the Cardinals stopped in Etowah, Tennessee. The entire population of that little town (except for four residents) waited at the station. The train was an hour late. No matter—Babe Ruth was on that train, and that was all that really mattered to the crowd. Interrupting his bridge game, the Great Bambino stepped out in the blinding rain onto the train platform, to be cheered by and to cheer his fans.

That day it was once again Yankees versus Cardinals, this time in Atlanta. Murderers' Row mauled a quartette of St. Louis hurlers, including the great Alexander, hammering the Cards, 15–8, and tying "the little World Series," 3–3. The Big Bam was at the top of his game, tossing out two runners at home and getting two hits.

In Knoxville, Tennessee, there was another huge crowd at the station and agape and agog an army of high schoolers in the lobby of the Farragut Hotel, downtown. The Yankees of New York were the top of the heap, the cream in the coffee, standing room only wherever they went.

So important were the Yankees that the Nashville, Tennessee, city legislature adjourned on April 7 so its members could see the game between St. Louis and Babe Ruth and Company.

But the star of stars that day was not the Sultan of Swat but a former New York Giant: Frankie Frisch. His two home runs and two doubles powered the Cards to a 10–3 triumph over the Yanks. Just as if the whole thing had been scripted, the Yankees and the Cardinals split their "little World Series" at four wins each.

Gate receipts for their total preseason exhibition games amounted to $600,000, virtually all the revenue needed to cover spring training expenses plus Babe Ruth's salary for the year

Heading to New York City for their final exhibition games—two contests against the Robins (as the Dodgers were known) in Brooklyn —the Yankees had committed no errors in their last 56 chances. Urban Shocker's 10 scoreless innings in spring training gave him bragging rights on the pitching staff. Ruth had batted .315 in the games in the Southland, but Ray Morehart had outdone all New York batsmen with a .373 average in 51 at-bats.

Frigid conditions were on parade at Brooklyn's Ebbets Field on April 9 and 10; nevertheless, fans were out in record numbers in "winter wraps and furs," in John Drebinger's phrase.

On April 9 before 15,000, Mark Koenig's single in the eighth inning broke a 5–5 tie and drove in Bob Meusel with the winning run. The Yankees nipped the Robins, 6–5.

The next day, seemingly gluttons for punishment, 25,000 showed and shivered in what Drebinger called "the ice palace," watching the Yankees nip Brooklyn, 4–3. Ruth, who had homered the day before, delighting almost everyone, stroked three singles. Herb Pennock hurled seven shutout innings. Wilcy Moore provided a little excitement, yielding three runs in the eighth inning, but held on to give the visitors their win.

The next game for the New York Yankees would be against the Athletics of Philadelphia, April 12, 1927, Opening Day at Yankee Stadium.

THE ROSTER

What visions burn, what dreams possess him,
seeker of the night. The packed stands of the
stadium, the bleachers sweltering with their
unshaded hordes, the faultless velvet of the
diamond. The mounting roar of 80,000
voices and Gehrig coming to bat.

—Thomas Wolfe

A range of individuals made up the 1927 roster of the New York
Yankees. The average age was 27.6. All white, they came from
diverse backgrounds, had very different personalities, professional
backgrounds, educations, interests, skills, and avocations.

There was a former teacher, a railroad fireman, a bartender, a sea-
man, a logger, a cardsharp, one who had studied for the Roman
Catholic priesthood, another who as a kid had climbed the tenement
stairs in New York City delivering laundry, swam in the Hudson River,
and knew his way around local pool halls. There was one who had an
almost royal aura who had attended the finest prep schools and wore

thousand-dollar diamond rings. There was a meat cutter and an ex-vaudevillian. There was a former full-time boilermaker, a talented painter, artist, writer, and singer, a skilled piano (jazz and classical) player, and several former farm boys and farmers.

And a few who had never known anything but playing baseball.

Baseball was what bound the 25 of them together. The total payroll for that 1927 team was an estimated $250,000, while the average salary was $10,000, compared to $2,699,292 for the 2006 Yankees. Salaries ranged from Julie Wera's $2,400 to Babe Ruth's $70,000.

The team had a pronounced German American flavor, from its owner, beer baron Jacob Ruppert, to Lou Gehrig, Babe Ruth, Mark Koenig, Bob Meusel, George Pipgras, and Dutch Ruether and half Germans Waite Hoyt and Earle Combs.

The 1927 Yankees

There was also a collegiate flavor: Lou Gehrig (Columbia), Miller Huggins (University of Cincinnati), Joe Dugan (Holy Cross), Benny Bengough (Niagara University), Earle Combs (Eastern Kentucky State Teachers College), Mike Gazella (Lafayette), Ray Morehart (Stephen Austin College, Texas), Myles Thomas (Penn State), Bob Shawkey (Slippery Rock and University of Pennsylvania), Ben Paschal (University of Alabama), and Dutch Ruether (St. Ignatius College, now San Francisco University)

One player received his education at St. Mary's Industrial School, and another had been in and out of one-room cotton county schoolhouses. A few had no true formal education at all.

Born in 1904, the youngest player on the roster was Mark Koenig. He, along with Joe Grabowski, Lou Gehrig, Tony Lazzeri, and Julie Wera were the only Yankees born in the twentieth century.

The shortest players were catcher Benny Bengough and utility man Mike Gazella. Bob Meusel was the tallest Yankee, at six-three, and Babe Ruth was the next tallest, at six-two. Other six-footers included pitchers Wilcy Moore, Herb Pennock, George Pipgras, and Dutch Ruether, infielders Lou Gehrig and Mark Koenig, and center fielder Earle Combs. The only Yankees who weighed more than 200 pounds were Babe Ruth and Lou Gehrig.

There was no roster shuttling of players from the minor leagues. The 25 players who began the season remained on the roster all season, tying a record for fewest players used by a major league team.

Only Lou Gehrig would start every game (155 in all) at first base. Tony Lazzeri appeared in 113 games at second base, Mark Koenig 122 at shortstop, and Joe Dugan 111 at third. Earle Combs would start all but 3 games. The final statistics on Ruth and Meusel would be misleading. The Babe would start 95 times in right field and "Silent Bob" 83 times in left field. But they flip-flopped positions at Yankee Stadium and in a few parks on the road. Six men accounted for almost 90 percent of the innings pitched.

There was an almost grotesque quality to the team collectively as well as individually. One player could only sleep sitting up. He had a heart condition he kept secret from his teammates. Another seemingly aloof, sometimes painfully quiet, was an epileptic whose condition was never mentioned by the press. One was taciturn, some would say miserable, a drinker, a scowler who looked at the world with anger. One worked off-season as a mortician. Another was a "mama's boy," allegedly a virgin, who was very uncomfortable in the presence of women, enjoyed fishing by himself for eels, and living with his parents in an apartment. There was one whose hearty belches sometimes rattled bats stacked in the dugout, who slugged down great quantities of beer and ate prodigiously. His prowess with women was the talk throughout baseball. Another was an uneducated dirt farmer, age 30. Or was it 40? There was also a Kentuckian, a churchgoer, a nonsmoker, nondrinker, a man who never cursed and read his Bible on the road in hotel rooms.

There were ten pitchers on the roster, three catchers, seven infielders, and five outfielders.

Through the decades, baseball team pictures have become—like family portraits or class graduation shots—collectibles, marker moments, archival records. The sheer act of assembling 30 or so individuals in clean uniforms, positioning them, being mindful of likes and dislikes, physical size, ego, and professional stature has always posed a challenge.

Various 1927 team photos that have come down through history. One shot features the players without baseball caps. Another has them with jackets on. Another, taken after the team won the World Series, has the identification banner "World Champions." Another version of the 1927 team photograph has an unidentified player in the back row. That was pitcher Walter Beall.

But the team photo shown in this book (see page 40) remains perhaps the most famous baseball team photograph ever—it is the iconic image of the 1927 Yankees. The complete 1927 team autographed photo is a rare piece in the world of sports collecting. It was offered in auction on December 14, 2006, by Memory Lane, Inc., and sold for a world record of $206,000: $176,000 plus 17.5 percent to the auction house.

All signatures were collected by pitcher George Pipgras. It took much persistence on his part to cajole, sweet-talk, and buttonhole his teammates, manager and coaches, and team mascot, but he got the job done. Even batboy Eddie Bennett, not the most camera-friendly of the bunch, posed and signed.

The only player in the 1927 team photograph who stands apart from the others is 24-year-old Henry Louis Gehrig, an anchor to the whole composition, smiling, hands linked behind his back.

"He's burly, broad-shouldered, deep chested, long waited, stout legged and muscled like a wrestler, Frank Graham wrote in the *New York Sun* of Gehrig "He walks with a rolling gait, chews tobacco, reads the funny papers and plays pinochle." That was just part of the story.

Gehrig's mother, Christina, came to America in 1899 at age 18. A year later she married a 33-year-old metalworker named Heinrich Gehrig, who had come over a dozen years earlier. They had four children; only one survived infancy. That was Heinrich Ludwig, later Americanized to Henry Louis.

Papa Gehrig had trouble holding down a job. Christina took over, working as cook, housemaid, or laundress in their Washington Heights neighborhood. Anything to keep the little family going—especially the big kid Lou, who had power, surprising speed, and terrific eye-hand coordination playing marbles, billiards, and baseball.

The 16-year-old Gehrig blasted a tremendous grand-slam ninth-inning home run over the right-field fence for his Commerce High School team in a special "national championship" game at Wrigley Field in Chicago.

"It was a blow of which any big leaguer would have been proud," wrote a *Chicago Tribune* scribe. The *New York Times* declared, "The real Babe Ruth never poled one more thrilling."

The youth then went on to star at Columbia University, where he launched more homers and was labeled the "Babe Ruth of Columbia."

"I did not go to Columbia to look at Gehrig," Paul Krichell, who became one of the greatest scouts in baseball history, recalled, "I did not even know what position he played, but he played in the outfield against Rutgers and socked a couple of balls a mile. I sat up and took notice. I saw a tremendous youth, with powerful arms and terrific legs. I said, here is a kid who can't miss."

Krichell told general manager Ed Barrow, "I think I've just seen another Babe Ruth." The Yankees offered the 20-year-old Gehrig a $2,000 salary for the remainder of the season, plus a $1,500 signing bonus.

After minor league stints in 1923 and 1924 with the Hartford Senators in the Class A Eastern League, where he bashed a total of 61 home runs, Gehrig came back to the Yankees to stay in 1925.

On June 1, 1925, Lou Gehrig pinch-hit for Wally Pipp, and for the next 14 years and 2,130 games, he was truly the Pride of the Yankees.

Bob Meusel stands next to Gehrig in the 1927 team photo. The younger brother of National League star Irish Meusel, out of San Jose, California, "Long Bob" had the best arm in baseball. Babe Ruth said: "I never saw a better thrower."

Veteran Meusel's 1927 salary was $13,000. He was paid well for his talent by the standards of the times. But he lacked good character. Miller Huggins said his attitude was one of "plain indifference." Others had nastier things to say about him.

James R. Harrison wrote about Meusel in the *New York Times*: "Bob hustles when he feels like it and doesn't care what any one else thinks about it. A strangely cloistered gentleman is Mr. Meusel. Impervious to pleas, threats or jibes, he moves serenely through the world in solitary splendor."

Bob Meusel played for a decade in the majors, nine of those years with the Yankees. He still ranks among the all-time Yankee leaders in doubles, triples, RBIs, and batting average.

Babe Ruth is easy to spot, standing tall in the back row. "One of the secrets of the Babe's greatness was that he never lost any of his enthusiasm for playing ball, and especially for hitting home runs," wrote Frank Graham. "To him a homer was a homer, whether he hit it in a regular game, a World Series game, or an exhibition game. The crack of the bat, the sight of the ball soaring against the sky—these thrilled him as much as they did the fans."

George Herman Ruth, as the story goes, was first called "Babe" by teammates on the Baltimore Orioles, his first professional team. He called most everybody "Kid," because he couldn't or wouldn't remember names, even of his closest friends.

He was called "Infant Swatatagy," "Jidge," "the Bambino," "the Wali of Wallop," "the Rajah of Rap," "the Caliph of Clout," "the Wazir of Wham," "the Maharajah of Mash," "the Sultan of Swat," "the Colossus of Clout," "the Home Run King," "the Behemoth of Biff," "the Prince of Pounders," "Bam," "Big Bam," "Bammer," and "the Goliath of Grand Slams." Those were just some of the positive names. Some of the negatives included "Baboon," "Monkey," "Big Monk," and several others that are unprintable.

Babe Ruth was a force unto himself for whom the superlatives outdid themselves. But first and foremost, he was the greatest slugger baseball had ever seen. Writers, sociologists, opponents, and teammates all took turns explaining what made Babe Ruth, Babe Ruth.

Joe Dugan, one of the best friends of the slugger on the Yankees, had a very earthy explanation. "Born? Hell, Babe Ruth wasn't born, he fell from a tree."

In the outfield he not only possessed a strong and highly accurate arm, he also could move, with those great instincts of his taking over, and he knew where to position himself.

Through his playing time pitchers lay in wait for him with spitters, shineballs, emery balls, and other slippery mound offerings, with brush-back pitches, with intentional and unintentional walks. He took their best and more than dealt with it.

George Herman Ruth was born in Baltimore in 1894. He once told a biographer, "I was a bum when I was a kid." A truant, he cursed, drank, and stole at an early age. His parents sent him to the Catholic brothers at St. Mary's Industrial School. It was there that he learned to play baseball very well. It was said that at age 13 he hit a baseball 400 feet. That was farther than any major leaguer of that time hit a ball.

In 1914 he signed a contract with the minor league Orioles and later that season joined the Red Sox as a pitcher. His stats from that experience are just incredible:

- 47 wins from 1916 to 1917
- .671 winning percentage, tenth best all-time
- fifteenth best lifetime earned run average

Then, in one of the great mistakes in baseball history, he was sold to the Yankees for $125,000 in 1920. His 54 home runs that year were more than any other team total except the Phillies. The 6-foot-2, 215-pound Ruth revolutionized the sport, changing it from a pitcher-dominated, small-ball game to home-run, big-boom times.

"I hit big or I miss big," Ruth said. "I could have had a lifetime .600 average, but I would have had to hit them singles. The people were paying to see me hit home runs."

The superstar Ruth and the rookie Wilcy Moore standing side by side made for an odd couple in the photo. Frank Graham in his *New York Yankees*, wrote of Moore, a slow-speaking, slow-walking, low-throwing dirt farmer from Hollis, Oklahoma: "Nobody knew how old he was. He said he was twenty-eight but nobody believed him. . . . For six years he had toiled in the minor leagues with no hope of getting to the majors. He had good years and bad ones. When he picked up a little money, he went home and put it in the bank or bought new tools for his farm. "

Born in Bonita, Texas, the veteran Moore, who had been everywhere and seen everything—even plying his pitching trade for a time in the old Indian territories—was acquired for $5,000.

The 6-foot, 195-pounder was the second-lowest-paid player on the 1927 Yankees. His deal was for $2,500 and included a $500 bonus if he stuck with the team for the entire year.

George Pipgras, who stands between Wilcy Moore and Earle Combs in the photo, was born on December 20, 1899, in Ida Grove, Iowa, and grew up on a farm in Minnesota. He liked to talk of his times rising at 4:30 A.M., and going out in all kinds of weather to care for and feed 150 head of sheep, milk cows, and minister to horses. By the time he was ready to play high school baseball, his dad had traded the farm for a hotel in the Schleswig-Holstein area of Germany. But baseball was the only sport for George, and pitching was the only position.

He was a big kid and able to throw almost hard enough to tear a hole through a barn wall. His only problem was control, a problem that dogged him for years.

The Iowan served in World War I with the 25th Army Engineers.

Discharged, Pipgras pitched for semipro teams for little money. He was "discovered" pitching for Madison in the Dakota League by head Yankee scout Bob Connery, but the Red Sox signed him.

The Yankees, always plucking when it came to the Red Sox, plucked Pipgras from the Boston organization prior to 1923. The former farm boy was now a 6-foot, 2-inch 200-pounder.

Pipgras, the man responsible for collecting all the autographs on the photograph, came up to the Yankees on June 9, 1923, and walked 25 batters in 33 innings. "That was the first season of Yankee Stadium," he recalled. "I didn't know a place could be so big. I liked New York, but you seem to like whatever city you're working in. In all, it was a good life."

He won only one game (while losing three) in that rookie season, and went 0–1 in '24. Miller Huggins sent him to the minors for two years to work on his control. "I knew I was terribly wild," he said. "But I pitched so seldom I had little chance to improve."

The solidly built righty won a total of a 41 games at Atlanta, Nashville, and St. Paul in more than 100 games in the minors.

"I was off stride all the time," he explained. "I kept falling toward first base when I pitched. Pennock fixed my stride and also taught me a curveball."

In 1927, the man they called the "Danish Viking" because of his size and roots was back with the Yankees, salaried at $4,500, tied with Cedric Durst as the fourth-lowest-paid player on the roster. The 27-year-old Pipgras was the hardest throwing hurler on the team. He also, according to Babe Ruth, had "the best knuckleball in the business."

The husky Earle Combs stands between Pipgras and Don Miller. "I was always assured a place on the baseball team," Combs recalled his growing-up years, "not because of my athletic ability, but because I always furnished the ball. My dad made them for me."

He lived on the family farm until he was 17 years old. "And from boyhood my brothers—Matt, Conley and Clayton—played ball with me, and frequently Dad would join us," Combs said. "He made us all our balls and bats. Many a time I've watched him make a baseball. He

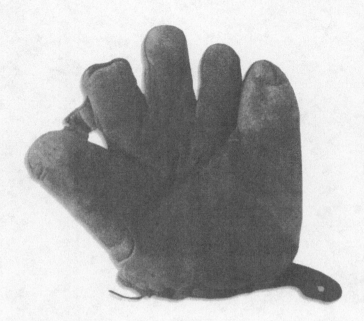

Earle Combs's glove

would get some old socks which mother had knitted . . . an old gum shoe and an old high-topped woman's shoe for his materials. He would unravel the socks, cut a ball from the gum shoe for the center, wind the yarn about this, and then cut a cover from the shoe top. He made bats out of hickory and poplar."

Combs began working as a teacher in a one-room Kentucky schoolhouse but learned quickly there was much more money in pro baseball. Batting .444 for the Harlan, Kentucky, lower minor league team, he was signed by the Class AAA Louisville Colonels of the American Association. In 1923 Combs batted .380 for the Colonels, and in 1924 the Yankees bought his contract for two players and $50,000.

Pictured near Combs in the back row, Waite Hoyt, out of Brooklyn, was called the "beau ideal of the Yankees" by a few writers. Going into his tenth big league season, the 27-year-old Hoyt had a 110–85 career record and was under contract for a salary of $11,000, plus another $1,000 if he won 20 games.

According to the Paul Krichell scouting report: "Hoyt had a good arm, meaning speed and stuff, smart head which meant control and pitching know-how. And he had guts. His physique was ideal—190 pounds, six feet tall, and he had width, bulk and power in the region of the sacroiliac, which is the hinge of the entire pitching business."

Always one looking for gainful employment, Hoyt was an artist, writer, singer, and vaudevillian. He also went into business as a mortician. He declared: "I'm knocking 'em dead on Seventh Avenue while my partner is laying 'em out up in Westchester."

The animated Hoyt had a way with words. They all talked about the stocky right-hander's run-in with an umpire and Hoyt's comment, "You should be a traffic cop so you could stand in the middle of the street and insult people with impunity."

Tony Lazzeri, head down, appears deep in thought, standing next to Hoyt and his buddy Mark Koenig. While his given name was Anthony Michael Lazzeri, he was also known in those politically incorrect times as "Tony the Wop," "the Walloping Wop," and "the diamond Mussolini."

Born on December 6, 1903, in San Francisco, Lazzeri worked with his blacksmith father, a full-time boilermaker, from age 15 on. That was where his powerful forearms were shaped.

"I was a pretty tough kid," Lazzeri recalled. "The neighborhood wasn't one in which a boy was likely to grow up a sissy, for it was fight or get licked, and I never got licked."

His father wanted him to stick to a boiler factory job, but he wanted to play baseball. In 1925, with the Salt Lake City Bees in the almost 200-game-schedule Class AAA Pacific Coast League, the supple second baseman hit .355, slammed 60 homers, and drove in 222 runs.

The Yankees were very interested in signing the young Lazzeri, but there were stories about his epilepsy.

"If he had not suffered from that disease," Yank general manager Ed Barrow wrote, "I doubt he would have ever come to the Yankee Stadium. As long as he didn't take fits between three and six in the afternoon, that was good enough for me."

Italians were an ethnic group in some disfavor at that time with the baseball hierarchy, but that also factored into Lazzeri's availability. According to reports, the Yankees purchased his contract for $55,000 and five players. The major league debut for the 5-11, 170-pound Lazzeri was on April 13, 1926. His 1927 salary was $8,000 plus round-trip train fare for him and his wife at the beginning and end of the season.

One scribe complained that venturing to interview Lazzeri was "like trying to mine coal with a nail file and a pair of scissors." Lazzeri's epilepsy made him almost painfully reserved, making him seem unfriendly and detached.

Seated next to Lazzeri, high-strung Mark Koenig committed a league-leading 52 errors in the 1926 regular season, plus 4 more in the 1926 World Series. But at 22 years old and the youngest of the Yankees, he would get much better.

Pitcher Urban Shocker was the least flamboyant of all the players on the 1927 Yankees. He stands between Koenig and reserve outfielder Cedric Durst.

"The life of a substitute outfielder in the days when the Yankees are mighty champions isn't a merry one," New York sportswriter James B. Kahn said. "For it means looking at the world from a dugout seat. It is only because he hasn't been more often in the lineup that Durst's splendid ability as a fielder isn't more generally appreciated."

On the left end of the middle row, Bob Shawkey, the second-oldest player on the roster, was born on December 4, 1890, in Sigel, Pennsylvania, in the Alleghenies. At age 15 he swung an ax from six in the morning until after dark and settled for his pay, $1.25 for the day's work. Way led onto way, and Shawkey managed to enroll for a semester at Slippery Rock State Normal School. Strengthened by his years of work outdoors, the always athletic Shawkey in 1910 became a pitcher for the semipro Bloomsburg team in the Mountain League.

One of Connie Mack's scouts observed Shawkey hurling with great speed for the Harrisburg Senators in the Tri-State League. In the spring of '21 Shawkey signed with the Philly organization. There was a season with the Baltimore Orioles of the Class AAA International

League, and in the latter stages of the 1913 season he joined the Athletics.

A very unassuming—some would say colorless—type, the strong-armed and wiry Shawkey joined the Yankees on July 7, 1915, coming over from Philadelphia for $18,000.

The former fireman on the Pennsylvania Railroad won 24 games in 1916, helping the Yanks enjoy their first winning season in six years.

A slow, deliberate worker on the mound, Bob Shawkey was given the honor of being the starting pitcher for Opening Day at Yankee Stadium in 1923. Sporting a red sweatshirt under his jersey, he pitched the Yankees to a 4–1 victory over the Red Sox. He also hit the second home run in Stadium history. Babe Ruth slugged the first.

The gentle and relaxed Shawkey had been in service as a Yankee pitcher for a dozen years, the longest tenure of any other player on the 1927 roster. Four times in his career he won 20 or more games. His 1927 salary was $10,500.

Joe Giard, out of Ware, Massachusetts, is seated next to Shawkey in the middle row. On December 17, 1924, Giard was traded by the Yankees along with Joe Bush and Milt Gaston to the St. Louis Browns for Urban Shocker. But on February 8, 1927, the 28-year-old Giard was traded back to the Yankees along with Cedric Durst for Sam Jones. One of the reasons why Huggins wanted the 5-10, 170-pound hurler back was to have three lefties on the staff, and one he knew well. Giard's 1927 salary was $5,000, near the bottom on the team.

In 1925, Giard's rookie season, he had gone 10–5 despite a 5.04 ERA and twice as many walks as strikeouts for the struggling St. Louis Browns. He was 3–10 with a 7.00 ERA in 1926. The 1927 season would be his final year in baseball.

Seated next to Giard, John Patrick Grabowski, one of the top throwing catchers in baseball, the player they called "Nig," was well liked by teammates. He was an important member of the team when the 1927 season began. At that time, catcher Benny Bengough was beset with arm troubles, not a good thing for a defensive catcher, and Pat Collins lacked confidence in his arm, also not a good thing for a catcher.

The intellectual motor of the 1927 Yankees—little Miller Huggins—is positioned in the center of the middle row, is flanked by his lieutenants Charley O'Leary and Art Fletcher.

Pictured near Huggins, Herb Pennock, 6 feet tall and 160 pounds, was approximately the same height as Gehrig, who outweighed him by 40 pounds. Pennock was generally regarded as the best left-hander in baseball in his time. But Miller Huggins went a bit over the top, calling him "the greatest left-hander in history."

With Quaker roots going back to William Penn, heading into the 1927 season Pennock owned a 156–115 record with a 3.45 ERA. He was the second-highest-paid player on the Yankees; only Babe Ruth made more. Pennock's salary was $17,500, with a bonus clause for another $1,000 if he won 25 games.

Born on February 10, 1894, in Kennett Square, Pennsylvania, into an independently wealthy family whose fortune had come from the sale of their farm and road equipment business in the late nineteenth century, Pennock, an outstanding athlete, went directly from high school to debut with the Philadelphia Athletics on May 14, 1912. Then he moved on to the Red Sox.

Pennock, with his just adequate 76–72 career record, was traded to the Yankees from Boston before the 1923 season. The graceful hurler was given the news of the trade when his ship docked after a 30-day tour of the Orient with Herb Hunter's traveling All-Stars, a touring baseball group. To celebrate, Pennock danced a jig with his wife on a San Francisco pier.

When Pennock received his first Yankee World Series check, he invested in a fox pelt farm. The aristocratic pitcher also collected antique furniture, built chrysanthemum greenhouses on his Kennett Square property, wore thousand-dollar rings, and led fox hunts in the off-season. Hence the nickname the Knight of Kennett Square.

Pennock was very durable, not expending a lot of energy. He did not overpower batters. He let them hit the ball, giving up more than a hit an inning in his career. Yet he still managed 35 lifetime shutouts.

His pitching pace was slow. He walked around the mound, fixing his pants and tugging on the bill of his cap between pitches. He was six

Herb Pennock

feet tall and thin, with an oval face atop a long neck. Grantland Rice wrote that Pennock pitched each game "with the ease and coolness of a practice session."

Featuring impeccable control, Pennock fit the stereotype of a crafty southpaw, constantly studying hitters—a habit gained from sitting on the bench of the old A's. It was said that he had an encyclopedic knowledge of the strengths and weaknesses of opposing hitters.

Huggins, who most times utilized Pennock's slow stuff in the third or second game of a series, not often matching him with the opposition big winners, said, "If you were to cut that bird's head open, the weakness of every batter in the league would fall out."

Cool and impossible to fluster on the mound, Pennock was intense and introverted in the clubhouse before a start. But he never swore and never drank, and those characteristics, coupled with his bearing and breeding, gave him an almost royal aura.

Pictured to the right of Pennock, backup infielder Julie Wera was but 5-8 and 164 pounds, the lowest-paid player on the roster at $2,400. The 25-year-old Wera was another of the little guys Huggins liked to have around. Everyone on the 1927 team had a nickname, some more than one. Wera was called "Flop Ears," for obvious reasons.

Pat Collins, seated next to Wera, was one of the three catchers Huggins carried that 1927 season. Out of Sweet Springs, Missouri, 30-year-old Tharon Leslie Collins had played half a dozen years with the Browns, and was picked up by the Yankees from the St. Paul Saints of the Class AAA American Association before the 1926 season. The private Collins was an enigma, one most of the players felt they hardly knew. His salary for the 1927 season was $7,000.

Seated on the left end of the bottom row, Californian Dutch Ruether began his major league career with the Cubs in 1917, then moved on to the Brooklyn Dodgers from 1921 to 1924. He pitched for the Washington Senators in 1925 and 1926 and came to the Yankees off waivers on August 27, 1926, for "cash well exceeding the waiver price." One possible explanation wrote Rud Rennie, "is that his salary may have scared them away. Another is that he had been unruly." Back then "unruly" was a code word for a boozer. Ruether's 1927 salary was $11,000.

Lively Joe Dugan is seated next to Ruether in the photo. Dugan's powerful throwing arm and agility and ability with a snap throw made him an expert handler of bunts. "The way he darts about," *Baseball Magazine* noted, "scooping up grounders with the full play of those long arms and legs of his reminds you of a toy jumping jack on a string. Not that Dugan is awkward, for he is not."

They called him "Jumpin' Joe." "I can't remember exactly why they called him Jumpin' Joe, whether it was because he jumped ball clubs so often or was always hoppin' mad," George Uhle, one of his contemporaries, said.

Pictured to the right of Dugan, Ben Paschal, out of Enterprise, Alabama, was 19 years old when he broke into the big leagues with the Cleveland Indians. Paschal had been out of the majors for three seasons when the Yankees obtained him in 1924. His 1927 salary was $7,000. A steady but sulking type, he rarely made an error. As a substitute he had a lofty .319 career average. Like Durst, Paschal probably could have been a regular outfielder on most big league teams.

Seated next to Paschal, likable gagster Benny Bengough had instant rapport with most of his Yankee teammates from the moment he joined the team in 1923. Born in Liverpool, England, Bengough grew up in Niagara Falls, New York, and had studied for the Roman Catholic priesthood. He attended Niagara University and made the majors after toiling for several minor league seasons with the Buffalo Bisons of the International League.

There was a mystery as to how Bernard Oliver Bengough lost his hair in an imitation of what today would pass for a shaved head.

"One day I went to sleep and woke up that way," he said. "I thought I had been scalped."

A talkative catcher behind the plate, he would get laughs and distract hitters by removing his baseball cap and running his fingers through his imaginary hair. Sometimes he used a comb as a prop.

Bengough became the regular Yankee catcher in 1925 and was considered the best defensive backstop in the American League. Heading into the 1927 season, the punchless Bengough had a .268 career batting average, no home runs, and but 43 RBIs.

Players in that era were generally paid based almost strictly on seniority; Bengough made $8,000 in 1927, $500 more than Hall of Fame-first-baseman-to-be Lou Gehrig.

Myles Thomas was nicknamed "Duck Eye" by Babe Ruth. In 1927 he earned $6,500 and won 7 of 11 decisions. He is pictured in the photograph seated between Bengough and Gazella.

Known as "Gazook," Mike Gazella was smarter than his nickname sounded. Of Ukrainian descent, out of Olyphant, Pennsylvania, a graduate of Lafayette College, in 1923 he was offered $500 by Yankee superscout Paul Krichell to sign. Gazella knew Connie Mack and told him of the offer. The owner of the A's countered with $5,000. But Gazella wanted to be with the Yankees and signed with them for $1,000.

The 165-pound Gazella played in eight games in 1923 with the Yankees and then was sent down to the minors. He returned to the big club in 1926. After the Yanks lost to the Cardinals in the '26 World Series, the 30-year-old Gazella was awarded only a quarter share. He had appeared in but 66 games, yet had been with New York the entire season. "Gazook" protested to Commissioner Landis and won. The judge ordered the Yankees to pay him a full share.

Gazella was salaried at $5,000 for 1927 and got into 44 games at third base, 6 at shortstop. All told, he would only play in 160 major league games and bat .241. But he did all right. His four years of World Series checks added up to more than $50,000.

Ray Morehart, second from the right on the bottom row, took over second base when Lazzeri was moved to short in place of Koenig, who needed some rest. He played in 73 games and was a handy guy for Miller Huggins to have around.

The team photo of the 1927 New York Yankees is not only a record of a peerless collection of players, but also is marked by several peculiarities.

Strangely, Don Miller, pictured in the middle of the back row, was not a member of the team. He had tried out but was unsuccessful. His role with the 1927 New York Yankees was primarily as a batting practice pitcher.

Strangely, pitcher Walter Beall is the only member of the 1927 team not in this photo. He does, however, appear in other team photos. In one he is referred to as "unknown."

Walter Esau Beall appeared in just one inning of one game for the Yanks in 1927. Born July 29, 1899, in Washington, D.C., he was dubbed one of the best players to come out of the sandlots. As a 15-year-old, his stocky build gave him a much older appearance. He had much success pitching in amateur baseball. In 1921 Beall used his nasty curveball to great advantage with the Norfolk Tars of the Class D Virginia League, winning 23 of 31 decisions. He was also a 20-game winner for the Greenville Spinners of the Class A South Atlantic League. Moving up to the Rochester Tribe in the Class AAA International League in 1924, he led the circuit in ERA. The Yankees bought his contract, and Beall made his major league debut with them on September 3, 1924.

Control problems had him shuttle between majors to minors. But his curveball never failed to tantalize all who saw it.

"It was a curve," Lee Allen wrote in *Hot Stove League*, "that simply exploded and when he got it over the batters would grunt, swing, miss and walk away, shaking their heads in wonder." Babe Ruth called Beall's curveball "The best I ever saw. He could make a baseball sit up and sing bass, no kidding. His curve broke down, and I'll swear he could break it three or four inches."

Curiously, 30-year-old "batboy" Eddie Bennett never played. However, he was as well known as the players on the team, perhaps better known than some. On the Yankees since 1921, he was considered a good luck charm and a mascot. Envied by the youth of New York, Bennett took his job being in charge of Yankee bats very seriously. "Eddie just minds bats and his own business," wrote Westbrook Pegler.

Although Yankee owner Colonel Jake Ruppert and the general manager, Ed Barrow, are not in the photograph of the 1927 team, there would have been no roster if they had not been on the scene.

In 1880, 13-year-old Jacob Ruppert was owner, manager, captain, and second baseman of a baseball club. Young Ruppert insisted that his players clean the cages of his private menagerie before he would bring his bat and ball down to the vacant lot where the team played. He fired any player who struck out. Everyone knew very early on that young Jake could not abide losing.

Born in New York City on August 5, 1867, the son and grandson of beer tycoons who founded the Ruppert Breweries, he lived with his family in a fabulous apartment on Fifth Avenue in Manhattan. His was a life of luxury replete with all that money could buy. A rabid baseball fan, the privileged youngster rooted for the New York Giants and as a teenager tried out for but couldn't make the club.

Ruppert attended the prestigious Columbia Grammar School and was accepted to the School of Mines of Columbia University, but his father wanted him to be part of the brewery business. At 19 he began by washing barrels, working his way through the ranks. At 23 he was general manager. At 29 he was president, succeeding his father, who retired.

Heir to the family millions, he was appointed a colonel in the New York State 7th National Guard Regiment. It was an honorary title, but Ruppert was pleased when people used it when addressing him.

Using his money to help get elected as a Tammany Democrat in a normally Republican district, Ruppert served as a four-time member of the House of Representatives from 1899 to 1907, representing the "Silk Stocking" district of Manhattan. The Teutonic, punctilious Ruppert lived within easy walking distance of his brewery in a fashionable 12-room apartment at 1115 Fifth Avenue (now 1119 Fifth Avenue), on the corner of East 93rd Street and Fifth Avenue, directly across the street from the Central Park Reservoir. Five full-time servants catered to his every whim.

In an office devoid of curtains, close by his desk were marble pedestals, a goldfish aquarium, and two bronzes of Native Americans.

Ruppert was an avid collector of first editions, jade, porcelain, fine art, trotting horses and racehorses, St. Bernard show dogs, yachts, Chinese porcelains, Native American relics, monkeys, all varieties of doves, rare books, and dress shoes. He also became enamored of purchasing choice parcels of Manhattan real estate.

One of the richest men in the United States, it seemed that the aristocratic and eligible bachelor always seemed to have one beautiful and desirable woman or another with him as he made the rounds of New York's high society. North of the city, at his large estate in Garrison, New York, Ruppert had St. Bernards and Boston terriers. Both breeds of dogs won him many prizes. He kept little monkeys on his property, calling them "friendly little things." He had a collection of Percherons, the large horses that had pulled the big beer trucks in the days before the automobile. They were at leisure on a nearby farm. His country place was a repository of one of the largest personal art galleries and libraries in the United States. At the country estate, Ruppert reconstructed the Manhattan room of his late mother, arranging furnishings there as she had left them.

Always acquiring, Ruppert was very much interested in purchasing the New York Giants but was told by his friend manager John J. McGraw that they were not for sale but that the Yankees might be.

On January 11, 1915, Ruppert and Tillinghast L'Hommedieu Huston paid $460,000 and co-owned the New York Yankees, a franchise that had a 12-year record of 861–937, with average attendance of 345,000 a season.

"I never saw such a mixed-up business in my life—contracts, liabilities, notes, obligations of all sorts. There were times when it looked so bad no man would want to put a penny into it. It is an orphan ball club without a home of its own, without players of outstanding ability, without prestige," Ruppert the fan and the businessman said.

He wanted to name the team the "Knickerbockers" after his best-selling beer, but the marketing ploy failed. Besides, it was said, the name was too long for newspaper headlines. Years later it would be short enough for basketball's New York Knickerbockers.

The initial years of ownership saw Ruppert and Huston lose almost as much money as they had paid to purchase the Yankees, who finished the 1915 season in fifth place and the 1916 season in fourth place, their first time out of the second division since 1910.

Miller Huggins was signed by Ruppert as Yankee manager for 1918 against the objections of Huston, who was stationed at an army base in France in World War I; he had wanted Brooklyn manager Wilbert Robinson.

On May 21, 1922, two weeks after construction of Yankee Stadium got under way, Ruppert paid Huston $1.5 million and bought him out.

Colonel Jake Ruppert, whose idea of a wonderful day at the ballpark was any time the Yankees scored 11 runs in the first inning and then slowly pulled away, and who said "there is no charity in baseball, I want to win every year," early on in his ownership tenure provided each Yankee player with three sets of uniforms—an unheard-of luxury at the time—so they would always look fresh. He was responsible for Yankee

Stadium and for the foundation of the Yankee aura and successes. He truly earned his nickname "Master Builder in Baseball."

Equally significant to the 1927 Yankees, general manager Ed Barrow was born in a covered wagon on what was the wastelands of Illinois. He grew up to be a 250 pounder, always clean-shaven, a consumer of everything written about baseball. He said, "A fellow with work to do doesn't need any." He played golf just once. He never played in a major league game.

Barrow's baseball roots stretched back to 1894, when he partnered running concessions for the Pittsburgh Pirates with "Score Card Harry" M. Stevens, who would become baseball's leading concessionaire and the one who coined the phrase "You can't tell the players without a scorecard."

Moving quickly up the rungs—minor league manager, owner, president of the Eastern League, and manager of the Detroit Tigers—by 1918 Ed Barrow was the manager of the Boston Red Sox, leading them to a world championship, helped by a young southpaw pitcher whom he converted to an outfielder.

Barrow wrote, "Many people have said that when I changed Babe Ruth from a left-handed pitcher into a full-time outfielder, I changed the whole course of baseball. "

In 1920, the young Ruth was sold to the Yankees, and Barrow joined him in New York at the end of the season. He was now the Yankee general manager and presided over their first three pennants, from 1921 to 1923. He also stripped talent from his old Red Sox team, getting players such as Wally Schang, Waite Hoyt, Sam Jones, Joe Bush, Everett Scott, Joe Dugan, and Herb Pennock.

When the Yankees won their first world championship in 1923, five of their six top pitchers were former Red Sox. In Barrow's first eight years with the Yankees, they won six pennants.

The bald Barrow was powerfully built and had an explosive temper. He was old school, a strict disciplinarian, a man who feared no one. Once he even challenged Babe Ruth to a fight. Salaried at $25,000 in 1927, for a time he was the highest-paid man in baseball next to Babe Ruth.

The very conservative general manager ran the affairs of the Yankees from the Stadium and his office on 42nd Street. Ed Barrow and Jake Ruppert might have been opposites in many ways, but their work ethic was the same and their relationship was very close.

Barrow took chances going after players that other teams shied away from. He was innovative in creating one of the top farm systems and scouting networks.

Baseball's first real general manager, Ed Barrow said:

"I had always run things pretty much myself. I had good men who were responsible for their jobs. Paul Krichell headed up the scouts, Charlie McManus was the superintendent in charge of the Yankee Stadium, and Mark Roth was the traveling secretary who took care of the ball club on the road. But I had never delegated much authority. I kept on top of everything myself, and knew what was going on at all times."

That he did.

Barrow and Ruth and Gehrig and Combs and Lazzeri and Hoyt and Pennock and Ruppert and Huggins—nine in all from the 1927 New York Yankees—are members of the Baseball Hall of Fame.

4

SPRING

> This isn't just a ball club! This is Murderers'
> Row!
>
> —Arthur Robinson

From what the majority of preseason predictions had been and from what the New York Yankees had accomplished in spring training, no one could have, would have, dared to predict what would take place for them that 1927 season.

John Kieran had written in the *New York Times*: "The Yankees are the toughest team in either league to 'dope.' . . . The team is practically the same as last year, with perhaps a slight favor age in the pitching staff."

All told, in the 18 spring training games played against the Cardinals, Braves, and Reds, the Huggins men posted a record of 10 wins, 7 defeats, and a tie. Adequate results, but not awesome.

Owner Jacob Ruppert was very upbeat about prospects for baseball in 1927 but was muted in predictions for his team. He did not seem to have a clue as to what tremendous accomplishments lay ahead for his Yankees.

"Everything indicates that 1927 will be one of the most remarkable in baseball history," Ruppert told reporters. Although born in New York, he had never lost the German accent inherited from his paternal grandfather. It was an accent that became thicker when he became emotional, usually when talking about the Yankees.

"Everywhere we have played this spring," he continued, "the crowds have been large and in cities nowhere we have been before the attendance has been doubled. There seems to be deep interest in the game, interest that baseball men have not seen so pronounced in recent years."

April

On April 10, a *New York Times* headline proclaimed, "Big League Season to Open on Tuesday: Yanks Will Greet Athletics, Picked by Many to Win Flag, at the Stadium."

"Well, it won't be long now," James R. Harrison wrote in the *Times*. "Only a few days more and the greatest show on earth will be on. Tired business men will lock their desks and go uptown for an important 'conference' at 3:30 P.M. The mortality rate among the grandparents of office boys will take an alarming jump."

Everything was in readiness for the Yankees of New York, beginning their fifth season at their majestic home field in the Bronx. But no one was prepared for the epic battle that would take place that season between the elder Babe Ruth and the younger Lou Gehrig for the American League home run title. No one could have predicted the assault the Babe would make on his own home run record and the new standard he would be setting. But incredibly—as a lot of things were that momentous season—right after New Year's Day 1927, the *New York Sun* asked premier athletes in different sports what promises they could make for their careers in the new year. Babe Ruth's caption proclaimed: "I promise 60 homers for Jake."

No one realized just how formidable an offense, a defense, a pitching staff the Yankees possessed. Theirs would be the best relief pitcher

Babe Ruth and Lou Gehrig

and the best rookie in the American League. No one could predict how the team from the Bronx would manhandle its competition. No one could have foreseen the career years several key players were primed to experience. No one could have realized what lay ahead for the 30-year-old pitcher Wilcy Moore. No one realized the impact the switching of the places of Ruth and Gehrig in the batting order would have on them and the Yankees. No one could have ever predicted the depth and range of adulation and praise the working press would heap on the Yankees that 1927 season. No one would have ever predicted the effect Miller Huggins had on the team, the work ethic displayed by the players, the relentless drive to bear down, the pride on parade game after game. No one would ever estimate the record outpouring of crowds wherever and whenever the Yankees appeared, how the Yankees were baseball's best in 1927.

They had an owner who would not predict a pennant, and a manager concerned about whether some of the players on his team were serious enough and who thought six teams had an almost equal chance to be contenders.

What would happen belonged to the future. What would happen were the story lines of the long season ahead. Now it was only April, when all the teams in baseball began on an equal footing.

"The big parade toward Yankee Stadium started before noon yesterday," Peter Vischer described Opening Day 1927 in the *New York World*. "Subways brought ever-increasing crowds into the Bronx. Taxicabs arrived by the hundreds. Buses came jammed to the doors. The parade never stopped."

"Yankee Stadium was a mistake, not mine but the Giants'," Ruppert had said. The site was chosen, among other reasons, to irritate the Yankees' former landlords, the Giants, whose home park, the Polo Grounds, from which the Yankees had been evicted, was in plain view across the Harlem River, in Manhattan. It was also selected because the IRT's 161st Street–Yankee Stadium elevated subway station was virtually atop the stadium's right-field wall.

Built at a cost of $2.5 million, "The Yankee Stadium," as it was originally named, was nicknamed "The House That Ruth Built," when the park first opened in 1923 by sportswriter Fred Lieb, who was always especially handy at coming up with a catch phrase. The stadium had a brick-lined vault storing electronic equipment under second base, making it feasible to have a boxing ring and a press area in the infield.

Yankee Stadium was the first ballpark to be called a stadium. A mammoth horseshoe shaped by triple-decked grandstands, the edifice had huge wooden bleachers circling the outfield. The 10,712 upper grandstand seats and 14,543 lower grandstand seats had been fixed in place by 135,000 individual steel castings upon which 400,000 pieces of maple lumber were fastened by more than 1 million screws. Sod from Long Island, 16,000 square feet of it, was trucked in.

Scattered throughout the stands and bleachers, the stadium had eight toilet rooms for men and as many for women, a nice touch for the time. A 15-foot-deep copper facade adorned the front of the roof, covering much of the Stadium's third deck, giving it an elegant, almost dignified air. This decorative and distinctive element was the ballpark's logo.

Seating capacity in 1927 was now 62,000, increased from 58,000. The admission price for the 22,000 bleacher seats (the most in baseball) was reduced in 1927 from 75 cents to 50 cents. Grandstand admission was $1.10. All wooden seats were painted blue. In right-center field there was a permanent "Ruthville" sign. Sometimes the area was also called "Gehrigville."

The left-field foul pole was but a short 281-foot poke from home plate. It was 415 feet deeper in left, 490 feet to left-center, 487 feet to dead center, 429 feet to right-center, 344 feet to right, and 295 feet down the right-field line. The 82 feet behind home plate made for plenty of room for a catcher to run and chase wild pitches, passed balls, and foul balls.

The park's dimensions favored left-handed power—read: Babe Ruth. Yet he complained: "All the parks are good except the Stadium. There is no background there at all. I cried when they took me out of the Polo Grounds."

Above the bleachers in right-center field was a manual scoreboard. The Yankee bullpen looked out on left-center field. The dark green Yankee dugout was on the third-base side of the field and remained there until 1946, when owner Larry MacPhail moved it to the first-base side, also installing lights for night baseball. Bats were lined up neatly at the top of the dugout stairs.

"By game time the vast structure was packed solid," Peter Vischer's article continued. "April 12, 1927, Opening Day at Yankee Stadium. Rows of men were standing in back of the seats and along the runways. Such a crowd had never seen a baseball game or any other kind of game in New York."

Yankee general manager Ed Barrow crowed: "No question. It was the greatest crowd to ever see a game."

The crowd was the largest in all the history of baseball, 73,206, breaking the previous attendance record of 63,600, which had been set in game two of the 1926 World Series. Another 25,000 were turned away on this Opening Day.

There were 9,000 guests of the Yankees, plus 1,000 who were able to get in with passes. They were all part of the record 1,164,015 who would come out during that 1927 season to see the team play ball in the Bronx, topping the million mark for the seventh time in eight years.

On this balmy, almost summery day, the 7th Regiment Band, dressed in gray outfits, began playing with vim and gusto. Red-coated ushers, really into their effort of trying to keep the level of behavior orderly, worked the crowd, seating people at 3:25 P.M. The stringbean manager Cornelius McGillicuddy (Connie Mack) of the Philadelphia Athletics, who was dressed in dark civilian clothes and a high stiff collar and featured on that week's *Time* magazine cover, and the wisp of a Yankee pilot Miller Huggins posed for photographs.

On the managerial scene since 1894, the 64-year-old Mack, Miller Huggins, and Bucky Harris of Washington were the only holdover American League managers. There were new pilots in place in St. Louis (Dan Howley), Chicago (Ray Schalk), Detroit (George Moriarity), and Cleveland (Jack McCallister).

Mayor Jimmy Walker, 45, typified New York City and the 1920s. A svelte, more dressed-up model of the gregarious Babe Ruth, Walker in 1927 was happily involved with Betty Compton, 23, an actress. The two of them, it was said, had a gay time of it in their Ritz Hotel suite. Largely ignoring public mention of the relationship, the press instead gave lots of attention to the way Walker dressed, the parties he attended, the stories he told.

Urbane and dashing, the mayor left his position in Ruppert's private box to throw out the first ball—twice, taking no chance to miss a photo op—to Eddie Bennett, referred to in newspapers of the time as "the hunchback batboy."

Bennett gave players their bats and presented baseballs to umpires. He let his cap and hump be rubbed by Yankees before games. He sat on the bench next to Miller Huggins, observing and pointing out things on the field, a kind of precursor to today's bench coaches. He would bring bicarbonate of soda to Babe Ruth before every game, generally during batting practice, after the big man had downed his massive quota of hot dogs and soda pop.

Always kneeling, sometimes chatting, next to the Babe in the on-deck circle, Bennett and the Babe according to Westbrook Pegler were "the two orphans on the Yankee ball club who made the baseball bat their weapon in life and achieved a lot of glory, each in his own way."

Ruth and Bennett would provoke laughs from early arrivals at the Stadium by engaging in a highly animated game of catch. Starting about 10 feet apart, they would toss the ball back and forth. Ruth would throw the ball after a while about a foot above Bennett's reach, and he would scamper after it. They would repeat the routine and the Yankee mascot would complain a bit to the Babe, who would feign total innocence. The game continued until Bennett found himself backed up against the screen behind home plate. To some, the whole ritual was viewed as cruel behavior on Ruth's part, a taunting, shaming of a cripple. It wasn't—it was just two guys playing around.

Celebrities and those who thought they were entering celebrity status came to Opening Day 1927 to see and be seen. The "A" list included Sir Thomas Lipton, of tea and boating fame.

On this day of days, the Yankees had two loud-voiced announcers using megaphones to inform the crowd of the on-the-field goings-on. Previously one megaphoner had sufficed. Now colorful Jack Lentz, a longtime announcer who wore a derby hat and sometimes mangled the king's English, was joined by George Levy, who had made a reputation as an announcer at the Polo Grounds. He wore a soft hat and used a smallish megaphone. The work of the announcers was simple: give the name of each player as he came to bat and keep silent after that, except when a new player entered the game.

The *New York World* reported that the Athletics wore "blue silk blouses, quite snappy." The team from Philly and the Yankees marched in columns of four to the outfield. The national anthem was played.

Knowledgeable fans noticed a significant change in New York's white wool flannel home uniforms for 1927. "YANKEES" rather than the name of the city was now on the front of the jersey. Navy blue vertical pinstripes and stirrups accentuated the uniform. Players wore navy blue caps with a white interlocking "NY" in script on the front. The V-necked shirts had a brief tapered extension around the neck. Sleeves extended over the elbows, and the knicker pants reached just below the knees. Belts and cleats were black. On the road, the team from the Bronx would wear a gray uniform with "YANKEES" in navy blue block letters across the chest, and two colored stirrups, navy blue on top and rust on the bottom.

By noon, a carnival-like atmosphere pervaded the area around Yankee Stadium. Swarms of hawkers, vendors, gawkers, and fans intermingled in a circus of sounds and colors.

By three o'clock, most unreserved seats had been snatched up. Lines of police were at River Avenue in the back of the park and also along the approaches in front of the Stadium. New York's Finest checked carefully, allowing only those with tickets to pass.

Standing at attention at the base of the staff, both teams watched as the American flag and the American League pennant the Yankees had won in 1926 were raised to the top of the flagpole. The national anthem was played, and then there was the cry "Play ball."

It was exactly three-thirty when the game got under way.

This was the Yankees' Opening Day lineup:

Earle Combs, cf

Mark Koenig, ss

Babe Ruth, rf

Lou Gehrig, 1b

Bob Meusel, lf

Tony Lazzeri, 2b

Joe Dugan, 3b

Johnny Grabowski, c

Waite Hoyt, p

"Picture yourself a pitcher trying to get by Murderers' Row," Frank Graham wrote in his book *Lou Gehrig*. "First up was Combs, a sharp-eyed hitter, long legged and fast as a whippet. One mistake and you'd have Combs sitting on first. Koenig was up next. A precision machine at getting a man along to second with a hit or a sacrifice. And by that time you were shaking anyway, because Babe Ruth was approaching. And if you got by Ruth you had to whip Gehrig who was even more dangerous because whereas Babe was just as apt to strike out as hit a home run, Lou was a wonderful all-around hitter. And then you still couldn't relax because you got Bob Meusel after Gehrig, and Tony Lazzeri who was also no slouch with his funny slouching swing that could park a ball in the bleachers. Then came Bengough or Collins, the catchers. All the Yankee pitchers could hit, especially Waite Hoyt. And then it started all over again."

The Opening Day pitcher for the Athletics was the legendary fast-baller Lefty Grove, who started off well in the early innings, fanning Combs, Gehrig, Lazzeri, and Ruth. The Yankees finished even better, scoring four runs in each of the fifth and sixth innings. Their 8–3 Opening Day triumph put them in first place, where they would remain day in and day out throughout the season.

Waite Hoyt, tabbed by Huggins to start the Yankee season, didn't disappoint, holding the powerful Athletics in check. Off and running, he would emerge as the best pitcher in the American League. Of his 32 starts that season, the Yankees would win 26. "The secret of success as a pitcher lies in getting a job with the New York Yankees," Hoyt said. It was more a truism than a brag.

Babe Ruth was the only real Opening Day negative. Hitless with two strikeouts, the Big Bam was removed from the game because he felt dizzy.

A fund of knowledge about all things, John Kieran was the first sports columnist for the *New York Times*. He wrote "Sports of the Times," the paper's first signed sports column. Kieran noted on April 14:

"Cornelius McGillicuddy is now exhibiting his white elephants at the Yankee Stadium. In addition to Ty Cobb, Mack has such brilliant side-shows as Eddie Collins, Zach Wheat, Bob Grove and Al Simmons. It's a team with which the manager hopes—only hopes—to win the AL championship of 1927. His pet pitcher, Bob Grove, was treated rather roughly by the Huggins Heavy Artillery in the opening game."

The second game was a 10–4 Yankee romp over a quartette of Mack's pitchers. Mark Koenig went an eye-catching 5 for 5.

The third game of the series against the Athletics was tied at 9–9 in the tenth inning, then called because of darkness. The Yankees won the fourth game, 6–3.

Philadelphia, a team that would bat .303 and win 9l games, a team that sported eight future Hall of Famers—Lefty Grove, Ty Cobb, Eddie Collins, Zack Wheat, Jimmie Foxx, Al Simmons, Mickey Cochrane, and Connie Mack—a team of tough losers, was just elated to skip town.

The powerful and versatile Yankee lineup was something to behold—except if you were on the opposing team.

Six different times that season of 1927 there would be five-game multiple-hit streaks. Gehrig would have three of them, and the others would be recorded by Combs, Koenig, and Lazzeri. On four different occasions a Yankee would rip five hits in one game: Combs twice, Koenig and Ruth once apiece.

The Kentuckian Earle Combs and the San Franciscan Mark Koenig served as table setters in the wonderfully balanced Yankee batting order. The southpaw-swinging Combs, one of the great leadoff batters in history, would hit .356 and lead the league in hits, singles, and triples.

The switch-hitting Koenig would bat .285 and strike out just 21 times in 586 at-bats. "Just putting on a Yankee uniform gave me a little confidence, I think," the shortstop said. "That club could carry you. You were better than you actually were. If I'd have been with a tail end club the year I came up [1925], I don't think I would have been around for 1927."

Locked into the third space was the man they called the "Mauling Monarch," Babe Ruth.

The cleanup hitter was the handsome Lou Gehrig. His power came from his big shoulders, broad back, and powerful thighs. He and Ruth gave the Yankees back-to-back left-handed power threats.

Batting in the fifth slot was the right-handed-hitting Bob Meusel, in his seventh Yankee season.

Tony Lazzeri, the team's main right-handed power hitter, batted sixth. He was in the second of what would be a dozen solid seasons as a Yankee second baseman.

"Jumping Joe" Dugan, at 30, was the old man of the infield. A right-handed hitter, he was one of the best seventh-place hitters in any major league lineup. He was salaried at $1,000 less than Meusel and $1,500 more than Combs. Only half in jest Dugan would complain:

"It's always the same. Combs walks. Koenig singles. Ruth hits one out of the park. Gehrig doubles. Lazzeri triples. Then Dugan goes down on the dirt on his can."

He also had a variation of that story that has come down through the decades. A tight game is under way. Combs triples to center, Koenig doubles to left. Ruth smashes one over the wall—a home run. Gehrig homers. Meusel doubles. Lazzeri triples. Dugan singles. Afterward, Huggins tells Dugan: "That will cost you a hundred dollars' fine."

"What for?"

"For breaking up a rally."

The eighth position in the batting order was for one of the right-handed-hitting catchers: Benny Bengough, Pat Collins, or Joe Grabowski.

Through the first three games of the season Gehrig collected 4 hits and 5 RBIs. Joe Villa in the *New York Sun* on April 15 wrote: "Huggins knew what he was doing when he benched veteran Wally Pipp in favor of the former Columbia University player."

The Red Sox were next on the Yankee hit parade, and the Bostonians went down to three straight defeats. On Easter Sunday, the Columbia strong boy Lou Gehrig slammed his first and second home runs of the season in a 14–2 Yankee rout of the Red Sox.

Then it was on to Philadelphia, where the Yanks took two out of three. Babe Ruth's second home run was recorded in the eleventh game the Yankees played, on April 23 at Philly, off lefty Rube Walberg.

Three days later, Ruth was quoted in the *New York Evening Journal*: "I don't expect I'll ever break that 1921 record. To do that, you've got to start early, and the pitchers have got to pitch to you. I don't start early and the pitchers haven't really pitched to me in four seasons. I got more bad balls to hit than any other six men—and fewer good ones."

Back in 1920, the Babe had blasted 54 round-trippers, which dwarfed the 15 hit by the Philadelphia Phillies' Cy Williams, the National League leader, that season. Ruth's 59 the next year easily surpassed the National League–leading 23 homers of George Kelly of the Giants the following season. The Bambino had never really had any competition for the home run titles.

"If I am to break my 1921 record, I believe I will do it this year," the Sultan of Swat wrote in his column in the *World*: "I'm getting a bit older now. I figure I have about five or six more years and I will have to step aside and retire. Unless I can break my record this year, I believe there are only two men in baseball who have a chance to do it. One of them is Lou Gehrig and the other is Tony Lazzeri."

It was rumored that Bozeman Bulger, a reporter for the *Evening World*, had a hand in writing the Babe Ruth column. Regarded as the clown prince of baseball writers then, the witty, large, and literate Bulger did not take himself seriously and had a cavalier attitude toward his responsibilities as a statistics-keeping official scorer. Bulger was commissioned a lieutenant colonel during World War I and was General Pershing's press officer in the Allied Expeditionary Force. Bulger also was a hero in that war, at Argonne. He made some good money, as did Damon Runyan, John Drebinger, and others who covered the Yankees, ghosting for various baseball celebrities such as Walter Johnson, John J. McGraw, Christy Matheson, and others.

Through the first 10 games, "Buster Lou" Gehrig had 19 RBIs, "Long Bob" Meusel had 14, and "Poosh 'em up Tony" Lazzeri had 13. With two weeks of the season gone, the Yankees were settled comfortably in first place. They had scored 86 runs. Gehrig, batting .447, had scored or driven in 32 of those runs.

The *Sporting News* claimed that the Yankees featured a "shoot-first, ask-questions-later attack." Primed to form the greatest one-two punch the world of baseball had ever seen, Babe Ruth and Lou Gehrig throughout a good part of the 1927 season would jockey back and forth for the American League home run lead.

"Larrupin' Lou" would be one of only five major leaguers to play in every Yankee game in 1927. He played in 155; Ruth played in 152. "Babe Ruth, Lou Gehrig, and Company" was newspaperspeak.

Damon Runyan plied his trade in the press boxes of New York City with grace and skill, always original, the main man who made the top dollars. He loved the colorful characters on the Broadway scene, the gangsters, the guys and the dolls. He also loved Babe Ruth and kept giving him nicknames. It was Runyan who coined perhaps the least famous and most colorful one—"Beezark of Kerblam"—and more famous ones, "Bam" or "the Big Bam."

"Babe Ruth was a cartoonist's dream, and his homeliness was classic," said Waite Hoyt. "No one failed to recognize Ruth, no matter where he was. Gehrig was a smooth-faced Atlas, an all-American type, a typical first boy in the seat in Sunday school."

Ruth was a wholehearted participant in the ritual and superstition that were major elements and a big part of the culture of the 1927 Yankees. But there were others with odd ways, too.

After hitting a home run, the Babe would notch his bat. But when he slugged his twenty-first four-bagger in 1927, the new notch split his bat. That ritual stopped then. Ruth always touched second base coming in from the outfield. Before games he would only warm up with catchers, and in 1927 that catcher was Benny Bengough. Ruth always said that when he saw a yellow butterfly there was big news coming—good or bad. And he claimed if he saw an empty barrel on his way to the ballpark that victory was in the offing.

Gehrig would fish for eels by himself or with his mother, who would pickle them. Lou would eat them, believing that doing so helped his batting eye.

The well-dressed Waite Hoyt, called by Ruth "a regular tailor's model," warmed up only with his starting catcher.

The least flamboyant Yankee, Urban Shocker, was very rattled if anyone ever threw a hat on a bed. He also had a fetish about his baseball glove, making sure to always keep it in a safe place, allowing no one to touch it. The Yankee hurler would especially go berserk if someone managed to lay a hand on his glove between innings when he was pitching.

Joe Dugan would always scratch out a mark at third base, a kind of security measure for him. He never threw the ball back to the pitcher, even in infield practice. He would toss the ball to the catcher or to another infielder—never to the man on the mound except for a putout. Sometimes Dugan would walk over and place the ball in the pitcher's hands. "Jumpin' Joe," who always sat next to the Babe on the bench and was one of his best friends, as the story goes, complained to Ruth for weeks about an annoying trick played on him during a game. A putout was made. Mark Koenig gave the ball to Dugan. Then Koenig, Lazzeri, and Gehrig walked to the outfield grass, turning their backs on Dugan. Frustrated, the Yankee third baseman wanted to toss the ball to Gehrig and called out his name. No response. Ditto Lazzeri. Nobody's fool, Dugan fired the ball at Koenig, hitting him in the derriere.

Probably the one who was the most superstitious on the Yankees was their 47-year-old leader, Miller Huggins, who called the 1927 club "the only team in history that did not need the breaks." He had messages delivered to the bullpen only by Mike Gazella. When Ruth batted, the little pilot sat next to the same man the Babe had sat next to before he hit his last homer. Huggins would often change his seat on the bench to change the luck of the Yankees.

Wilcy Moore, whom Huggins characterized as "cool as a cake of ice," threw his first warm-up pitch only to Eddie Bennett. Many of the players allowed nobody else but Bennett to handle their bats. Bennett, Westbrook Pegler explained, "raised the job of batboy from a summer pastime to a solemn and responsible business."

Throughout 1927 most fans talked about the Yankee offensive muscle, which was something to behold. But pitching also was paramount in the team's success. For 25 straight games, from April 29, when Dutch Ruether hurled his second shutout of the season, to May 28, Yankee pitchers allowed no home runs. Their relievers that season would make 21 different appearances, allowing no hits.

April was not the cruelest month for Yankee fans. But it did not end quite the way they wanted it to. The New York American League club wound up tied for first place with the Athletics, both having won 9 of 14 games. The White Sox, too, who finished the month in third place, seemed to have the right stuff.

And despite the ecstatic and unabashed rooting of such writers as John Kieran of the *New York Times*—"I'll lay five bucks against one thin dime there was never a team came crashing through like Ruth and the rest of the Yankee crew, like Combs, Lazzeri and Buster Lou"—the predicted runaway by Murderers' Row had not happened.

Not yet.

May

Jack Quinn, age 44, who would finally quit pitching in the majors six years later, was on the mound on the first day of May 1927 for the Athletics. A grandfathered spitball hurler, Quinn served wet ones and other exotic offerings to the Yankees that day. No matter. The New Yorkers socked him good, winning 7–3. The Babe popped two homers, one off the elderly Quinn and another off Walberg. Buster Lou smacked one, too.

The next day Wilcy "Master" Moore earned the first save of his major league career in relief of Waite Hoyt as the Yankees defeated the Washington Senators, 9–6. The 30-year-old Moore would make 38 relief appearances, record 13 saves, start 12 games, and post a splendid record of 19–7 in 1927.

It was said that one of the chief strengths of the 1927 Yankees was that they did not beat themselves. In fact, they would play 47 errorless games in 1927. But on May 5, in a loss at Washington, the Yanks committed six errors. That was atypical Yankee baseball.

When Colonel Ruppert's "Rough Riders," as some called them, were not going head to head against their American League competition, they were playing exhibition games in Buffalo, Omaha, Rochester, Columbus, Dayton, Indianapolis . . .

Everyone in the little cities and small towns wanted to catch a glimpse of the Babe, Lou, and the others. Wherever the Yankees went, there were always packed ballparks and playing fields. The team was a magnet, a syncopated jazz band playing a baseball song with the Babe leading, striking up the band with his home run baton, his bat. Whole towns came out early and stayed late, studying the moves of "the Colossus of baseball"—how he walked, how he ran, how he swung a bat, how he caught and threw a baseball, how he joked and wrestled with kids on the fields of play, how many different kinds of home runs he hit. Demand for the Yankees came from all over. Murderers' Row even played exhibition games in Pittsburgh and Cincinnati, National League cities.

In Omaha, Nebraska, Ruth—"the King of Clout"—and his protégé, Gehrig—the "Prince of Pounders"—seemed genuinely happy to make the acquaintance of one "Lady Amco" who was known as the "Babe Ruth of chickens." She was a world champ at laying eggs. The morning the Babe and the Buster met her she produced on cue, laying an egg for the 171st straight day.

In Indianapolis, the Sultan of Swat failed to homer or even swat the ball out of the infield in his first at-bats. Each time the smattering of boos and heckling became louder—all good-natured, of course. According to reports, Ruth in his fourth at-bat tagged the ball, and it leaped over the fence in right field into the street, bouncing into boxcars in a nearby freight yard. That was the story.

And its punch line: "I guess I did show those people something, make fun of me, will they," the Big Bam boomed going into the dugout.

In a dilapidated park in Fort Wayne, Indiana, before 35,000 spectators and against the Lincoln Lifes, a semipro team, the scene was all too familiar. Hundreds of kids screamed, ached to ogle, to get an autograph or just to be close to their idol, Ruth.

The Bambino, to save his legs, played first base, as was his custom many times during those exhibition games. Gehrig played right field. Going into the tenth inning, the score was tied, 3–3. Mike Gazella was on first base when Ruth stepped into the batter's box. Always the showman, signaling to the crowd that they might as well start going home, the Big Bam poked the ball over the right-field fence, giving the Yankees a 5–3 win. Hundreds of boys who had been relatively controlled and contained mobbed their idol as he crossed home plate. It was quite a while before Ruth and the Yankees could clear out of the park.

Wherever the exhibition games were staged, overflow crowds sat in the outfield, watching the action. Attendance records were broken. Mobs cheered. They roared and howled and jumped to their feet, marveling at the power and magic of the mighty Yankees and especially of George Herman Ruth.

"God, we liked that big son of a bitch. He was a constant source of joy," Waite Hoyt said. "I've seen them kids, men, women, worshippers all, hoping to get his name on a torn, dirty piece of paper, or hoping for a grunt of recognition when they said, 'Hi-ya, Babe.' He never let them down; not once. He was the greatest crowd pleaser of them all."

In a game played at Sing Sing, New York, against the prison team, Ruth slugged a batting practice home run over the right-field wall and then another over the center-field wall. "I'd love to be riding out of here on those balls," one of the prisoners joked.

During the game the Sultan of Swat turned to the crowd of cons in the stands and bellowed in that big, booming baritone voice of his: "What time is it?"

Many of the cons shouted back the answer.

"What difference does it make?" the showman Ruth yelled. "You guys ain't going anyplace, any time soon."

The Yankees were going anyplace they could play baseball. On May 26 they were at West Point. Entering the mess hall at noon to dine with the cadets for lunch, the team from the Bronx received a standing and enthusiastic ovation from the 1,200 West Pointers. Before the baseball exhibition game began at West Stadium, "Jidge" Ruth presented members of the Army nine with autographed baseballs and a specially autographed baseball to the leading ballplayer of each of the twelve companies.

The Yankees used virtually their regular lineup, except that Ruth and Gehrig switched places in the field. Earle Combs walked to start the game. Mark Koenig singled. Ruth was struck out by Army pitcher Tim Timberlake, and that got a mighty rise from the cadets.

James Harrison described the time in the *Times*: "'Aw, he didn't try to hit the ball,' said one of the cadets. 'He was just trying to make us feel good.'

"However, the truth of the matter was that the Big Bam was so eager to hit a homer for the Hudson folks that he went after bad balls which he couldn't have reached on a stepladder."

No matter. A good time was had by all, until lightning, thunder, and a soaking rain brought the festivities to a quick conclusion after just two innings. The Yanks, as usual, won another, 2–0.

It was said that the Babe got a big kick playing in exhibition games, that he liked that time to show off his skills, play without pressure, and have fun. But there was also the unpublicized financial benefit. At the beginning of his participation in exhibition gigs, Ruth received 10 percent of the gate receipts. That arrangement ballooned later to a guaranteed $2,500 against 15 percent of gate receipts.

Just how many became fans of the Yankees after attending those exhibition games cannot be measured. Just how many heard about the dramatic doings of the team and became lifelong fans of the team they were calling "Murderers' Row" is also beyond calculation.

The nickname "Murderers' Row" actually was a 19th-century reference to an isolated row of prison cells that housed some of the worst criminals of the infamous Tombs prison in New York City. But baseball-wise, the term surfaced in 1918 to characterize that year's Yankee team, one that led the league with 45 homers. It had hitters such as Frank Baker and Wally Pipp.

A newspaper story of the time explained: "New York fans have come to know a section of the Yankees' batting order as 'murderers' row.' It is composed of the first six players in the batting order—Gilhooley, Peckinpaugh, Baker, Pratt, Pipp, and Bodie. This sextet has been hammering the offerings of all comers."

The Yankees that season of 1927 had another, even more appropriate nickname: "Five O'clock Lightning." Games at Yankee Stadium began at 3:30 P.M. and were over in a couple of hours. Actually, a third of the Yankee games were played in two hours or less that season. Dutch Ruether especially helped his team keep their "time of game" average down. Among his speedy efforts were an 89-minute, 3–0 complete-game triumph over Boston on April 18; a 91-minute, 2–0 nine-inning win over Detroit on June 2; and a 92-minute, 4–1 complete-game victory over Cleveland on September 14.

Early on, opponents dared to dream of victory against the Yankees, thinking that if they got ahead early in the game, they had a good chance. More times than not, their hopes were smashed by a Yankee offensive barrage that erupted sometime around five o'clock.

"We'd beat you in the late innings," said Miller Huggins, "if not before."

Many times the Yankees had to come from behind, starting rallies, scoring many of their runs in the eighth inning, which was generally around five o'clock.

"Almost every day," Waite Hoyt recalled in his introduction to Gordon H. Fleming's *Murderers' Row*, "whether we were behind or in front, before our time at bat in the eighth, Earl came trotting in from center field yelling, 'C'mon gang. Five o'clock lightning, five o'clock lightning!'"

It was a reference to Yankee power coming into play in the late innings. It was also a reference to the five o'clock blowing of a factory whistle close by Yankee Stadium, signaling the end of the workday. The Yankees were fond of the sound of the whistle.

"It was like when I was a kid," Paul Gallico reflected in Richard Bak's *Lou Gehrig*, "and there used to be a lot of blasting going on down on Park Avenue where they were digging out the cut for the New York Central tracks.

"There would be a laborer with a plunger handle, and they would spread the mats and get ready to dynamite. There would be a nerve-wracking suspense and what seemed liked an interminable wait. But then there would be one hell of a big boom, and chunks of Park Avenue would go flying through the air. Well, it was just like that with the 1927 Yankees. You never knew when that batting order was going to push the handle down."

"The phrase 'Five O'clock Lightning' caught on," according to sportswriter Frank Graham, "spread through the league and seeped into the consciousness of opposing pitchers. They began to dread the approach of five o'clock and the eighth inning."

The Yankees could just as easily have been called "First Inning Lightning." That happened to be the most productive inning for the team, one where they would score 131 runs in 1927. The second inning, with 85 runs scored, was their least productive. The Yankees scored the most at home against Detroit, in 44 percent of their innings. At Shibe Park in Philadelphia they scored in 38.6 percent of their innings played, most on the road.

No matter the inning, no matter the nicknames, no matter where games were played and who they were played against, no matter the day or the month, the constant for the Yankees was that they were the center of the baseball universe, the team to beat, the team with Babe Ruth, Lou Gehrig, and Company, all first class, number one.

The wonderful world the team lived in was one of adoring fans, a circus of reporters, a whirl of porters and bellhops falling over each other, all anxious to please the fabled and mighty Yankees.

In their regular-season merry-go-round through the American League circuit, Yankee road hotels included Boston's Buckminster, Chicago's Cooper-Carlton, Philly's Aldine, Washington's Raleigh, Cleveland's Hollenden, Detroit's Book Cadillac, and St. Louis's Chase, where players enjoyed dinners at the Zodiac restaurant, on the top floor of the hotel.

There was a successful sameness season after season, even though there were changes in the Yankee roster. The spring training games, the regular season of 154 games playing in seven cities in 77 games on the road and 77 games at Yankee Stadium, the exhibition games bringing more cash for the Jake Ruppert coffers, the postseason World Series and afterward for some.

The leave-taking by train would be out of Grand Central Terminal or Penn Station in midtown Manhattan. The airplane belonged to the future, and there was disdain for lengthy trips by automobile or bus, which were bouncy and arduous adventures. To get to Philadelphia from New York City was an ordeal via ferry to Hoboken and then five hours over poor stretches of roads, sometimes behind very slow drivers or horse-drawn wagons. Getting from Manhattan to Washington or Boston by car was exhausting and could take up the better part of a day. Buses were not much better.

Trains were the way to go. There was the Orange Blossom Special to Florida. There was the overnight train to Boston. To St. Louis, the 24-hour trek began with a five o'clock New York City departure, and dinner at sunset. Plenty of time to talk, to sleep, to drink, to walk around, to play cards, to forge friendships.

The first Yankee road trip of the season to midwestern cities began on the sixth of May—first stop Chicago and on to Michigan Avenue and the Cooper-Carlton Hotel, called by some of the players the Cooper-Carlstein. It was a place that always had a lot of Jewish guests, and a kosher kitchen as an attraction.

Against the White Sox, the team they scored the least runs against that season, 111, the efficiency of the Yankee pitching staff was on display from May 7 to 9. New York hurlers logged 25⅓ scoreless innings. On May 7, a day on which all who spent it outdoors in Chicago shivered, the Yankees matched up against the White Sox at the remodeled Comiskey Park. The word on the street was that no one would be able to hit a home run over the heightened right-field stands.

But Babe Ruth was not no one.

A banner headline in the *Chicago Tribune* of May 8 declared, "35,000 See Yankee Stampede Sox, 8–0."

The story under a huge photograph of the packed ballpark began:

Anyone skeptical of the drawing power of George Herman Ruth, the home run king of the American League, must have been convinced yesterday. For the presence of the mighty slugger and his pacesetting colleagues was sufficient to draw 35,000 into the refurbished stands of Comiskey Park. Ruth failed to live up to his reputation as a home run hitter, getting nothing that smacked of a four base hit. But in the batting practice preparatory to the game, which the Sox lost, 8–0, the Bambino lifted a ball clear over the second tier of bleachers in right field. The crowd cheered. The architects had said that no one would ever hit a ball out of the park. But they had not counted on Mr. Ruth.

An exuberant Marshall Hunt in the *New York Daily News* went over the top in his comments: "Whang! . . . Higher, Higher! My gosh, it disappeared over the roof!"

Baseballs hit by Ruth disappeared. Players on the same team with

Babe Ruth too often disappeared in his big shadow. Sam Jones, who had played for the Yankees, knew firsthand about the shadow: "People forget that the Yankees," he told Lawrence S. Ritter in *The Glory of Their Times*, "were more than a great offensive club. They were the best defensive club in both leagues, as well. That outfield, terrific pitching, a great infield. It was a well balanced ball club in every way. Everybody played in the shadow of George Herman Ruth, of course, so a lot of people don't even remember who else was on that team."

Ludwig Heinrich Gehrig, after averaging a relatively scant 18 homers in each of his first two full seasons as an everyday Yankee, was now a superstar power hitter. He was asked how he felt playing in the shadow of the Bambino all the time.

"Babe Ruth," the diplomatic first baseman said, "has a pretty big shadow, it gives me lots of room to spread myself."

Nowhere was the Babe Ruth shadow more apparent than on that seventh day of May at Comiskey Park, the day of a Yankee romp in two hours and four minutes over the White Sox. Lost in the shadow of Ruth was a fine performance by the 32-year-old Herb Pennock, his only shutout of 1927. And lost somewhat in the shadow of Ruth was the very first home run ever hit in the made-over park, a ninth-inning grand slam off Louisianan Ted Lyons into the right-field pavilion by Buster Gehrig.

The next day, Sunday, May 8, the Yankees drew a record 52,000 to Comiskey Park. Waite Hoyt, who "appeared almost casual on the mound, never creating the impression that he was bearing down with any great amount of sweat or strain, games when the chips were down brought out the best in him," in the view of sportswriter Tom Meany, spoiled the party for the loyal Sox fans, twirling a 9–0 beauty, New York's second straight shutout of the home team. Hoyt was 5–1 with a 1.56 ERA in May, his best month. A Pat Collins seventh-inning homer and two triples by Gehrig in the game were a couple of Yankee offensive highlights.

Departing Englewood Union Station, near the corner of 63rd and State streets, the Yankees moved on to St. Louis. In one of the games Ruth struck out. Then Gehrig homered.

"There was just as much noise when Ruth struck out in the fifth as there was when Gehrig hit his home run with the bases full in the ninth. They don't pay to see Gehrig hit 'em. The fans applaud Ruth's home runs, that's his business. Not so Gehrig's. He's just a first base-man," wrote Rud Rennie, a courtly type who began writing about sports in 1925 for the *Herald Tribune*. He was a journalist skilled at writing simple, declarative leads that at times were masterpieces of understatement.

Rennie's writing about the home run duo had a similar theme all season long. "They were on the bench recently," he wrote, "Ruth squirting tobacco juice and advising the other team's catcher who had just missed a foul ball to look on the ground for it; Gehrig at the other end explaining to a friend how he speared eels at night. A group of pho-tographers approached the dugout and said they wanted a picture of Lou and the Babe. They asked Lou. 'It's all right with me,' said Lou, 'if it's all right with the Babe.'"

Outstanding baseball prospect Bill Werber had completed his fresh-man year at Duke and was able to spend a month with the 1927 Yan-kees courtesy of head scout Paul Krichell. Just 150 pounds and 5-7, Krichell's major-league playing career, as a reserve catcher with the St. Louis Browns, consisted of just 243 at-bats.

The outspoken Werber recalled in 2006,

Mr. Krichell told me to keep my eyes and ears open and learn. I lived in the Colonial Hotel in downtown New York. It was a modest place. The only other Yankee there was coach Charlie O'Leary. I suppose he stayed there because his salary was mod-est, and I suppose he was a frugal man. He had played in the majors. He was very helpful to me batting fungoes to me, taught me how to slide with my right foot.

I had no knowledge of where the other players lived. When the game was over I would take the subway and go back down-town to the hotel and have dinner. I was too damned scared to go out on the street.

The clubhouse at Yankee Stadium didn't have any food, and

there wasn't anything to drink other than water. The players never let me get into the batting cage. I was a stranger on their territory. They were rough, a hard-nosed, tobacco chewing crew. If I got in at shortstop to field a ball in batting practice they would run me out of shortstop. And when they told me to get out of the infield or outfield, well, I was observant, I did what I was told.

But I didn't feel I was in the presence of greatness, although that '27 team is considered by many to be the greatest team of all time. I did understand they were pretty rough people and they were absorbed with their own business which they should have been—and they didn't have time for me. But I can't say that I was awed. I guess you could have called me a pretty cocky kid. I didn't call myself cocky.

I liked Babe Ruth. He was a kindly man, he had a lot of things in his favor. He was lavish with his money. He was kind to kids. I had no conversations with Babe Ruth in '27. He wasn't unfriendly. He was just absorbed with what he was doing and didn't have any time for a kid.

Babe Ruth, however, did have time for kids. At the exit gates after games, kids, like bees after honey, were all over the Bambino, shoving scorecards, pieces of paper, autograph books, anything that could accommodate an autograph. He was the last Yankee to leave. Ruth obliged all. Gehrig exited. No one paid him much attention. He walked away.

"Lou Gehrig was not very convivial," according to Werber. "I don't want to say anything derogatory about him but he was all business. He was not a very friendly fellow. He was a loner. But I don't take any credit away from him for that—he was a good hustler and a great ballplayer, good to his mother."

On Wednesday, May 11, in a 4–2 win Yankee win over the St. Louis Browns, the Caliph of Clout belted a tremendous shot off Ernie Nevers that landed to the left of the center-field flagpole in the newly refurbished Sportsman's Park, at Sullivan Avenue, Dodier Street North Grand Boulevard, and Spring Street.

"Homeric Herman," gushed Martin Haley in the *St. Louis Post-Dispatch*, "careened the animated leather for a sky-scraping bulls eye into the distant center-field bleachers, the ball clattering up the icy seats at the point where the left-center and dead-center field sections conjoin."

St. Louis was one of the Babe's favorite stops. The Yankees stayed across from Forest Park at the Chase Hotel, built in 1922 and named for businessman Chase Ullman. It was a destination for upscale business and leisure travelers and baseball teams. Since electric fans did not help much to subdue the summer heat in St Louis and other hot cities and air conditioning belonged to the future, players, as a matter of course on extremely hot nights, would bring blankets out on the lawn of Forest Park, sit and talk under the stars, and finally fall off to sleep.

One of Babe Ruth's ways to keep cool off or on the ball field was to take a cabbage leaf that had spent some time in an ice cooler and spread it on his head. He taught other Yankees how to do it.

St. Louis had the Anheuser-Busch brewery, and that was one reason why the city was a favorite place for Babe and some of the other Yankees. Another was a famous whorehouse dubbed strangely enough "The House of the Good Shepherd." The word, according to Urban Shocker, was that the Babe exiting the whorehouse would always stop off next door at a bakery at about five in the morning and gulp down a dozen freshly baked doughnuts. He could never get his fill.

When the team took its leave from St. Louis from the suburban station at Brandon Avenue, "Ruth knew some people," Waite Hoyt recalled, and he'd always have a few gallons of home brew delivered to the train plus about 15 or 20 racks of spare ribs. We'd get on the train and since we had our own car," the headstrong and tempestuous Hoyt continued, "and nobody used the ladies', Ruth would take over the ladies' room and set up shop and for 50 cents you could have the beer and all the spare ribs you could eat."

Oh, what a time it was. Out of the windows of the train went empty bottles and bones from the ribs. Train tracks were littered with the debris.

There was also time for all who wanted it in the Babe's drawing room to chew on the tasty ribs, down the fresh beer, and listen and smile as the portable phonograph played Ruth's favorite talking record—the blackface comedy team Moran & Mack's "Two Black Crows." Music was always part of the drill on the long train rides, recorded or sung.

Ruth, befitting his celebrity status, traveled in a far different manner than any of his Yankee teammates. But no one had a jealous word to say—he was all the time putting money in their pockets and bank accounts. The Babe luxuriated in his private drawing room, the only player with that privilege. Fond of playing his portable Victrola or his ukulele, the big man lounged about in a satin smoking jacket and slippers, entertaining visitors.

"I never made a single trip that I didn't take with me a portable phonograph with a couple of dozen records," the superstar wrote in *Babe Ruth's Own Book of Baseball*. "And from the time we get on the train to when we leave the phonograph is working overtime."

Miller Huggins and the traveling secretary, Mark Roth, each had a drawing room. On the Yankee scene since its initial game, Roth served as the team's first traveling secretary from 1915 to 1942, and later as its first historian. When Roth was a young sportswriter for the *Boston Globe*, he and Sam Crane of the *New York Journal* were instrumental in having the team name Highlanders changed to Yankees—to better fit the needs of newspaper headline space.

Another drawing room was shared by the two coaches, Fletcher and O'Leary. And Doc Woods, whose business card stated that he was a "Trainer of Big League Baseball Clubs," had his own private space and usually a companion—his pet poodle. It was known that Woods was proficient in "forging" many Babe Ruth autographed baseballs at the slugger's request because the Big Bam found it almost impossible to keep up with demand.

The Ruppert effect—that of affording first-class treatment to his team whenever possible—showed itself in the sleeping accommodations for players. Most other teams had players, dependent on seniority, given berths, upper or lower. The players on the New York Yankees all slept in upper berths.

The whole traveling operation generally took up two cars at the end of the train. And there was many a summer day when the players, wearing only underwear (Babe Ruth, it was said, favored the silk kind), lolled about, had extended conversations, or played cards.

Without a coat, a tie, collarless, open-shirted, and having fun, a relaxed Ruth, who was partnered with Lou Gehrig, enjoyed a serious game of bridge on the train, pitted against batting practice pitcher Don Miller and utility infielder Mike Gazella.

Little guys always were favorites of Ruth. He was fond of kidding with them and pushing them around playfully. He especially liked Gazella, a Catholic like he was, and a man whose size he considered just right for playful manhandling. But "Gazook" was no push-around. Fiery and scrappy, he once chewed out the entire Yankee team at a meeting when he felt they were playing poorly.

The way the Sultan of Swat and Columbia Lou played bridge reflected their personalities. Ruth was reckless, while the Yankee first baseman took no chances. Gehrig was annoyed with the top bids of his partner. With a quart of Seagrams at the ready, Ruth felt no pain, even increasing his nipping as the card game progressed.

"We used to play poker on the trains with the Babe," John Drebinger recalled. "Five card stud. The Babe would bet like the devil, just taking wild gambles. He wouldn't drive you out, but he never folded. Always down to the last card. Most of the time we'd clean up on him. Gehrig would be sitting across the aisle, watching the game. The Babe would be throwing his dough around in this fine style and Lou would look at him and say 'My God, isn't that wonderful.'"

Gazella had a big-time reputation as a cardsharp. His salary was kind of meager, so he looked forward to any way he could pad his wallet. Ruth once played a hand of poker with "Gazook" and wound up $60 poorer. The mighty Babe never played poker with Gazella again.

George Pipgras, who was good friends with Ruth, liked to play hearts with Wilcy Moore. And there were always blackjack games that Meusel, Ruether, Lazzeri, Koenig, and Bengough and others enjoyed playing.

On those long train rides Benny Bengough sometimes played his saxophone, an instrument he tried without much success to teach Ruth to play. The slim Pennock did a lot of letter writing. Hoyt was a very serious reader, always packing a few books for road trips.

Miller Huggins smoked away on his pipe and spent a lot of time spinning old stories, checking out the business sections of newspapers for stock market insights, poring over sports sections for any new information he could glean about American League teams, complaining, and making plans with his coaches, O'Leary and Fletcher.

Bob Meusel

The Babe liked to skim the sports pages, but no one on the team was more a reader of things dealing with baseball than Urban Shocker. Newspapers were his passion. Litter from them was all over his berth most of the time—more than a dozen sports pages with parts torn out. Though dismissed by some teammates as a "newspaper hound," the crafty pitcher knew what he was doing. In Chicago he purchased newspapers from Cleveland, Detroit, and other major league American cities. He was a true student of the game and especially hitters, a one-man sports center.

"I used the time reading the papers from the next city on our schedule," he explained, "and that way I could keep book on the streaky hitters. Gave me a little edge," he explained.

Sleeping on the Pullman train rides sitting up because of a serious mitral valve disorder that prevented his sleeping lying down, Shocker told no one on the Yankees about this serious health issue. His road roomie, Eddie Bennett, kept the big pitcher's ailment a secret.

Shocker started the season slowly, splitting his first six decisions; he turned around his year on May 11 in a route-going 4–2 win over the Browns, helped by Ruth's two-bagger and eighth home run, off Ernie Nevers. Shocker, a former nemesis of the Yankees, would go 5–0 against his former Browns team (with a 2.07 ERA), tying him with Hoyt for best record against an opponent on the staff.

Getting by on guile, grit, and guts, Shocker would record only 35 strikeouts in 200 innings. But when he had to be on, he was. One of four Yankees to pitch at least 200 innings in 1927, Shocker would win 15 of his final 18 decisions, posting the third-best ERA in the league (2.84) and the second-best winning percentage (.750), a career high. A control pitcher, Shocker only allowed 1.85 walks per nine innings, lowest on the Yankee staff.

In Detroit, on May 16 it felt like a winter day, but not for Bob Meusel, who put on a running show in the third inning, swiping second, third, and home. That 1927 season his 24 stolen bases would place him second in the league. "Long Bob" was a heavy drinker, a scowler, a grunter, a bad guy. But on the move in the outfield he was a talented, graceful, and supremely competent performer. There was talk that he was turned off by fans and most of the players on the 1927 Yankees. The talk was true. But he could play baseball with the best of them, sometimes better if he felt like it.

On that May day in Detroit, Gehrig's two doubles and a homer powered the 6–2 Yankee win. Dutch Ruether pitched a complete game. Projected as the Yanks' fourth starter in 1927 and eligible for an additional incentive bonus of $1,000 if he won 15 games, Ruether seemed a shoo-in for the extra cash when he started the season 3–0 with a 1.59 ERA. But he would slump late, finishing with a 13-6 record and missing out on getting the extra grand. A handy man with a bat (.263, one home run, 19 RBIs in 1927), Ruether was the only pitcher Huggins would use as a pinch hitter, appearing 7 times and batting .333. Ruether said half kiddingly: "Do you know that I believe my whole career has been a mistake? I have had good years . . . but for all that I believe my natural position was at first base."

At Cleveland's prosaically named League Park, Babe Ruth on May 22 hit his tenth home run of the season. It was a high fly ball off righthander Benn Carr that barely made it into the stands. "George actually blushed as he loped around the bases," reported James R. Harrison in the *New York Times*. The shot was atypical for the Sultan of Swat, who generally put a charge into any ball he hit.

On May 23 Washington prevailed over New York, 3–2. The baby-faced Ruth and the dimple-cheeked Gehrig pumped back-to-back homers off Sloppy Thurston. It was one of five times that season that they accomplished back-to-backers. In a decade together, the greatest one-two punch in baseball history would homer in the same game 72 times.

The *New York World* declared: "They cheered for the two sluggers and other happenings meant little." That comment was not exactly true, but it was not that far from the mark. Up and down the lineup, the Yankees had professional hitters, clutch performers, sluggers, hit-and-run batsmen, effective bunters, gap hitters—but the Buster and the Babe that 1927 season were in a class by themselves. They knew it. So did everyone else.

Relaxed Herb Pennock, number two in the rotation, possessed of a quirky sense of humor, kept Ruth and Gehrig loose. But Pennock was not relaxed or May 27, when he lost to the Senators, 7–2. He began the season a victor in his first five games, but he just did not have it that day.

A Yankee pitching streak—one whole month, more than 25 consecutive games without allowing a home run, April 29 to May 27—ended on May 28 as Wilcy Moore gave up a homer in his first starting assignment, a 3–2 loss to the Senators in the second game of a doubleheader. The Yanks won the opener, 8–2, as Ruth ripped his 12th homer of the year, a three-run shot off Sloppy Thurston.

Although one streak ended for the Yankees on May 28, two days later they started another—the team's longest road winning streak of the year, nine games that included four straight wins in Philly, May 30 to June 1, and five in Boston, June 21 to 23.

The *New York Times* had dubbed the Ruth-Gehrig race the "Great American Home Run Derby." Like two mighty boxers, they slugged home runs, trying to outdo each other and everyone else.

"There has never been anything like it," Paul Gallico wrote in the *New York Daily News*. "Even as these lines are batted out on the office typewriter, youths dash out of the AP and UP ticker room every two or three minutes shouting, 'Ruth hit one! Gehrig just hit another one!'"

Ruth's business manager, Christy Walsh, born in Los Angeles in 1891, coined the phrase "the Babe and the Buster" for Ruth and Gehrig. Hillerich and Bradley, manufacturer of Louisville Sluggers, supplied their dealers with posters that had places for fans to mark off the homers hit by Ruth and Gehrig and keep track of their progress.

It was the reserved, young and muscular, dimpled and handsome college-educated Gehrig versus the flamboyant, older, moon-faced, in-and-out-of-trouble Behemoth of Swing, Ruth.

"There will never be another guy like the Babe," Gehrig said. "I get more kick from seeing him hit one than I do from hitting one myself."

In Waite Hoyt's view Gehrig was "A smooth-faced Atlas, an All-American type, typical first boy in the seat in Sunday school."

The Babe had that wink—he'd wink at fans in the stands, people on the street, at the opposing pitcher, at fielders on the opposition as he circled the bases totting out a home run. The winking Babe said: "This is easy. This is a lot of fun."

Babe hated authority.

Lou accepted it.

Babe loved people.

Lou was a loner, shy, suspicious.

Babe left a ten-dollar tip for a five-cent cup of coffee—sometimes a fifty-dollar tip if he was in the mood to do so, where fifty cents would have been generous.

Lou left dimes.

The good guy and the bad guy. You paid your money and you made your choice.

Crowds like never before were everywhere the Yankees went—the home run race between Ruth and Gehrig, the powerhouse that was the 1927 team, the mystique of New York in the Roaring Twenties. The Yankees were New York, and New York was the Yankees. It all was a package.

Richards Vidmer, a former minor league baseball player who wrote with style and grace for the *New York Times*, was a sophisticate and an adventurer. It was Vidmer who came up with the term for the Ruth-Gehrig battle: "The Great American Home Run Handicap."

And great it was. It was the first time Babe Ruth had ever had any real competition in a home run race. And the competition was the man who batted behind him in the potent Yankee order, who watched him from up close from the on-deck batting circle, who shook the Bambino's hand when he crossed home plate finishing the home run trot.

It was also Gehrig who was getting the publicity, who was becoming a fan favorite and a media darling.

"Holy shit, holy crap, holy moley, it was like two Babe Ruths," were the lines going around the American League. "One was bad enough but Gehrig, too."

"Babe Ruth and Lou Gehrig," Bill Werber noted, "were entirely different disposition-wise, but they both had an intense desire to win. And you'd better have the same disposition if you were on that ball club, or they were on your ass. Eating or drinking during the course of the game, you'd better not do that."

Although there were members of the fourth estate such as Bill McGeehan, the sports editor of the *Herald Tribune* who had been an impassioned and sometimes unfair critic of Miller Huggins for years, there was a closeness, a friendship, a kinship, even an affection in some cases between the writers and the players as they traveled through the summer game months on trains, in cabs, ate breakfast and dinners together, played cards in hotel rooms, or just hung out in speakeasies, in lobbies, in clubhouses.

The journalistic jock sniffing, the malice, the distrust, the crossing of the privacy line—all that belonged to the future. For good or bad, there was a community then of players and press. Baseball teams picked up the expenses of all writers traveling with the team. Players hired writers to ghost for them.

But there also was competition. Writers competed to tell the story not only of Yankee baseball, but also vied with each other in coverage of the battle for the home run title. There were arguments in the press box.

Fred Lieb had moved from the *New York Telegram* to the *New York Post*. A native of Philly, he was big on stats, inside baseball. And he knew his way around the game and its characters. He wrote later in *Baseball As I Have Known It* that there were two camps among the sporting fourth estate when it came to George Herman Ruth and Henry Louis Gehrig.

Ford Frick, Bill Slocum, and Marsh Hunt rooted for Ruth, while Lieb (who was friends with Gehrig's 220-pound mother, Christina), Arthur Mann and Will Wedge of the *New York Evening World*, who dreamed of being a poet and was very detail-oriented, openly cheered for Lou Gehrig.

Most of the baseball writers wanted Ruth to prevail. He was older, more familiar, much more likable, was how Richards Vidmer summed it up. Gehrig, for quite a few of the sportswriting guys was a Johnny-come-lately, suspicious, and not nearly as likable as the lightning rod Babe.

It was rare for more than two days to pass when a Babe Ruth or a Lou Gehrig home run was not being described in detail in a New York newspaper's sports pages. Daily pools were organized in the press box by the reporters covering the Yankees. Nine slips of paper, each one with a number signifying an inning, were deposited in a hat. Nine dollars were collected, and then the slips were picked out of the hat.

Home run, Ruth!

Bam 'em, Babe!

Home run, Gehrig!

Bust 'em, Lou!

The entire pot would be collected by the happy scribe who had the correct home run inning. There would be cheering and grumbling. And then the game would start all over again.

"I'd rather see Babe Ruth than Lou Gehrig in a tight place," manager Dan Howley of the Browns said. "Sometimes you can figure out what the Babe is going to do. But you can never tell about Gehrig. He is likely to hit any kind of ball to any field."

There were the casual and professional observations from such as Howley, and there were the pseudo-scientific comments by such as Austen Lake in the *Boston Evening Transcript*: "The Bambino does not wave it [his bat] as others do when addressing the pitcher. He flicks it with a switching motion, in his hands it becomes as responsive as a baton. . . . His combined leg, shoulders, arms and wrists motion is almost 100 per cent efficient as far as it concerns getting weight behind the swing. Ruth's bat on a missed strike usually fills a full circle and three-quarters of another. . . .

"Ruth also has that famous 'brown eye' which oculists say is unrivaled for sharpness of vision. . . . And lastly comes his co-ordination of eye, mind, and muscle, and action that is so synchronized as to be instant and accurate."

The stride of Gehrig was short, out of a stance that was like a man standing at attention. Using a compact, tight swing, holding the bat down near the knob, swinging with much force, Gehrig hit line drives straight to the seats or out of the park. Early in that magic season of 1927, he attempted to adjust his swing to make it similar to Ruth's. But he gave up on that, saying, "I'm going back to just try and meet the ball." Gehrig's was more a businesslike swing, much less fluid than that of the Colossus of Clout.

Ruth's swing was graceful, corkscrewlike. Pulling power came into it from the Babe twisting his skinny ankles. His home runs generally took a longer time to get out and had more air under them, making for high-rising drives.

"He had that uppercut swing so he never hit a hard grounder," Charlie Gehringer of Detroit recalled in Richard Bak's *Cobb Would Have Caught It*. "Gehrig would knock your legs off. But Ruth, the only thing he hit hard would be the air. But Gehrig? He'd hammer 'em."

"I use a golfing swing, loose and easy with a slight upward movement," the Babe said, comparing his approach to that of his home run twin in *Babe Ruth's Own Book of Baseball*. "Lou hits stiff-armed. Lou stands with his feet farther apart, and takes a comparatively short stride with his swing. I stand with my feet fairly close together, the right foot a little further in than the left, and take a long stride with the swing. Lou hits with his shoulders. I hit with my entire body coming around on the swing. Swinging stiff arm, too, Lou usually hits a ball on a line. The hardest balls he hits are those which travel twenty or twenty-five feet above the ground and on a line to the outfield. Any time he lifts a ball into the air (a fly ball) he loses some of the power. The balls I hit most squarely and with most power are apt to go high into the air. My home runs, for the most part, are usually high flies that simply carry out of the park. That's because I take a loose swing with a slight upward angle.

"I'm paid to hit home runs," the Babe continued. "In a way that's a handicap. I've got to swing from the heels with all the power in my body. Which isn't a good batting style."

The batting styles of Ruth, Gehrig, and the other Bombers were on display on Memorial Day in Philadelphia. And Connie Mack's Athletics made a batch of money from that display in a doubleheader at 18-year-old Shibe Park, the major leagues' first concrete-and-steel stadium. There was a morning game and a later game. Mack, always looking for the extra buck, charged separate admission prices for each game. The total attendance was 80,000.

Philly took the opener, 9–8. In that game, chunky Walter Beall saw his only action of the year for the Yankees, one inning, pitching to four batters and giving up one run. The Yanks won the second game, 6–5, and the mighty Ruth, despite his claims that he did not have such a good batting style, swung with such gusto at a pitch that he ripped the horsehide cover off half of the baseball's circumference.

May ended with another doubleheader. The weather was getting hotter and so was Murderers' Row. They slugged the third-place Athletics silly, 10–3 and 18–5. It made for a Yankee string of 23 wins in 33 games. The nightcap was a showcase for the Yankee crew as they pounded out an incredible 24 hits. Ruth homered in each game, winding up the month with a dozen homers, 16 total for the season. Gehrig singled twice, doubled, tripled, and homered in the opener. Mark Koenig and Tony Lazzeri hit home runs in the second game.

"I shouldn't say this," said Timmy Connelly, "being an umpire, but the young Eyetalian is a ball player. When things get tough over there, the others don't look to Ruth or any of the other veterans. They look to Lazzeri."

Even the great sportswriter Grantland Rice, an eloquent, dedicated, lyrical, knowledgeable and critical writer who wrote for the *Herald Tribune* and whose "The Spotlight" column was read nationally and with anticipation, was impressed with Gehrig and Lazzeri and Koenig, whom he described as "still only a trifle more than baseball kids. Two of them have less than two years experience under the big top. So here is three quarters of an infield with ten or twelve more years to go. And there is no other combination so valuable to baseball in spite of their brief experience."

The *New York Times* was especially smitten with Tony Lazzeri calling him "[one of] the craftiest, quickest-thinking players in the major leagues and a settling influence on the jittery Koenig on one side of him and the yet uncertain Gehrig on the other."

And Huggins also sang the young second baseman's praises: "I've seen a few better second basemen, but not many. He has a phenomenal pair of hands, a great throwing arm, and he covers acres of ground. He can play anyplace in the infield, can probably play the outfield, and

Babe Ruth signing balls for Japanese officers

if not restrained by force will undoubtedly attempt to pitch and catch before he is much older."

For a time in the spring of 1927, ships from the Japanese navy docked in New York Harbor. Some of the officers were invited to Yankee Stadium as special guests of the team. Babe Ruth smashed two homers, one with the bases loaded. The visitors from Japan were much taken with the colossal slugger. They had never seen anyone before who had hit a baseball the way the mighty Babe did. Seven years later, Ruth spent time in Japan and became a superhero, "the father of Japanese baseball," and whom they called "Baby Roos! Baby Roos!"

As the 1927 baseball season moved toward summer, there was a rhythm to the New York Yankees, a pace, a pride in full bloom.

"It was just a wonderful club. We could be five or six runs down and still pull out a victory. With the hitting we had, we could be six runs down in the eighth and still win," said Mark Koenig.

"It was murder," Babe Ruth bragged justifiably. "We never even worried five or six runs behind. Wham! Wham! Wham! And wham! No matter who was pitching. Wham!"

No matter the month, no matter the conditions, trampling and humbling the opposition was a way of life for the Yankees. At times, running late on the road, the team was accompanied by a police escort and rushed from train station to ballpark. Tired, hungry, the players wolfed down hot dogs, soda, peanuts, beer. Dressing quickly, they skipped batting practice and warm-ups and took the field. And they were ready.

St. Louis hurler Milt Gaston said with a sigh, "I would rather pitch a doubleheader against any other club than one game against the Yanks. There isn't a moment's mental rest for a pitcher against that batting order."

The Yankees played a game against Cleveland. Somehow, a decision was made to pitch outside to the New York left-handed hitters. That was a very bad decision, especially as far as Indian third baseman Rube Lutzke was concerned. A Ruth blast hit him in the shoulder, sinking him to the ground. A Gehrig shot smashed into the third baseman's shins. He writhed in pain. A Meusel liner made contact with Lutzke's stomach. The third baseman's teammates ran over to him as he lay on the ground.

"Are you okay?" "Are you hurt?"

The groggy and banged up Wisconsin native Lutzke responded slowly, "Hurt? Hell, a guy was safer in the Great War." That was Lutzke's final major league season. Perhaps the physical beating he took that day from the Yankees had something to do with it.

Through that fabled season, the Yankees would bat in 1,357 innings, scoring in 477 of them. That meant that 35.2 percent of the time they batted in an inning, they scored. Oddly enough in one-run games, the Yankees were just average, going 22–19. But when they were beating up on the opposition by four runs or more, they would win 54 of 63 games. In games where they beat the opposition by five runs or more, the men of Miller Huggins would post a 42–7 record.

There was so much offensive activity that the Yanks would strand 1,137 runners that season of 1927, an average of 7.34 per game. No matter; the team would outscore opponents by nearly 400 runs, average 6.3 runs and 10.6 hits per game. That was offensive firepower personified.

"When we got to the ballpark," pitcher George Pipgras said, "we knew we were going to win. That's all there was to it. We weren't cocky. I wouldn't call it confidence either. We just knew. Like when you go to sleep you know the sun is going to come up in the morning."

Even the nervous Miller Huggins was coming around as May was ending and June was looming. "I have a much better club than last year," he informed reporters, "and if we don't run into misfortunes we ought to stay on top . . . it's possible for us to take a slump at any time, but just now I'm not worrying a great deal. You see my boys are hitting the ball consistently and my pitchers are working very smoothly. The Yankees, as a team, have improved in every way."

June

The Yankee were busting out all over as June got under way. In first place on June 1, they had won 28 games and lost 14, for a .667 percentage.

On June 2, Dutch Ruether, who had been slumping, held the heavy-hitting Tigers to two hits. He had a one-hitter through eight innings. The Yanks won the game, 2–0.

"The first crooshial series to poke its nose above the placid surface of baseball will arrive this afternoon at Colonel Ruppert's Stadium," wrote James R. Harrison in the *New York Times*.

The White Sox of Chicago were coming in for a four-game series and were only a game out of first place despite all the accomplishments of the Yankees to that point in the season. Two mite managers would be pitted against each other: Miller Huggins and 5-9, 165-pound Ray Schalk of the Windy City. The ChiSox mentor had top pitching talent primed and ready for the battles: Alphonse Thomas, Red Faber, Ted

Blankenship, and Ted Lyons. Huggins was countering with prime pitching of his own. The series was promoted as a matchup of the best staffs in the American League, which it was. But the Yankees had the Sox beaten hands down when it came to offense: their team batting average was 25 points higher than that of Chicago.

Alphonse "Tommy" Thomas was the top pitcher in the American League at that point in the season with a record of 10–2 and a five-game winning streak. Entering the Stadium with a smile, Thomas asked: "Where is the fellow named Ruth? I am anxious to meet him."

He met Ruth. He also met Gehrig. Both sluggers slugged back-to-back homers in the fourth inning off him, pacing the 4–1 Yankee victory that increased their lead over Chicago to two games. Waite Hoyt scattered seven hits, struck out four, and picked up the win.

The next day, Wednesday, June 8, both "five o'clock lightning" and Tony Lazzeri were on big-time display for the 20,000 attendees at the Stadium. Things looked good for Chicago for a while. Ruether, Moore, and Giard had taken their lumps on the mound. The Yankees came to bat in the ninth inning needing five runs to tie. It was a bit late in the day for five o'clock lightning, but better late than never. The inning was typical of so many the Yankees had and would put forth all season long: Combs singled. Dugan fouled out. Ruth singled. Gehrig doubled off the right-field screen, Combs scoring. Durst, filling in for the injured Meusel, ripped the ball past second, both Ruth and Gehrig scoring.

Lazzeri had already pumped out two home runs in the game. The heavily tanned second baseman came up now in the ninth, digging in. The crowd was screaming for Tony to produce. And they were not disappointed.

Lazzeri smacked a two-run home run, his third dinger that day. The game was tied. In the eleventh inning, the Yankee bench prevailed. Durst tripled. The White Sox had had enough of Tony Lazzeri, and walked him. Morehart singled home Durst. Final score: Yankees 12, White Sox 11.

Game three of the series took place on a beautiful and breezy Bronx day, June 9. Two Yankee runs in the sixth inning, Ray Morehart's three-run homer, and Ruth's triple and steal of home in a six-run seventh inning put the game away for the home team. Pennock stayed the distance in the 8–3 victory.

The White Sox limped out of Yankee Stadium on June 10 with but one win in the "crooshial" four-game series. Chunky Ted Lyons, 26, in the fifth year of what would be a 21-year career with Chicago, scattered five hits, gaining his eighth straight win, his eleventh in 13 tries, after a trio of his team's best hurlers had tried and failed. Urban Shocker, who took the loss for the Yankees, was not as nifty.

Losing three of four to the Yankees in the big ballpark close by the Harlem River, enduring the shouts and squeals of their fans, Ray "Cracker" Schalk was just happy to get out of town. His parting shot: "Yankee Stadium was a trick field." Translation: it favored all the sluggers of Murderers' Row.

Baseball fans in general thrilled to the daily doings of the master swatters of the age, as some journalists called the Yankees. But to be an opponent of the New York Yankees and to feel like a punching bag sometimes got to be too much.

Too much happened for the Indians on June 11. Ruth poked two consecutive home runs (numbers 19 and 20) off southpaw Garland Buckeye. One shot was classically Ruthian, landing behind the 461-foot mark and six rows back, in center field. Cleveland catcher Luke Sewell was dismayed and angered. When the Babe came to bat again, the backstop suggested that perhaps it might be a good idea if the umpires checked out the Bambino's bat for lead that somehow might have gotten inside the wood. They checked. And so did Sewell, balancing and even smelling the big bat. Nothing illegal was found by Sewell or the umpires. But Ruth's home run show was over for that day. And as was generally the case, another Yankee took up where the famed clouter left off.

This time it was Tony Lazzeri, who hammered away at a ball that, in the words of James Harrison of the *Times*, wound up "beyond the cinder track and fled into the bull pen, hiding coyly under a green bench." New York won, 6–4.

On Sunday, June 12, the Bam thrilled the Stadium faithful yet another time, smashing his 21st homer in his 53rd game. Righty George Uhle, a friend of the Babe's, was the victimized hurler.

The next day, June 13, was one of the great testimonial days in the history of New York City. Millions cheered as a ticker-tape parade welcomed Charles A. Lindbergh, who had defied death and gained immortality flying the *Spirit of St. Louis* solo across the Atlantic Ocean to Paris.

Once an unknown, the 25-year-old "Lucky Lindy" was now too well known for some tastes. It was claimed in some quarters that the young aviator was a bigger star than Babe Ruth, if one could believe that.

Mark Koenig did not. The Babe, the Yankee second baseman argued, was larger than Charles Lindbergh, larger than life. "My God, the way people would come from all over to see him. You had to be there to believe it."

You had to be in New York City that day to believe the fuss made about the peerless pilot. "Colonel Lindbergh, New York City is yours," Mayor Jimmy Walker told him at the City Hall lovefest. "I don't give it to you. You won it."

Lindbergh rode bareheaded in an open automobile in what in later times was to be called the "Canyon of Heroes." There were estimates that 4 million people were there to see him and that many tons of confetti were showered on him.

At the Stadium that day, the Yankees were pitted against Cleveland. Lou Gehrig, with a .394 batting average, 14 homers, and an incredible 60 RBIs, torqued the Yankee dynamo. The 20,000 diehard fans who definitely cared more about their team than about seeing Lindbergh had a good time seeing New York pulverize the Indians, 14–6. Native Alabaman Ben Paschal had one of his greatest days in baseball, ripping two homers (he had but 24 in his career), a triple, and a double, and scored five times. Lazzeri and Dugan also homered, while Collins contributed a grand slam. The victory triggered the longest Yankee winning streak of the season: nine games.

June 14 was a rainy day, and the Yankees did not play. Their lead over the second place White Sox was five games. At this point in their sensational season, the Yankee lineup caused extreme stress to any pitcher who had the misfortune to face it. It was truly Murderers' Row, a killing squad with thunder aplenty. As the admiring members of the

New York press kept pointing out, if one of the Yankees sluggers didn't hurt the opposing team, another one would. You could count on it.

Big bats and pitching paraded at Jake Ruppert's big ballpark on June 15. Southpaw Tom Zachary, pitching for the St. Louis Browns, felt the sting of the Yankee bats. Ruth slashed his 22nd homer, a two-run shot. Gehrig followed with his 15th. Waite Hoyt went the distance in the 8–1 triumph.

The next day, Charles Lindbergh was scheduled to be the honored guest at Yankee Stadium for the game with the Browns. Three field boxes had been specially primed, painted, and prepared for his visit. The atmosphere was anticipatory for the 15,000 fans. A brigade of police were in the aisles and more men in blue were in the bleachers. But as game time approached, no sign, no word about "Lindy."

Game time, start time, came.

Game time, start time, went.

Umpire George Hildebrand, who had broken into the majors as a pitcher with the Brooklyn Superbas (later the Dodgers) in 1902, held up the first pitch for 25 minutes. Finally, at 3:55 P.M., he decided he could wait no more and ordered the game to start.

"I feel a homer coming on," Babe Ruth had told everyone who would listen. "My left ear itches. That's a sure sign. I had been saving that homer for Lindbergh and then he doesn't show up. I guess he thinks this is a twilight league."

In his first at-bat in the first inning, with two strikes on him, the Bambino clouted number 22 off the 31-year-old Zachary. Ruth seemed to always have the North Carolinian's number. The monster shot wound up halfway up the left-center field bleachers. Gehrig followed Ruth with a home run to almost the same spot.

"I held back as long as I could," the Babe said later. "But it had to come. When you get one of those things in your system, it's bound to come out."

The Yankees prevailed once again, this time 8–1 over the hapless Browns.

A headline the next day in the *Times* blared: "Lindbergh Got to Paris on Time but Was More Than an Hour Late to See Babe Ruth Hit a Home Run Yesterday."

Lindbergh reached Yankee Stadium after the game was over, according to the *Times*. Six police on motorcycles flanked his car, and the whole motorized party drove right onto the playing field, and aided by a wedge of 500 police, slowly made its way through hundreds of supercharged fans. The car stopped before owner Jacob Ruppert in his field box. According to the *Times*, the crowd boomed out "Lindy, Lindy, Lindy!"

The colonel and the aviator shook hands. Lindy rushed back to his car, and it moved slowly behind walls of police, who cleared the way out of the stadium for him. It was reported that Lindbergh offered no apologies or excuses for his lateness.

Another report, this one in John Mosedale's *The Greatest of All*, claimed that when "Lindy" finally arrived at the stadium, Ruth was showering and Ruppert told Lindbergh, "It's too bad you couldn't have gotten here earlier."

And Lindbergh's reply: "Who won?"

Another report, in Leigh Montville's *The Big Bam*, claimed that Lindbergh's "motorcade did not reach the stadium until 5:30 P.M. and then he decided they should skip the visit and get back to the Hotel Breevort, where he picked up a $25,000 prize.

The Yankees had their eyes on another prize, pulverizing the competition with their power. But the versatile and talented team had other ways to win aside from the long ball. They also won with pitching, "small ball," defense, unlikely heroes, their supporting cast.

The defense was on parade on June 17 in a 3–2 Yankee win. "Six times Earle [Combs] chased far into the distance to pull down long drives and turn seeming runs into putouts," Ford C. Frick wrote in the *New York Evening Journal*.

One of those who was an unlikely Yankee hero was Myles Thomas, the best-hitting hurler on the Yankee staff in 1927, with a .333 batting average, including .357 at Yankee Stadium. But with a surfeit of top-drawer pitching on the roster, the stubby Thomas was not given much opportunity to work. The 30-year-old got the bulk of the little work he did get in June, when he posted a 5–1 record with a 4.19 ERA in six starts and three relief appearances. He was the victor in a game against the Browns at Yankee Stadium on Saturday, June 18, aided by Lou Gehrig, who belted two home runs and drove in five runs in the 8–3 triumph.

"Lou Gehrig has made it inadvisable to walk Ruth," Rud Rennie wrote in the *New York Herald Tribune*. "There is no percentage in walking Ruth, when Gehrig, the next man up, is hitting 50 points or so better that Ruth is and just as likely to place the ball in the stands."

The Babe and the Buster copped the headlines, but the supporting cast sometimes did much more than just support. Examples of this were evident daily.

Cruising in a doubleheader at Fenway Park on June 21, the Yanks were victors by 7–3 and 7–1 over the BoSox, the team they would score the most runs against that season (171). That made it 6 straight, 17 of 21. Pennock in the opener allowed six hits, and Hoyt with his 10th win in 13 decisions gave up just five hits and cruised in the nightcap.

Before the second game, Tony Lazzeri was honored by Boston's Italian American community and presented with a special ring. That night a testimonial dinner was staged. Speechmakers placed the young Yankee second baseman in the same company as Mussolini and Columbus. The *New York Times* reported: "He didn't discover America but Columbus never went behind third for an overthrow to cut off the tying run in the 9th inning."

Time magazine called Lazzeri "the craftiest, quickest thinking player in the major leagues."

"Tony was a nice kid," his keystone infield partner, Mark Koenig, said. "He didn't say much but he had a temper. You couldn't say anything against him. Once I was in infield practice and I called him a Sicilian. Boy, he got madder'n hell. He was gonna kill me."

"Lazzeri had epileptic fits," Koenig remembered, "but never on the ball field. He'd be standing in front of the mirror and combing his hair. Suddenly the comb would fly out of his hand and hit the wall."

The Yankee second baseman rarely shaved in the bathroom, fearful of falling backward and hitting his head on the floor. One time Koenig, who roomed with him on the road, recalled he did shave in the bathroom and fell backward. Koenig dashed out of the hotel room rushing to get help from trainer "Doc" Woods, who got things under control.

Tony Lazzeri was usually under control, a magnet for more and more new fans of Italian extraction who made their way to Yankee Stadium and other parks to see one of their own background. They brought along wicker baskets loaded with fruit, sandwiches, cheese, and bottles of wine.

"He was tall, lean, square-shouldered, and for all his comparatively slight build, extremely strong and durable," noted sports writer Frank Graham Jr. Born in Harlem, Graham worked for the *New York Sun* from 1915 to 1934, moving on from there to other newspapers and magazines. "[Lazzeri] had a face," Graham continued, "like those in the paintings of the Italian Masters—olive-skinned, oval, with high cheekbones and smoldering eyes. He spoke seldom."

But he did have a playful way about him and especially enjoyed giving hotfoots to teammates when they were reading a newspaper or otherwise killing time. Or he'd set fire to the corner of a newspaper.

June 1927 was a month when the Yankees and Tony Lazzeri were on fire. It was also a month for doubleheaders. The Yanks played 4 of them in six days, from June 21 to 26. All told that season, they would play 18 doubleheaders, 10 at Yankee Stadium and 8 on the road, 4 of which were at Fenway. They would win 8; lose 1 to Philadelphia; and split 9.

On June 22, Ruth homered twice off lefty Hal Wiltse of Boston, moving his total to 24. The second homer was a jackhammer shot sending the ball out of Fenway into a vacant lot, where it banged against a garage wall; two boys and six men battled for the souvenir.

The next day, June 23, Lou Gehrig took over, triggering the ninth-straight Yankee victory, an 11–4 romp over the Red Sox. The Yankees had 15 hits and 26 total bases. Their record was now a glittery 44–17. The Yankee strongman slammed three home runs, becoming the 20th player in history to accomplish that feat. There was a two-run shot in the second inning, and solo homers in the sixth and eighth innings. It was also the first time anyone had ever slugged three dingers in one game at Fenway Park. "Columbia Lou" now had a season total of 21 and was just 3 behind Ruth.

Baseball's first true home run race was under way.

James R. Harrison's story in the *New York Times* the next day began: "On a balmy summer afternoon in Boston, Henry Louis Gehrig, son of Columbia, scaled the dizzy heights by hitting three home runs in one game, the second Yankee to turn the trick this season." Lazzeri was the other one. "They were as handsome and as far as any man has ever hit in one game," continued Harrison, describing the work of the Iron Horse that day.

Winning was the Yankee way. There were, however, a couple of small glitches along the way that season, but there always was a correction. They had one three-game losing streak (June 25–26) and one four-game losing streak (August 19–22).

But in that magic and momentous season there were many more highs than lows for the Yankees, including a longest home winning streak, of 14 games—3 over Philadelphia and 4 over Boston (June 26–July 2), 3 over Washington (July 4 and 5), and 4 over St. Louis (July 26–28).

In the July 26 game at St. Louis, the Yankees scored nine runs in the eighth inning in a 12–3 cakewalk, equaling the nine-run sixth inning they put up on July 4 in a 21–1 whacking of Washington.

Along the way some of the players had to cope with minor injuries, nagging aches and pains. Tending to a sore right knee, the Babe missed his third straight game, on June 28. John Grabowski also did not play that day against Philly. But fans from his hometown of Schenectady, New York, presented him with $1,500, showing their appreciation for his Yankee accomplishments. Grabowski took the money gladly— he made only $4,000 more in salary that entire season. Despite an eight-run ninth-inning rally by the Athletics, the Yanks won, 9–8, pushing their lead to 10 games. Gehrig homered for the 23rd time in 1927.

In 1926 the Babe had first taken up residence in a twelve-room suite at the Ansonia Hotel, a posh New York City residence at 2109 Broadway, at 73rd Street. The odd-looking, cavernous edifice was a destination for visiting baseball teams, gamblers, loose women, bootleggers, celebrities, and assorted characters. To accommodate this assemblage, many exits and entrances to the hotel were available. That pleased the hyperactive Ruth immensely, because it enabled him to leave and return attracting only as much attention as he wished. In New York

City—the city that never sleeps—George Herman Ruth was right at home.

Helen Woodforth Ruth, a waitress he met in Boston and married in 1921, was the Babe's first wife. They had adopted a baby girl named Dorothy. It was rumored that Dorothy was Ruth's biological child, the product of an affair between him and a longtime family friend.

By 1927 his marriage to Helen was virtually finished, and Dorothy was in boarding school. More footloose now than ever, wheeling around in his 12-cylinder Packard up and down Riverside Drive to and from Yankee Stadium, cruising carefree about town, winding up at the Ansonia in the early morning hours when his carousing was complete, the Bambino was having a hell of a time.

Most of the other Yankees rented apartments in big buildings along the Grand Concourse, not far from the stadium. Benny Bengough, it was reported, had a nifty apartment on 181st Street and Broadway. Ed Barrow also lived on the Upper West Side, in a home on Riverside Drive. "Jumpin' Joe" Dugan was an exception to the rule. He lived out of the city in ritzy Scarsdale, in New York's Westchester County. "Of course, what else? I was a Yankee," the wisecracking third baseman said.

"Nobody with the Yankee club seems to know much about the Babe's unofficial activities," wrote Westbrook Pegler. "He runs alone and what he does are of no interest whatsoever so long as he shows up at the yard no later than 1:30 P.M. and hits home runs."

He was known to consume half a dozen hot dogs and drink half a dozen beers at a time. He had his own cigar company, "Babe Ruth Cigars," with his picture on the wrapper of each stogie.

It was claimed that he was the top slugger of all time when it came to flatulence and hearty belches. Frank Graham wrote: "He was a very simple man, in some ways a primitive man. He had little education, and little need for what he had."

Joe Dugan may have put it best about Babe Ruth: "To understand him, you have to understand this. He wasn't human. No human being could have done the things he did and lived the way he lived and been a ballplayer. Cobb? Could he pitch? Speaker? The rest? I saw them. I was there. There was never anybody close. When you figure the things he did and the way he lived and the way he played, you got to figure he was more than animal even. There was never anyone like him. He was a god."

Ruth arose when he felt like it; most times he was the last Yankee to arrive in the clubhouse. Trainer Doc Woods or Eddie Bennett always had bicarbonate of soda at the ready. Still in street clothes, the spindly-legged six-footer would quickly measure out a mound of bicarb, mix, gulp, and be ready to go.

Led by the Babe, the Yankees were also always ready to go. Powering their way through the season, pounding all comers, personifying the mood of the times, the Yankees basked in their celebrity status. They sang, they roared "Roll Out the Barrel." And they let the good times roll on. They were the 1927 Yankees!

After victories there would be singing in the showers and noisy celebrating continuing in upscale restaurants or speakeasies, depending on what the players were in the mood for. Prohibition banned commerce in liquor. But liquid was there for the taking for those who wanted it, needed it, in more than 100,000 venues in the city.

Nicknamed "the Peter Pan of baseball" because of his lively ways, Benny Bengough liked after-hours activities. "We liked to go out at night," the catcher said. "But we all went out together."

George Uhle was a 27-year-old Cleveland pitcher in 1927, and he hobnobbed a lot with the Babe. "Ruth had good connections," Uhle said in *Cobb Would Have Caught It*, by Richard Bak. "Everybody liked him. He liked a lot of fun. And of course, the places that were cheating, the speakeasies, they were tickled to death to have *Babe Ruth* come there. They'd put us in a side room so the public wouldn't know he was drinking there. There was a place in New Jersey, for instance, that had an upstairs room where they served good beer and had really good food. Babe would invite a player or two from the other ball clubs and take them over."

As the story goes, according to a writer of the times, the Babe would summarize the entire history of the United States this way:

"Columbus, Washington, Volstead, two flights up, and ask for Gus."

Voluminous mail was the order of the day for the players on Murderers' Row and especially for the one some called "the Behemoth of

Bust." And there was less and less room to contain the flood of mail, so an extra locker especially for all correspondence addressed to Ruth was brought in. Many letters were just vulgar. Many letters contained outlandish requests or crazy get-rich schemes. The Babe ignored many letters, but some he answered, especially those that came from young boys seeking an autograph.

"Open these for me, will ya?" the Yankee icon would ask anyone who was handy. "Keep the ones with the checks and the ones from the broads. And throw out the rest."

Once trainer Doc Woods went through a garbage basket loaded with dumped mail. He discovered $6,000 in checks and endorsements.

Women were one of life's top priorities, some said the most important priority, for the Yankee slugger of sluggers. There were "Babe Ruth Suites" in hotels where liquor, women, partying, and sex were always present in one way or another, in one order or another, and where George Herman Ruth was always on top of his game.

At one of the wild parties where the joint was jammed with a crowd of attractive young women and players, as the story goes, seizing the moment, savoring the time, perhaps a bit tipsy, the Babe climbed atop a piano and bellowed at the women:

"Okay, girls, anyone who does not want to get fucked now can leave!"

There was another widely circulated story that the Bammer laid eyes on a pretty woman, an admirer, who had an infant cradled in her arm.

"You'd better watch out," he told her, "or I'll put one on the other arm, too."

"Babe," wrote Fred Lieb, "was inherently a Phallus worshipper. It cropped up regularly in his conversation. His phallus and home run bat were his prize possessions in that order."

Bill Werber, a wide-eyed college kid, was astonished peering once through the transom into Babe Ruth's suite to discover the Yankee icon simultaneously and happily involved with both a cigar and a woman.

One of the more widely circulated stories about him was that he once broke a batting slump by staying out all night and partying, and in the game the next day hit two home runs.

The life Babe Ruth led was not the way of life for all Yankees, for most, even if they wanted to, never would have kept up with his appetites, excesses, and exploits.

Actually, there were three groups on the 1927 team: the movie set, the late-night set, and Babe Ruth. The movie set was composed of those players who displayed a conservatism when it came to sex, cursing, and liquor. Charter members were Wilcy Moore, Lou Gehrig, Earle Combs, Cedric Durst, Ben Paschal, and Herb Pennock.

The life of Pennock, whom sportswriter Will Wedge called "the aristocrat of baseball," was one of normalcy, especially compared to quite a few others on the team. Happily married since 1915, he and his wife, his former high school sweetheart, and their children lived in an apartment on the Grand Concourse during Yankee summer home stands. Mrs. Pennock often traveled with the team and was with "the Squire" in spring training.

Controlled, in charge, philosophical about his pitching craft, the veteran Pennock even had his own "Ten Commandments for Pitchers":

1. Develop your faculty of observation.

2. Conserve your energy.

3. Make contact with players, especially catchers and infielders, and listen to what they have to say.

4. Work everlastingly for control.

5. When you are on the field, always have a baseball in your hand and don't slouch around. Run for a ball.

6. Keep studying the hitters for their weak and strong points. Keep talking with your catchers.

7. Watch your physical condition and your mode of living.

8. Always pitch to the catcher and not the hitter. Keep your eye on that catcher and make him your target before letting the ball go.

9. Find your easiest way to pitch, your most comfortable delivery—and stick to it.

10. Work for what is called a rag arm. A loose arm can pitch overhanded, side-arm, three-quarter, underhanded, any old way— to suit the situation at hand.

Unlike Pennock, Babe Ruth was often out of control, doing things his way, alone, away from the playing field. It was rare that the Yankee slugger shared his play time after dark with other Yankees. He had his own way to make. If good friends were not around to drive him, he usually took a taxi by himself to a hotel, a ballpark, or a railroad station. The hotel dining room or a soft chair in a hotel lobby were favorite places for most players, but not for Ruth. He was seldom seen in either location.

Fred Lieb wrote that the kind of girls the Babe selected as his favorite playmates were "Mostly prostitutes, who in the 1910s and 1920s spoke of themselves as sporting girls." They were certainly sport for Ruth, who had telephone numbers of girls in all the big cities. He also knew intimately the red light districts in even the smallest of towns. "Some of his visitors," wrote Lieb, "were semi-pros, bored women who came to him out of curiosity, and some were amateurs."

They weren't exactly an odd couple, but for a time—which ended in about midseason—Babe Ruth and Dutch Ruether were roommates on the road. Then, in an attempt to brake—or break—some of the late-hour mayhem and carousing on the part of the "Goliath of Grand Slams," Yankee officials gave the guy who loved the high life what was referred to as a "sumptuous suite" in the team's hotel.

It seemed like a good idea, but it didn't quite work out. The suite stimulated the Babe's social doings. It was estimated that on some nights as many as 250 visitors came a-calling, to hobnob, talk baseball, drink, party, whatever.

Waite Hoyt recalled, "Ruth would retire to his suite and change into a red moiré dressing gown and red Moroccan slippers." A long 60-cent cigar protruded from his lips, making the big slugger look, in Hoyt's phrase, "for all the world like the Admiration Cigar trademark." He also smoked pipes, cigarettes occasionally, and used enough snuff for any other two players. Author Robert Creamer wrote: "He had the constant need to placate his mouth with food, drink, a cigar, chewing gum, anything."

As June moved toward its end, the Yankees hit a little bump in the road. Against the Philadelphia Athletics, off whom they hammered 26 home runs that season, the most off any opponent, they lost three in a row for the only time that season, June 25–26 at Yankee Stadium.

Snapping out of it, the Yankees closed out the month with their 5th straight win in their 70th game of the season on June 30. Just 3,000 fans showed as the home team sent the Red Sox to their 12th straight defeat, 13–6. Lou Gehrig stroked his 25th homer in the first inning, one that bounced into the stands off righty Slim Harriss. Gehrig wound up with a three-hit day and stole home.

Ruth also did Harriss in, golfing his 25th circuit shot in the fourth inning. The win, one in which they tallied 19 hits, gave the Yankees a 49–20 record.

One of the big hit songs of 1927 was George and Ira Gershwin's "'S Wonderful." Everything 's wonderful was the way the New York Yankees and their fans felt as the season turned into July.

SUMMER

It isn't a race in the American League, it's a landside.

—John Kieran, *New York Times*

July would be the best of all months for the 1927 Yankees. They would win 24 of 31 games and stitch together their longest winning streak of the season, 9 games.

In first place, where they had been all season, flying, unstoppable, cocksure, determined, and proud of what they were accomplishing, they played on.

And Gehrig and Ruth especially played on. Ruth played off Gehrig, and Gehrig played off Ruth. They both gave opposing pitchers fits and the fans delight. The pennant race was over. It had actually been over before it began.

But the home run derby was in full throttle, mesmerizing more and more baseball fans day after day. Gehrig and Ruth, Ruth and Gehrig. Neither man could gain significant separation from the other as they took those mighty swings that baseball summer. And what separation there was, was never more than two home runs for much of the season.

JULY

On the first day of July, the Yankees faced the hapless Red Sox. The Buster and the Babe were tied, with 25 home runs each. Gehrig slammed a home run to pace the 7–4 Yankee win, the 13th straight defeat for Boston. That game was a marker moment for the Bammer—the first time since 1922 that he trailed a rival on that date in the home run race.

"There's only one man who will ever have a chance of breaking my record, and that's Gehrig. He is a great kid," the King of Clubbers said.

Whenever Ruth hammered a homer, Gehrig waited at home plate to shake his hand as he rounded third and touched home plate. If Gehrig homered with Ruth on base, the two would trot around the bases. The Babe waited for Lou to touch home. Then the happy pair, like two schoolkids, smiling all the way, would enter the Yankee dugout to the cheers of their adoring fans, to the congratulations of their teammates.

The younger Gehrig said: "There will never be another guy like the Babe. I get more of a kick out of seeing him hit one than I do from hitting one myself. I'm just fortunate enough to be close to him."

The older Ruth said: "Gehrig is one of the greatest fellows in the game and a real home run hitter."

But Tony Lazzeri, who knew the score all too well, noted: "They didn't get along. Gehrig thought Ruth was a big-mouth and Ruth thought Gehrig was cheap. They were both right."

Despite Lazzeri's comments, there was no public animosity, no obvious jealousy, no enmity evident between the pair. Ruth even had a kind of big-brother, semipaternalistic interest in Gehrig. "This college kid," the Babe said, "is one of the queerest ballplayers I ever knew. It seems he never feels the cold weather. The coldest day in winter he'll come swinging down Broadway without an overcoat, his coat open and no vest. Never wears gloves and half the time goes bareheaded. Some of the boys claim he never had an overcoat on his shoulders until he joined the Yankees."

They were known in the media and by the fans as the "home run twins." But when it came to who was the favorite, it was no contest.

Ruth struck out in a game, and Gehrig followed with a homer. Afterward, at the exit gate, kids swarmed all over the Big Bam with adoring looks and cheers, scorecards, pieces of paper, autograph books. Ruth obliged all of them. No one paid Gehrig much attention. Seemingly content, he walked away and down the street.

"Babe and Gehrig were entirely different dispositionwise," Bill Werber said. "But they both had an intense desire to win. And you'd better have the same disposition on that ball club, or they were on your ass. Eating or drinking during the course of the game, you'd better not do that."

Their lockers were just a few feet from each other, and like all the rest at Yankee Stadium, their names were printed in white chalk near the top. The Yankee first baseman's locker was orderly. The Yankee outfielder's locker was the opposite and overflowing with telegrams, letters in the hundreds, salves and balms and toiletries, phonograph records of "Babe and You." The top of the locker had a green gourd about five feet long on it. After games ended, Gehrig sat on a stool in front of his locker, dressed quickly, and left. Ruth hung around. Sometimes he sat on a stool but most times he stood, enjoying the give-and-take with reporters.

Gehrig's style was totally opposite Ruth's. Although "Columbia Lou" was salaried for 1927 at $7,500, he drove a used $700 Peerless Packard and lived on West 133rd Street in a spare but pleasant apartment with his cheerful mother and his sluggish father, who had sustained a head injury while employed in a steel mill. Pop Gehrig became a caretaker in a tenement house. Because he suffered from epilepsy, Mama Gehrig frequently attended Yankee games without him.

A powerful presence, strong-willed, the heavy-set Christina Gehrig packaged her pickled eels for clubhouse gorging for her son and other Yankees. Her delicious spreads featured specialties such as stuffed pig, turkey, and goose replete with all the trimmings. These feasts brought

Lou Gehrig with his mother, Christina

"Mom's boys"—Babe Ruth, Benny Bengough, Joe Dugan, Tony Lazzeri, Mark Koenig, and others—to the apartment. They all shared a love for Lou's mom and for her home cooking and homemade beer. Ruth enjoyed speaking German with Mom and Pop and Lou.

Mama Gehrig made it clear that she did not want her "Louie," who was always "a good boy," to associate with what she thought were bad characters. She also sought to keep him away from single young women.

Ill at ease in the company of women, viewed as a virgin by reporters and teammates, the young Gehrig spent as many nights as possible with his parents. He enjoyed fishing by himself or with his father. He also was content to spend hours by himself riding the roller coaster in Rye Beach, in nearby Westchester County. On the road, Gehrig's roomie was catcher Benny Bengough, five years older than he. The pair had become Yankees in the same year: 1923.

Now, four years later, on July 2, 1927, they were still teammates. On this day, Dutch Ruether nipped Boston, 3–2, for the seventh straight Yankees win. A BoSox killer, the veteran Ruether would defeat them four times in 1927, half of them shutouts. Boston's manager, William Cardigan, saddled with a very losing team, was still upbeat. "A new week will dawn tomorrow," said he.

Cardigan was correct. Tomorrow his club did not have to play the Yankees.

In an odd bit of scheduling, the Yankees headed to the nation's capital to play a single game against Washington on July 3, and then back to Yankee Stadium for a Fourth of July doubleheader. In the July 3 game, the Babe cracked number 26 off righty Hod Lisenbee. It was the mightiest homer to that time at Griffith Stadium, deep into the center-field bleachers, a dozen rows from the top. But Washington was able to eke out a 6–5 win.

The Senators had now won 10 straight, leapfrogging the Philadelphia Athletics and the Chicago White Sox and taking possession of second place, 10 games behind the Yankees.

D.C. buzzed with talk that its team was making a push.

The Yankees were disdainful of such banter.

At the Fourth of July doubleheader, the largest baseball crowd in history to that time—72,641 plus 1,500 "deadhead" (nonpaying) patrons—surged into the huge ballpark. Before the game, thousands had clogged the avenues and streets around Yankee Stadium, hoping to purchase the few remaining standing-room only tickets. Most were turned away. Every seat in the grandstand and bleachers was sold.

"The crowd ringed itself four and five deep at the back of the stand," wrote James R. Harrison. "Intent on seeing the Yankees in action, spectators overflowed into runways and aisles, forsaking comfort and safety squishing themselves into "the House That Ruth Built."

The Yankees clubbed Washington, 12–1 in the first game. That was just a warm-up. The Yankees humiliated the Senators, 21–1 in the nightcap. Headlines in the *New York Times* the next day summed up what had happened: "74,000 Watch Yankees in Double Victory: Record crowd at the Stadium in Delirium of Joy as the Senators are Crushed 12–1, 21–1."

And "Gehrig Hits Two Homers: Gets No. 27 in Opener with Two on, Passing Ruth; No. 28 in Final with Bases Full."

George Pipgras and Wilcy Moore went the distance in each game. Joe Dugan stroked four hits in four at-bats in game one. Julie Wera hit the only home run of his major league career. Tony Lazzeri rapped out four hits in the nightcap. Not only did Lou Gehrig with two homers in the first game move past Ruth in their personal home run derby, but Washington hurlers were also unable to retire the Iron Horse until his ninth and final at-bat in the double bill.

Jumping to conclusions the next day, the *New York Telegram* headlined, "The Odds Favor Gehrig to Beat Out Babe in Home Run Derby."

The Yanks had racked up 69 total bases in the two games, which took just a total of 4 hours and 27 minutes to be played. But the games did not end soon enough for the ball club from the nation's capital. Sadly, they had to play the Yankees again the next day. The Yankees won, 7–6.

"Never have pennant challengers been so completely shot to pieces as the Senators. There hasn't been such hitting this year or any other year. It was record hitting for a record crowd," was the sentiment expressed in the *World*.

Washington first baseman Joe Judge was more emotional: "Those fellows not only beat you, but they tear your heart out. I wish the season was over."

But the season was anything but over for the Yankees and for Babe

Ruth and Lou Gehrig. They just were rolling along, rolling over teams. As in the team's theme song, it was the time of "roll out the barrel, we'll have a barrel of fun!"

The mystique and drawing power of the Yankees were such that a second big-voiced man shouted out the names of the pitchers and batters on a megaphone at Yankee Stadium. And the mystique and drawing power of Murderers' Row were such that more than ever before, fans came to the ballpark with baseball gloves, hoping to catch a ball smashed by Ruth or Gehrig or one of the other Yankee sluggers.

There was a culture in place for all the sluggers, for all members of the Yankees. Miller Huggins had schooled each player about attitude, disposition, bearing. If they didn't get it the first time, there was always time for lectures and lessons in Hug's spartan Yankee Stadium office, which consisted of a desk for him and a desk chair and a leather couch for all others.

Players were required to report for games at 10:00 A.M. at the Stadium—to sign in, not to practice. It was designed to cut down on late-night goings-on. No food or beer was allowed in the clubhouse between games of a doubleheader. There was a machinelike way about the Yankees: a precise, orderly, ritualistic rhythm that was repeated game after game. When the team was at bat and there were two outs, the regulars stood at the ready, poised at the second step of the dugout, primed to rush out to their defensive positions on the field when the final out of the inning occurred.

There was to be no backslapping, no flamboyant displays, no noise-making or razzing, no teasing of players on the other teams.

"We were never rough or rowdy," Waite Hoyt said, "just purposeful."

Throughout that long 1927 season, no Yankee ever had a fight on the field. And only once was a player—Joe Dugan—thrown out of a game by an umpire.

Unseen by the fans and the opposition, the only emotional show at Yankee Stadium after a victory was players exiting the dugout into the clubhouse and chanting "Roll Out the Barrel!" all the way.

"Roll Out the Barrel."

Waite Hoyt explained: "When we were challenged, when we had to win, we stuck together and played with a fury and determination that could only come from team spirit. We had a pride in our performance that was very real. It took on the form of snobbery. And I do believe we left a heritage that became a Yankee tradition."

Yankees who were not in the day's starting lineup were expected to pay attention to everything that was happening on the field. There was no slouching in the dugout and no conversation about anything but baseball despite Waite Hoyt's famous lines, "In the daytime you sat in the dugout and talked about women. And in the nighttime you went out with women and talked about baseball. It's great to be young and a Yankee."

The Yankee bullpen was in left field, on an embankment that was slightly graded. Huggins called down when he needed to, and when the phone rang it was usually a signal that a pitcher should get ready. Ed Barrow sat in his mezzanine box at Yankee Stadium observing all that took place on the field. If there was any lolling around, anyone trying to sneak a snooze, any food being consumed, "Cousin Eggbert" used the telephone in his box to get things in Yankee order, usually blending profanity with annoyance and with questions like "What the hell do you think we are paying you for?"

On July 11 Gehrig blasted number 29. The next day Ruth clubbed his 30th home run, off the Indians' lefty Joe Shaute. No one at that point in time would have guessed that the Big Bammer was at the midpoint of the total he would have for the year.

Four days later, "five o'clock lightning" struck again—seven runs scored in the last two innings to overcome Cleveland, 10–9. Richards Vidmer really got carried away the next day in the *New York Times.*

"You may sing of the ancient Orioles. You may chant of the glory that was the Cubs a score of years ago. You may harken back to the Athletics before the wreckage. But before anyone starts making any broad statements concerning those teams of a past baseball era, let him consider the frolicking, rollicking, walloping Yanks of the present."

They were frolicking Yankees and rollicking Yankees and walloping Yankees, of course. But they were also pitching Yankees. As of July 19, through 87 games, New York hurlers had posted victories in 40 of 45 complete games they pitched.

The ritual of winning was part of the Yankee package, as was the playing of exhibition games whenever there was a spare day. No matter the weather or the time of day, the ritual continued month after month through the long season.

Joe Giard started only one game for the Yankees all season. On July 25, he was on the mound in an exhibition game in Johnstown, Pennsylvania. Giard would appear in 16 games in relief in 1927, and wind up with no decisions and an 8.00 ERA. The Yankees had a 5–11 record in games in which he appeared. His negative stats would be more a result of rust from lack of work and his generally coming into games that were lost causes. But somebody on the staff had to have that mop-up role.

On a July night in St. Paul, Minnesota, despite a threatened storm, about 15,000 came out to watch the Yankees compete in an exhibition game against their home team. And although the visitors prevailed, 9–8, a good day was had by all, especially for those who got a good look at Gehrig and Ruth, whose personal score in their home run sweepstakes was now 31–30, in Lou's favor.

Richards Vidmer in the *New York Times* captured the time: "Last night as the special train carried the Yanks through Hannibal, Keokuk, Burlington and other rural regions, it was met at every stop by throngs who demanded a look at the Babe. The Babe never failed to step out on the platform with a few words and a smile as an added thrill. But only when the Babe went in and dragged him out did the Buster appear.

"He was bigger than the president," Vidmer wrote. "The train stopped to get water or something. It couldn't have been a town of more than 5,000 people, and by God, there were 4,000 of them down there standing in the rain, just wanting to see the Babe."

"We're all one big gang together," the Bammer wrote in *Babe Ruth's Own Book of Baseball.* "We know each other, trust each other, like each other. Baseball has its share of wonderful friendships and most of them have started aboard rattling, old Pullman cars when the boys get a few hours to be themselves and have a chance to act natural."

"It was a good bunch of fellows," said George Pipgras. "They were all friends. There were no cliques. We all got along real good. And when we got to the ballpark we knew we were going to win. That's all there was to it. We weren't cocky. I wouldn't call it confidence either. We just knew. Like when you go to sleep you know the sun is going to come up in the morning."

"Funny story," Bill Werber recalled. "During a ball game Urban Shocker was walking up and down the dugout and when he passed second-string catcher Pat Collins, a mouthful of tobacco juice squirted right past his shoulder, landing on his uniform, giving it a new pinstripe from shoulder to wrist.

"So Shocker looked at him with an ugly face. I was sitting beside Collins," Werber continued, "and I thought there was going to be a fight. But Shocker went on back down the dugout. About three innings later he came back, he had a mouthful of water and tobacco juice and spit it right in the face of Collins. And Collins took a towel and wiped his face and all the ballplayers laughed—they thought it was all very funny. And so did Pat Collins and Urban Shocker. Those guys were rough.

"If I got in at shortstop to field a ball in batting practice they would run me out of shortstop. They would run me out of there. They were rough and tough."

They may have been a rough-and-tough bunch, but in the dugout of the Yankees, no matter the situation, with their little cerebral manager Huggins in charge, nothing was ever out of hand. Fidgety, bouncing his legs nervously, he sat there, spitting, chewing tobacco, offering comments out loud about players on the Yankees as well as the competition.

"Huggins was almost like a schoolmaster in the dugout," Waite Hoyt said. "There was no goofing off. You watched the game and you kept track not only of the score and the number of outs, but of the count on the batter. At any moment Hug might ask you what the situation was."

Mark Koenig said: "He was a good manager. But he didn't have to be much of a strategist with that club. Lots of times, we'd be down five, six runs, and then have a big inning to win the game."

"I have always been strong for Miller Huggins," Bob Shawkey said. "I doubt if the public has ever properly appreciated Huggins. He is not the type that seeks the limelight and many people do not really know him. Huggins is fair at all times. If any player has had trouble with Huggins, it is his own fault."

Skillfully utilizing the talent on his roster, moving players around, saving them for the long season, maximizing strengths and minimizing weaknesses, Huggins held sway over all.

Miller Huggins used Pennock, Shocker, Ruether, Pipgras, and of course Moore in relief, and there were 21 different hitless appearances.

Bob Shawkey had served in the navy during World War I aboard the battleship *Arkansas*, obtaining the rank of yeoman petty officer, and was called "Bob the Gob" and "Sailor Bob." He was not effective in April as a starter, so Huggins moved him to the bullpen. In 17 relief appearances, the tall and slender hurler responded, going 2–2, with four saves and a 1.67 earned-run average. Huggins also rested Shawkey for the entire month of June. Despite his early-season futility, overall for the season Shawkey was 2–3 with a 2.89 ERA, fourth best on the team, seventh best in the league. So Huggins knew how to maximize the efforts and efficiency of his players.

According to George Pipgras, Miller Huggins eased him into the starting rotation as a replacement for Ruether, who was supposed to start one day but wasn't feeling well. What a marvelous move that turned out to be as the Iowa native won his first five decisions before suffering a 6–4 loss to Cleveland on July 29. He wound up with a 10–3 record, the highest winning percentage on the team. He was at his best pitching at Yankee Stadium, where he won eight of nine decisions. Pipgras fanned 4.38 batters per nine innings pitched; that was fourth best in the league, seventh best in the majors. Perhaps most important, the Yankees would win 16 of his 21 starts.

The legendary Damon Runyon wrote in the *New York American* about George Pipgras: "He takes a tremendous windup before letting the ball fly. He turns with his back to the batsman, then he comes 'round to deliver the ball, and all of his corn-nurtured one hundred and ninety some odd pounds are packed back of that delivery. And he carries on his open countenance an expression of great seriousness."

Some claimed one of the few weaknesses of the Yankees was the team's lack of depth. A chess master, Huggins always found the depth. When there was an injury, he improvised. Koenig missed a month. Dugan had a knee problem. Ruth had some aches. Combs was smacked by a ball in the temple. Adversity was managed. The Yankees more than coped, they rolled on. A way was always found to be great.

Herb Pennock opened 1927 with an 8–2 record, pitching his only shutout on May 7, winning 8–0 at Chicago. In July, Huggins gave him a lot of downtime, starting him on 8 and 10 days' rest. The rest helped. Pennock completed 69 percent of his starts in 1927, second on the team behind Hoyt. Going 9–2 on the road with a 2.56 ERA, Pennock was also a perfect 2–0 with two saves in eight relief appearances.

Smooth, graceful, and throwing out of an almost effortless motion that was deceptive to hitters, Herb Pennock was a slow worker. Between pitches he would walk around the mound, fixing his pants, playing with the bill of his cap.

His "out" pitch was the curveball, not the fastball. He employed three curveballs and a tailing fastball, a waste pitch. His curves were "big" and "bigger." His sweeping sidearm version was often used against lefties.

In 46 different games, Miller Huggins made no changes to his starting lineup. He used 89 pinch hitters, 47 times for pitchers and 42 times for position players, mostly catchers. Dutch Ruether was the only pitcher Huggins used as a pinch hitter; he batted .333. A pinch runner was used on 22 occasions. Wera ran for Ruether 3 times; the 19 other times the runners were for position players, again also mostly for catchers.

There was greatness on that Yankee team, but the sense of community Huggins helped forge made it even greater. Complimenting and complementing each other's strengths, compensating for each other's weaknesses, pushing each other to be even more successful, the Yankees marched on.

With Bengough, who would have been the main catcher if he had not been hindered by a sore arm, Huggins early on decided that he would have to catch Pat Collins one day and Grabowski the next, rotating them as much as possible throughout the season. Neither one worked two days in a row except for illness or injury.

The depth some critics said the Yankees lacked was there for all to see on August 27. Johnny Grabowski, badly spiked the day before in Detroit in an 8–6 Yankee victory, was sent back to New York with a split hand. He would miss the next three weeks. Huggins had said: "The Yankees got something of value when they got him. John is cool."

Ironically, Bengough, for whom Grabowksi had substituted, now took his place. In his fifth year with the Yankees, Bengough could have easily been mistaken for a batboy, at 5-7 and 145 pounds. He had missed most of the season with arm problems. Pressed into service, he lashed a bases-loaded triple. Although Bengough played in only 31 games and batted just .247, he was experienced, deep insurance and a highly capable defensive catcher.

The bald Bengough felt that a pitcher's wildness could be kept under control if he threw as many as 60 pitches a day to a catcher. That was the routine he set up with George Pipgras, whom he caught in nine starts and whose wildness was significantly reduced.

"He was like a box back there," Pipgras told Leo Trachtenberg in a 1985 interview, referring to Bengough. "He couldn't throw very good after he hurt his arm, but he was a great receiver."

"Grabowski," the New York American noted, "with more work behind the plate thrives on it. Collins works better when not asked to do all the work."

"The Yankee catchers are methodical, mere plodders, but brother, these types are the salt of the earth, the backbone of the game," Baseball Magazine observed. It was an apt observation, for although the rest of the lineup was smothered with praise, the three Yankee catchers were largely under the radar. Yet they all worked well with the pitching staff and would hit a combined .271, with 7 home runs and 71 runs batted in. Not bad for the maligned backstops in the shadow of Murderers' Row.

"A good catcher," Huggins said, "is the quarterback, the carburetor, the lead dog, the pulse taker, the traffic cop, and sometimes a lot of unprintable things, but no team gets very far without one."

By the end of July, the Yankee runaway lead was 15 games. Their team batting average was .314. Lazzeri's average was two points higher at .316. Earl Combs was at .338. Meusel had a .362 mark. Ruth was at .377. Gehrig was out of sight, at .389.

"Break up the Yankees!", the cry that had been out there most of the season, was now being heard more often, and it was louder.

AUGUST

The Yankees were an august presence throughout major league baseball as they began the eighth month of the year with a record of 73 wins and just 23 losses, and a gaudy .760 winning percentage.

But the month did not get off to the start they wished, as they lost two close games, 2–1 to the Indians on August 1 and 6–5 to the Tigers on August 3. Still, their record at Yankee Stadium was now a glossy 36–13. The Yankees would wind up with a 57–19 mark (with one tie) at Yankee Stadium in 1927, tying the American League record for home wins. They would win every season series against American League teams at Yankee Stadium, going 10–1 against St. Louis and 9–1 over Boston.

Nervous types among the Yankee faithful were a bit rattled on August 6 when Chicago nipped the Yanks, 6–3, behind star hurler Ted Lyons, known in some circles as "Sunday Teddy." The defeat was the fifth loss in nine games for the New Yorkers.

Departing New York City on August 8, Murderers' Row embarked on its most grueling stretch of the 1927 schedule: Philadelphia, Washington, Chicago, Cleveland, Detroit, and St. Louis. Back in New York on August 31—for one game against the Red Sox—they would then take leave of the Big Apple again, for seven more games in Philadelphia and Boston. Talk about living out of suitcases.

Wilcy Moore

Hod Lisenbee, a 28-year-old rookie Washington pitcher from Clarksville, Tennessee, was having a season against the vaunted Yanks. On August 11, the submariner pitched a beauty, defeating the team from the Bronx, 3–2 in 11 innings. It was his fifth consecutive triumph over New York. In that 1927 season, 22 different pitchers won games against the Yankees, but no one had the success of Horace Milton Lisenbee, who finished the 1927 season with an 18–9 record, including four shutouts for the third-place Senators. He never had another winning season.

Wilcy Moore pushed his record to 12–5 on August 13 in Washington, nipping the home team, 6–3. A wonder of wonders on the Yankee pitching staff, he was almost untouchable away from Yankee Stadium, posting a 1.77 ERA on the road and limiting the opposition to a .217 batting average. With the magnificent Moore on the mound as starter or reliever, the Yankees had a 36–13–1 record in 1927.

He was called a lot of names, including the "Ambulance Man," for all the emergency work he performed out of the Yankee bullpen. Dubbed "Doc" by sportswriters, Moore, according to one scribe, "specialize[d] in treating ailing ball games and putting them back in a healthy condition."

The best rookie in the league, the best relief pitcher in baseball, Moore was able to keep cool under pressure, and this ability was one of his strong suits, along with that deadly sinkerball. Inducing mostly ground balls, Moore would be touched up for just 2 home runs in 212 innings pitched in 1927, lowest in the majors. Overall, he would wind up 19–7, the third-best winning percentage (.731) in the league. He also would have a 2.28 earned-run average, while holding opponents to a league-low .234 batting average. He won 13 games in relief, leading the league, and saved another 13, tying for the league lead.

On August 15, Gehrig was ahead of the Babe, 38–36, in the home run derby. More and more were claiming that he would outhomer George Herman in 1927.

But the Buster would manage just 9 more home runs the rest of the season. His beloved mother was ill and in the hospital. Anguish over her health had him fretting during games, and at the hospital after each home game. The reckless abandon he once had that allowed him to sometimes play baseball until darkness in the streets of his neighborhood with a bunch of kids was no longer something he could do. His nonbaseball playing moments were totally reserved for thinking about and being with his mom.

Gehrig faltered. The Babe forged on.

What Babe Ruth could do, few others could. Earlier in the season, the Big Bam had become the first player to bash a ball out of the made-over Comiskey Park. But that was during batting practice. On August 16, he duplicated the feat—this time in an official game, the 114th for the Yankees.

The *New York Times* headlined the next day, "Ruth Clears Park with 37th Homer: Is First Ever to Put Ball out of White Sox Field.

Richards Vidmer's story had these tidbits: "the scores Yankees 8 White Sox 1, Ruth 37, Gehrig 38 . . . probably more interest in the twin thrillers [home run battle] than in the cut-and-dried contest between the two teams."

Vidmer reported that the Babe's fifth-inning shot off a fastball from Alphonse Thomas was one of the hardest "Ruth has ever hit in any park, but the distance it traveled will never be determined. . . . When the game was over," the *Times* sportswriter said, "5,000 representatives of American boyhood surrounded the Babe and left him black and blue from hearty slaps on the back. The game lasted but two hours and four minutes, but the former Red Sox pitcher had quite a time collecting a double, two walks and showing off his arm cutting down young White Sox shortstop Ray Flaskamper at home."

Throughout that momentous 1927 Yankee season, every aspect of the great Bam's game was given the up-close treatment in the media and among fans and players. However, the one aspect of his game that never was truly given its due was his powerful and accurate arm. He liked to show it off during batting practice, throwing balls from the outfield and hitting a towel near home plate.

Yankee coach Arthur Fletcher who had begun his major league playing career back in 1909, said: "I have seen a lot of accurate throwing by outfielders, but I never saw a man who had even a slight edge over Ruth in pegging."

Babe Ruth, who had 14 assists that 1927 season, was "still one of the best outfielders in the league," according to John Kieran of the *Times*, "and had a marvelous throwing arm."

A very accomplished outfielder with surprising range for a man of his heft, Ruth had a brilliant baseball mind and rarely made a mental mistake on the field. Throwing to the wrong base was just not part of his game.

But his true calling as a baseball player was hammering home runs. He shattered records, going from 29 home runs in 1919 to 54 in 1920 and 59 in 1921. On August 16, Ruth racked numbers 37 and 38. Reporters were more and more using the expressions "Bam 'em, Babe!" and "Bust 'em, Lou!"

On August 22, despite Ruth's 40th homer, New York lost to the Indians, 9–4. For the first and only time that season the Yanks lost four in a row, August 19–22. Urban Shocker made a relief appearance that day, his 37th birthday, and became the only Yankee to pitch on his birthday during the season.

A running sideshow for the Yankees all season was a bet that Babe Ruth had made in spring training with Wilcy Moore, who he said was "the lousiest hitter in history" and who wound up with the worst batting average on the heavy hitting Yankees: .080. Huggins pinch-hit for Moore on nine different occasions, most on the team.

Ruth put up $15 at 20–1 odds against Moore recording three hits that whole season. On August 26 the Yankees won in Detroit, 8–6, pushing their first-place lead to 15½ games, their largest cushion of the season to that time. But the big news of the day was a weak grounder by Moore that came to rest just fair in the grass after slowly dribbling down the third-base line, giving him his third base hit of the season.

Bingo, jackpot! $300! Payup time for the Bambino.

"This is just an easy park to hit in," a smiling Moore said. It was not so much about the money for the rookie hurler as it was about his desire to win the bet that had him going all out for those three hits.

"The Yankee camp tonight teems and thrills at the feat of Wilcy Moore," wrote Richards Vidmer in the *New York Times*. Winding up with not only the 300 bucks but also with six hits in 75 at-bats that season, Moore claimed the Babe inspired him. With Ruth's money, Moore would purchase two mules for his cotton patch of a farm. One mule he named "Babe"; the other, "Ruth."

While some in the Fourth Estate devoted a lot of ink to Wilcy Moore's hitting histrionics, Grantland Rice preferred to focus on "the slugging race between Ruth and Gehrig." Writing in the *New York Herald Tribune*, Rice made the point that "Ruth and Gehrig opened their act back in April, and they have been spilling climaxes all along the route for four months. The horsepower of their rival punch is so well matched now that the accruing climaxes may carry to the last day. All of this may be considered destructive to team play, but it is even more destructive to the other team's defensive system."

Southpaw Ernie Nevers of the Browns, in his second major league season, a future National Football League Hall of Famer, felt the fury and destructiveness of the Big Bammer on August 27 in St. Louis, when the Bambino socked number 41. A true home run machine, the Babe would smash 24 homers in his last 42 games.

On August 31, a Wednesday, the Yankees pounded the Red Sox, 10–3. Ruth hit number 43. Gehrig had 41. The Bombers, with 89 wins and just 37 losses and a .706 winning percentage, moved into September with a 17-game lead over the second-place A's, the team most had favored to win the American League pennant. It was a long way for Philly from April to September.

SEPTEMBER

At the start of the month, rumors abounded that Lou Gehrig was going to be traded to the Detroit Tigers. They may have abounded, but they were just rumors. The real truth was how the Yankees were doing.

For the team and their fans, September would be a month to remember. Babe Ruth had 43 homers as the month began. His September surge would see him club 9 homers in two weeks and 17 home runs in his last 29 games. Yankee hurlers would post a 2.48 ERA in September, their best month.

In Philadelphia, the Bambino swatted his 400th career home run on September 2, number 44 for the season. His junior home run partner crashed the next pitch for a towering dinger. In his next at-bat, in the second inning, Gehrig pounded number 43. In all, the Yankees clubbed 20 hits. Gehrig went 4–4. Combs had four hits, one of them a three-bagger. Yankee might strutted in full stride. The Bombers slugged at least 19 home runs off each American League team, with the most against Philly, 26.

About 25,000 Philadelphia rooters rejoiced on September 3 when Lefty Grove spun a four-hit, 1–0 masterpiece, his only shutout that season. The effort bested Wilcy Moore. Incredibly, it was the only time that the powerhouse Yankees were shut out all year.

Humid Boston was the scene of a doubleheader between the last-place Red Sox and the high-flying Yankees on September 5. For weeks the game had been a very hot ticket—not because Babe Ruth in the long ago had played for the BoSox, but because he was now baseball's biggest draw. Oddly, Ruth with eight and Gehrig with six would be the only Yankees to homer at the Fens in 1927. More than 70,000 wanted to get into Fenway, and half of them were turned away.

"The weak spots in the wooden barricade on the Ipswich Street side of the park were rushed and several holes made through which the human flood poured in a merry torrent," observed Burt Whitman in the *Boston Herald*. The Associated Press reported that "hundreds stormed the gates after ticket sales were stopped."

Fans were pressed 15 to 20 feet against the outfield wall by police on horseback and then roped off. Umpires ruled that any ball hit into the mass would be a ground-rule double. Atop fences, alongside outfield foul lines, from underneath the grandstand and nearby rooftops, fans seized whatever space for viewing they were able to get.

There were 26 games in 1927 where the Yanks lit up the opposition for 10 or more runs, posting a 25–1 mark. That lone defeat came in the first game of the Fenway doubleheader, an 18-inning, 12–11 heartbreaking loss. It was also the longest game of the season for the Yankees, 4 hours and 20 minutes. The second game was speed baseball, 55 minutes, called because of darkness. The Yanks were 5–0 winners.

Still slugging, Gehrig tied Ruth at 44 home runs with 23 games left in the schedule. His shot was a blast into the bleachers in right field off 22-year-old Charles Herbert ("Red") Ruffing, who three years later would be traded to the Yankees and would pitch 15 seasons for them. The Babe in seven at-bats managed a double. Incredibly, 23-year-old Hal Wiltse, who had pitched three innings for Boston and was the victor in the first game, was the losing pitcher in the second game.

The next day the teams were at it again—another doubleheader. The Bambino was ferocious, blasting 3 home runs. Two innings after Gehrig popped number 45, that man Ruth slugged what many called the longest home run ever at Fenway.

"This long one yesterday was the daddy of all others," the *Boston Globe* proclaimed. "The ball was still climbing when it went high over the highest part of the high fence in center field, just to the left of the flagpole. Nobody at the park could tell where it landed, but when it disappeared it was headed for the Charles River basin."

That gargantuan shot was an exclamation point delivered by George Herman Ruth, marking the last time that season he would be tied in home runs with his "junior partner." In his next at-bat Ruth parked the ball deep into the right-field stands. In the second game's ninth inning, he slammed still another long-ball homer.

On September 7, in the final road game of the season for the Yankees, the day after Babe had hit the trio of homers in the second doubleheader, the mighty Ruth hit 2 more, one off "Deacon" Danny MacFayden and the other off Slim Harriss. With the record 5 home runs in three games, the tally sheet showed Babe Ruth 49, Lou Gehrig 45 in the home run race.

During the season, Tony Lazzeri days had been staged in Boston and Detroit. His legion of fans, especially the Italian ones, had pushed for a day for him at Yankee Stadium. They got one scheduled for September 8 there.

"I suppose," the 23-year-old second baseman said, "they will give me a huge floral wreath just before the game and jinx me at bat. But I will fool the jinx. One home run is the least I can make to show my appreciation."

True to what Lazzeri had predicted, just before the game a delegation presented him with a floral horseshoe to the accompaniment of much cheering, and the band played on. The crowd roared "Push 'em up, Tony! Poosh 'em up, Tony!"

Lazzeri indelicately explained where the phrase came from: "When I was playing in San Francisco, there were these old wops who used to sit together in the bleachers and didn't speak English very well."

Another version of the derivation of the expression was that it came from a restaurant owner in Salt Lake City in the Pacific Coast League who generously supplied free pasta to the slim young ballplayer, always exhorting him to eat and "poosh 'em up"—hit home runs.

On Tony Lazzeri Day on the playing field, the Yankees, behind the stellar hurling of Waite Hoyt who yielded but three hits, nipped the Browns, 2–1, for their 19th straight success against the challenged club from Missouri. And not true to what he had predicted, Lazzeri, "the foremost spaghetti farmer," in the indelicate phrase used by some of the sportswriters of the time, went hitless, striking out twice. The Yankee win triggered an end-of-season spurt that sent them to 17 wins in their final 21 games.

"Tony Lazzeri Night" at the Hotel Commodore's grand ballroom in Manhattan followed his day. A lavish dinner was served, and all manner of Italian Americans from finance, the arts, and the world of sports showed up. Delegations from Boston, Providence, Jersey City, and other locales were on hand. They heard speeches from Babe Ruth, who it was claimed was first called "the Bambino" by people in New York's Little Italy, Lou Gehrig, Ed Barrow, Miller Huggins, and Jacob Ruppert, all tributes to the soft-spoken native of the Cow Hollow district of San Francisco. Lazzeri got the floral horseshoe at the game; at the dinner he was presented with a silver service valued at $1,000.

The grand that Lazzeri got was double the bonus money Wilcy Moore was in line to get, according to his contract terms for finishing the season with the Yankees. On September 10, the hurler from Oklahoma, who had so much sink on his ball that Yankee catchers moved up on the plate to keep the ball from getting too much dirt and having umpires call those pitches balls, had the sinker humming. Spinning a 1–0 shutout before 25,000 at the Stadium, Moore was instrumental in the 21st straight Yankee win over the Browns.

In his newspaper column Babe Ruth lauded Moore: "He's the type of pitcher who's a mystery to any club the first time they face him. He's different from any one in either league. For a single game pitcher, I'd rather see old Cy out there than any pitcher I know of."

"No pitcher ever came up from the minors," wrote Bill Slocum in the *New York American* "to do as much for his club in a single season . . . baffling low delivery, a sinker ball and control deluxe."

Mark Koenig said: "Wilcy had one of the first good sinker balls. "He'd go in with three on base and they'd never score."

Sportswriter Dan Daniel was born Daniel Markowitz, but was refused a byline early in his career because of his Jewish name. So he did double duty with his first name and kept on writing all the way to age 91. In 1927, he worked for the *New York World Telegram* and was proud of the fact that he was one of the pioneers in using the new portable typewriter. Daniel wrote that Wilcy Moore "owed his relief success to his strange sinker, which he never could explain. It was a natural delivery and he really did not know how to throw it."

The sinker was Moore's money pitch. But he was enamored of his curveball and begged Huggins, to let him use it in games. "No"—the mighty mite manager was adamant. "Your curveball won't even go around a button on my vest."

Dan Howley, manager of the St. Louis Browns, was known as "Howling Dan." Throughout 1927 he, along with lots of other members of the competition, was howling at what the Yankees did to them. "Those birds should be in a league by themselves," he complained. "Or if not that, each Yankee batter should only be allowed two strikes."

On September 11, a Sunday, the Browns of St. Louis, who had suffered not so silently through 21 consecutive defeats at the hands of their Yankee tormentors, finally got the monkey off their back in the final season meeting of the teams. Pennock, Shawkey, and Pipgras could not hold them back. St. Louis prevailed, 6–2, behind righty Milt Gaston, who pitched a five-hitter. The Yankees of 1927 did all kinds of remarkable things. But no team ever swept a 22-game season series—not even that bunch. A bright note for Yankee fans was Ruth slugging number 50. No other player had ever reached 50 before; for Ruth it was the third time.

Winning pitcher Gaston, who was touched up in 1927 by the Babe for four home runs, whose moving forkball caused problems for his catchers, would be traded in the off-season to Washington. The story in St. Louis was that Browns' owner Phil Ball was annoyed by and tired of ducking Gaston's wild pitches.

On Tuesday, September 13, the Yankees swept a doubleheader from Cleveland and clinched the pennant, bringing their season win total to 98 in 140 games. The Sultan of Swat swatted 2 home runs, 1 off 21-year-old right-hander Willis Hudlin, the other off 27-year-old south-paw Joe Shaute. Ruth's homer total was now 52. Both games, won by an identical score, 5–3, were played in less than two hours each. George Pipgras and Waite Hoyt methodically went the distance in each contest. Hoyt became the only 20-game winner for the 1927 Yankees and locked in his $1,000 bonus for those wins. His breakthrough year would actually see him win 22, tying him for the league lead in wins and winning percentage. Hoyt would finish second in league ERA, third in complete games, and fourth in innings pitched. Five of his seven losses were by one run.

"Hoyt's pitching has been a treat," the *Herald Tribune* declared, "a treat for those who can appreciate something other than hitters murdering the ball. Such control, such transition from one speed to another, such art in the pleasure of his slow curve."

Although the Yankees clinched their second straight pennant, there was not much celebrating to mark the clinching. For the Yankees, who had been in first place all season long, their eyes were on the prize that had eluded them the year before: a world championship.

With the clinch, Miller Huggins now had won his fifth pennant, tying him with Connie Mack. Now a bit more relaxed, Hug encouraged all his regulars to ask for a day off when they wanted as the regular season marched to its ending—for sleeping, fishing, resting, whatever. But virtually all played on, including the Iron Horse, Gehrig. Neither he nor others realized the consecutive games–played streak that was in progress.

"I particularly rooted for Lou to bat in 200 runs," Fred Lieb wrote in *Baseball As I Have Known It.* "But by mid-September he had almost all of the 175 runs batted in that he ended with. All his thoughts were on Mom. As soon as he finished the game he would rush to the hospital and stay with her until her bedtime. Lou just stopped hitting for the closing fortnight."

Mama Gehrig had been diagnosed with an inflammation of the thyroid that would require surgery. "I'm so worried about Mom that I can't see straight," Gehrig said with a sigh.

He batted just .275 over the final 22 games of the season with just two home runs. Gehrig also made four errors. He was, for sure, not what he had been.

But the Yankees were.

Although a team clinching a pennant would have a tendency to coast, the Yankees kept on charging, winning 12 of 15 games after the clinch. Huggins, like his team, never let up. He let the season play out without employing a pinch hitter or pinch runner in the final 13 games.

From September 16 to 21, the Yankees received six straight complete games from Moore, Shocker, Pennock, Pipgras, Hoyt, and Ruether. That was how honed in they were.

Wilcy Moore's route-going performance on September 16, the day the Yankees recorded their 100th victory, saw him scattering seven hits, trimming Chicago, 7–2, in the first of a five-game series at Yankee Stadium. The player they were calling "the King of Emergency" singled in the first inning, his first hit at Yankee Stadium. Then he slugged a homer into Ruthville in the fourth, smiling as he made the unfamiliar route around the bases. Ruth smacked number 53, a third-inning dinger into the right-field stands. The home run positioned the Babe just three behind his 1921 pace, with a dozen games remaining.

The next day was another good one for the Yankee star of stars. In a Manhattan court, "Mr. Ruth, stood behind the bench with his arms folded, a giant immobile figure," the New York Times reported. He had been accused by Bernard Neimeyer, a cripple, of punching him in the eye on the Fourth of July near the corner of Broadway and 74th Street. Neimeyer claimed that Ruth was walking with two women and then came up and asked him if he had insulted one of the women and then hit him. Ruth's attorneys proved that their famous client was not even in Manhattan at the time, and he was exonerated. Fans of the Yankee star burst into applause at the verdict. The legal doings were just another example of the celebrity distractions, the nuisance moments that hounded Babe Ruth throughout his career, but nothing seemed to slow him down, especially in 1927.

Nothing slowed down Earle Combs either. On September 17, between games of a doubleheader, fans from the right-field bleachers showed their appreciation for the great center fielder, presenting him with a gold watch. Five days later, the day when Jack Dempsey was defeated attempting to regain his heavyweight crown from Gene Tunney in Chicago, Combs tripled three times in an 8–7 Yankee win over Detroit. He would finish with 23 three-baggers in 1927, most in an American League season to that time.

Ty Cobb had scolded Combs: "You're crazy! Those two big guys just stand out there and point out the ball so that you can go after it. In another season you'll have your legs worn off clear up to the knees."

Although he was bookmarked by the burly Ruth and the lanky Meusel in the outfield, Combs was totally different from these men and from most of the other Yankees. The graceful center fielder was a man without vices. Early in his Yankee career pressure was put on him to drink. He refused. He did things his way.

"If you visit Earle in his hotel room some night after a game you are likely to find him reading his Bible," Fred Lieb wrote in the *New York Post*. "And he doesn't try to hide it when anyone comes into the room. . . . This does not mean that Earle Combs is a gloomy, praying Colonel. . . . He loves his pranks and his jokes; he loves his hits and winning ball games.

"If a vote," Lieb continued, "were taken of the sportswriters as to who their favorite ballplayer on the Yankees would be, Combs would have been their choice."

Miller Huggins had even more lavish praise: "If you had nine Combses on your ball club, you could go to bed every night and sleep like a baby."

With three days left in the season the only suspense around the Yankees was how many home runs the chief assassin of Murderers' Row would wind up with.

Jack Dempsey and Babe Ruth

Number 57 came off Philadelphia's Lefty Grove on Tuesday, September 27, a grand slam. Gehrig poked number 46. The Yanks trimmed the A's, 7–4.

On September 29, at Yankee Stadium, the Big Bammer homered twice to his favorite spot there—"Ruthville," the right-field bleachers. The shots came off two different Washington pitchers, Hod Lisenbee and Paul Hopkins, in a 15–4 Yankee rout. The Babe now had 59 home runs, tying his record set in 1921. He also set a record of most grand slams hit in consecutive games.

"I was out in the bullpen at that time," Hopkins recalled. "The bullpen in Yankee Stadium was perched deep in left field and you couldn't even see how the game was going. Well, the call came down that they wanted me to relive and I could see that the Yankees had three men on base. I guess I would have been nervous if I knew who the next batter was. It was Babe Ruth. It was Babe Ruth with the bases loaded.

The rest is history. I threw him a series of curveballs and he finally hit one into right field at least five rows in. "

John Drebinger wired the *Times*, "The ball landed halfway up the right field bleacher, and though there were only 7,500 eye witnesses, the roar they sent up could hardly have been drowned out had the spacious stands been packed to capacity. The crowd fairly rent the air with shrieks and whistles as the bulky monarch jogged majestically around the bases, doffed his hat, and shook hands with Lou Gehrig."

The shot off Hopkins was number 59. The one off Hod Lisenbee was number 58. After the game ended Lisenbee had somehow gotten possession of the home run ball and came around to the Yankee clubhouse dressed in street clothes, wanting Ruth to sign it. The Babe, always ready with an autograph, obliged, not even knowing who Lisenbee was.

On September 30, in the second-to-last game of the season, only 8,000 were in attendance at Yankee Stadium for what would prove to be one of the great moments in baseball history. The Sultan of Swat needed one more home run to break his former record. So capacious was Yankee Stadium back then that the top deck was never opened on a weekday, so with the small crowd in the park, there was an odd feeling in "the House That Ruth Built."

New York and Washington were tied, 2–2. Southpaw Tom Zachary, a Quaker, was on the mound.

"I had made up my mind," the Senator pitcher bragged, that he would not "give Ruth a good pitch to hit."

Bottom of the eighth. One out. On third after tripling, Mark Koenig stared at his buddy the Babe as he stepped in. Ruth had two singles in the game.

Home run number 59 had been hit with the bat the Bammer called Black Betsy. His other bats were the ash blond Big Bertha and the reddish Beautiful Bella. Much coverage had been given to Ruth's bats, which were so unlike the 34-inch, 38-ounce Louisville Slugger models swung by the more sedate Gehrig. Like the big fish stories, the Babe's bats kept getting heavier and heavier. There were claims that he used a bat that weighed 52 ounces. But the heaviest bat the big man ever used was 42 ounces, about the weight of Beautiful Bella, which he carried up with him as he stepped into the batter's box, lusting for home run number 60. The count was one and one.

"I don't say it was the best curve I ever threw, but it was as good as any I ever threw," Zachary, who also gave up home runs 22 and 36 to Ruth that season, said later.

The Babe reached out for the ball with the reddish Beautiful Bella. The shot was a gigantic and dramatic exclamation point to an incredible, miracle season and all that the 1927 New York Yankees had accomplished. No steroids, no performance-enhancing substances, no corked bats, just the Babe. The ball landed in the first row of the stands near the right-field foul pole, fair by about 10 feet.

In the Yankee dugout players leaped to their feet, watching the historic shot go into the stands. Fans scaled the screen there, charging out after their hero.

Slowly trotting out the historic home run, in "a triumphant almost regal tour of the paths," according to the *New York Times*, Ruth doffed his cap a few times to the small crowd in the stands, who cheered him as he carefully touched each base.

Another who doffed or rather tossed his baseball cap and jumped all over it, swept up in this moment of moments, was Charley O'Leary. It was an unusual bit of behavior for the Yankee third-base coach, who was always careful about not baring his bald head in public.

As he crossed home plate, a very happy Ruth was greeted by a double line of Yankees. In the dugout later his teammates banged their bats on the floor and stamped their feet, celebrating the moment. It was like New Year's Eve, only better.

The image of the big man with those measured, mincing steps going around the bases, the cast of characters waiting as he stepped on home plate: Washington catcher Muddy Ruel, home plate umpire Bill Dinneen, Eddie Bennett, and Lou Gehrig—a dramatic end to a magic season for the Prince of Pounders and Murderers' Row.

When Ruth took his defensive position in right field, his ecstatic fans in "Ruthville" tossed confetti, hats, and programs onto the field, applauded and screamed at him, and waved handkerchiefs. Playful in return, the Babe acknowledged them, snapping back a series of fancy and exaggerated military salutes.

In the ninth inning, in one of those special moments that baseball always seems to have, the legendary pitcher Walter Johnson made his final appearance as a player, pinch-hitting for Zachary, and flying out to Ruth. The Yankees won the game, 4–2.

"It is doubtful," Fred Lieb wrote, "if anyone in that crowd will ever live to see another baseball player hit his 60th home run in a 154-game season. I saw Ruth hit his 59th in 1921 and never thought I would score the game in which that record would be broken."

The news of what the Bam had done went out on the wire across America. In small towns in New Hampshire, rural Texas, down in Mississippi, there were many who ran out of cigar stores or gas stations shouting, "He hit sixty! Babe hit sixty!"

In the clubhouse after the game was over, Ruth bellowed, "Sixty! Let's see some son of a bitch try to top that one!"

The clubhouse was strangely reserved. What he had done, what they had done, was expected.

"See the funny thing about it is," Benny Bengough explained, "we never figured 60 was going to stand. We felt Babe Ruth might hit 65 the next year because, see, he was the only real home run hitter. And Babe never really thought about it. He never figured I'll hit 90 home runs this year or 60 or whatever. He just hit the home runs. He hit 60 and I imagine the next year Babe figured, well, I'll probably hit 65 or 70—who knows? He never hit that many again, but we thought he might. So it wasn't that important."

The day after Ruth set the record of records, the *New York Times* reported in headlines and an unsigned article: "Babe Crashed 60th to Set New Record."

"Babe Ruth scaled the hitherto unscaled heights yesterday. The first Zachary offering was a fast one, which sailed over for a called strike. The next was high. The Babe took a vicious swing at the third pitched ball and the bat connected with a crash that was audible in all parts of the stand. . . . Boys, no. sixty was some wallop a fitting homer to top the Babe's record of 59 in 1921."

The first player to reach 30 homers, to reach 40, 50, and 60, a record that stood for 34 years, Babe Ruth would wind up in his fabled career homering once every 11.76 times at bat.

Later Zachary explained: "I gave Ruth a curve, low and outside. It was my best pitch. The ball just hooked into the right field seats and I instinctively cried 'foul.' But I guess I was the only guy who saw it that way. If I'd a known it was gonna be a famous record, I'd a stuck it in his ear."

Paul Gallico was the highest-paid sports editor in the country, earning $25,000 a year from the *New York Daily News* from 1923 to 1936. A native New Yorker, born in the Big Apple in 1897, he graduated from Columbia University in 1921. His first job with the *News* was as movie critic, but too much attitude in his writing led to his removal. Moving on to the sports department, by 1923 he was the sports editor, with a daily column. Of the Ruth record-setting home run, Gallico wrote:

"They could no more have stopped Ruth from hitting that home run than you could have stopped a locomotive by sticking your foot in front of it. Once he had that 59, that number 60 was as sure as the rising sun. A more determined athlete than George Herman Ruth never lived. . . . A child of destiny is George Herman. . . . I even recall writing pieces and saying that Gehrig would soon break Babe Ruth's cherished record and feeling kind of sorry for the old man, having this youngster come along and steal his thunder, and now look at the old has-been.

"Succumb to the power and romance of this man," Gallico wrote, all journalistic objectivity gone. "Feel the athletic marvel that this big, uncouth fellow has accomplished."

Babe Ruth hammered 28 of his 60 home runs in Yankee Stadium, while Lou Gehrig hit 24 of his 47 there.

"I don't think I would have established my home run record of 60," Ruth reflected later in life, "if it hadn't been for Lou. He was really getting his beef behind the ball that season. . . . Pitchers began pitching to me because if they passed me, they still had Lou to contend with."

Frank Graham wrote in *The New York Yankees*: "One of the secrets of the Babe's greatness was that he never lost any of his enthusiasm for playing ball, and especially for hitting home runs. To him a homer was a homer, whether he hit it in a regular game, a World Series game, or an exhibition game. The crack of the bat, the sight of the ball soaring against the sky—these thrilled him as much as they did the fans."

The Babe played in 151 of the 155 Yankee games (one game was a tie replayed). His home-run dossier had all kinds of interesting stats. A third of his 60 home runs were hammered in his final 32 games. After 123 games, Ruth had just 40 home runs. September's 17 slams, a record for the time, put the Babe over the top. He homered most against the Red Sox, 11 times, least against the White Sox, 6 times. The 60 home runs came off 33 pitchers, and 16 hurlers gave up one or more homers. The Babe hit 1 inside-the-parker, 16 home runs in the first inning, 1 in the second, 4 in the third, 5 in the fourth, 7 in the fifth or sixth, 5 in the seventh, 9 in the eighth, none in the tenth, and 2 in the eleventh. There were 29 bases-empty homers, 22 with one runner on, 7 with two on, and 2 with the bases loaded. Nineteen dingers came off lefthanders. Two were grand slams. The 60 homers accounted for 100 RBIs.

Nearly 40 years after Tom Zachary gave up the 60th home run to Babe Ruth and four years after Roger Maris broke the Ruth record, in 1965 a still unhappy Zachary wrote: "Tied 2–2 in 8th. 2 outs, one man on and a count of 3 and 2 strikes on Ruth. I threw him a curve, but I made a bad mistake. I should have thrown a fast one at his big fat head. Lost game, 4–2. It was a tremendous swat down right field foul line. At that time there were just bleacher seats in right field with foul pole. But since (at first) It went so . . . far up in bleachers that it would be difficult to judge it accurately. I hollered 'foul ball' but I got no support, very little from my team mostly so it must have been a fair ball—but I always contended to Ruth that it was foul."

On October 1, the Yankee played their final game of the 1927 regular season, game 155. There was nothing really at stake. But Babe Ruth and Lou Gehrig played on. The United German Societies staged "Lou Gehrig Day," and the Yanks eked by Boston, 4–3. Ruth did not homer. Gehrig did. But the shot by the Iron Horse, anticlimactic after Ruth's 60, which were more than every other team in the league, drew only muted reactions from fans.

Nevertheless, "the guy who hit all those home runs the year Babe Ruth broke the record," in the words of columnist Franklin P. Adams of the *Herald Tribune*, still managed a record-setting 175 runs batted in and a batting average of .373, surpassing Ruth's numbers in both categories. His 47 home runs were more in a single season than any player other than Babe Ruth had ever hit. Gehrig's home run total was greater than that of the White Sox, Red Sox, Indians, and Senators combined.

"I don't know," Ruth said as the Yankees prepared to go to the World Series, "if anyone will ever break my record of 60 home runs. I don't know and I don't care. But if I don't, I know who will. Wait 'til that bozo over there— he pointed to Gehrig—"wades into them again and they may forget that a guy named Ruth ever lived."

Years later he commented: "My 60 home runs in 1927, they were made before many of the parks had been artificially shortened so as to favor the home run hitter. I hit them in the same parks where, only a decade before, 10 or 12 homers were good enough to win the title. They said they livened up the ball for me. Well, if they put some of the jack in it around the 1927 period, they put the entire rabbit into it in 1947 and at the same time shortened a lot of the fences."

Babe Ruth and Lou Gehrig were the most devastating and exciting power batting tandem in all the history of baseball, finishing one-two (Ruth-Gehrig) in the league in home runs, runs scored, batting, strikeouts, and walks. Winding up one-two (Gehrig-Ruth) in the league in runs batted in, total bases, and extra-base hits. Almost 25 percent of all the American League home runs in 1927 were hit by Gehrig and Ruth.

Ruth's 60 homers represented 13 percent of all the homers in baseball that season. His 60-home-run record stood as the single-season record for 34 years, nearly as long as 714 lasted as the career record, 39 years.

The Babe's 1927 line of .356 batting average, 164 RBIs, and a league-best .772 slugging percentage was just part of his story. Scoring the most runs, drawing the most walks, recording the most total bases, and compiling the highest on-base percentage, Ruth outhomered all

American League teams, all major league teams except for the Giants, Cubs and Cardinals.

The 1927 New York Yankees were so free of serious injury that six of the eight position players logged more than 500 at-bats. The 1927 Yankees went through the entire season with no changes in the batting order. When substitutions were made due to illness, injuries, fatigue, or the manager's decision, the position of the regular in the lineup was the position the substitute occupied. This was a very unusual sidebar to that remarkable campaign. The final American League standings clearly showcase the extent of the Yankee runaway:

Team	Wins	Losses	Winning Percentage	Games Behind
New York	110	44	.714	—
Philadelphia	91	63	.591	19
Washington	85	69	.552	25
Detroit	82	71	.536	27½
Chicago	70	83	.458	39½
Cleveland	66	87	.431	43½
St. Louis	59	94	.386	50½
Boston	51	103	.331	59

The men of five o'clock lightning pounded 158 home runs, batted .307 as a team, and held opponents to 599 runs, outscoring them by 376 runs. Setting major league records for runs (975), home runs (158), RBIs (908), and slugging percentage (.489), the 1927 Yankees were the only team to have the top three home run leaders: Babe Ruth, Lou Gehrig, and Tony Lazzeri, who finished with 18.

The team's 158 home runs were 36 percent of the eight-team American League's 439. The next-best Philadelphia Athletics had 56 home runs. Eighty-three Yankee home runs were hit at the Stadium, 75 on the road—the most, 16, at Philadelphia's Shibe Park; the least, 5, at Cleveland's Dunn Field. When a Yankee homered, the team's record was 77–16. When Ruth hit a four-bagger, the Yanks were 43–9, when Gehrig homered, 33–7.

The Yankees scored 100 runs more than their nearest competitor, allowed 100 less than anyone else, and hit three times more homers than any other club. They were the fourth team in the history of their league to have the highest batting average (.307) and the lowest ERA (3.20) in the same season. They were the first club in major league history to reach triple figures in doubles, triples, and home runs.

The Stadium was a privileged playing field for the Yankees. Their 57 wins at home tied an American League record. They batted .312 there as a team, paced by Ruth's .372. Of their team-record 158 home runs, 83 were slugged at the Stadium. Their pitchers compiled a splendid 2.75 ERA at home, while the opposition was held to a mediocre .251 batting average and 30 homers at Yankee Stadium. The Bombers' won-lost record in the big ballpark in the Bronx was 83–30 in 1927.

In addition to his league-best 175 RBIs and 52 doubles, Gehrig batted .373 (third in the American League), and his slugging percentage of .765 was second only to that of Ruth. The 30-year-old Bob Meusel batted .337, drove in 103 runs, and stole 24 bases. The 28-year-old Earle Combs led the league with 231 hits and 23 triples; he also stole 15 bases. The 23-year-old Tony Lazzeri stole 22 bases. Overall, about the only weak spot in the Yankee arsenal was base stealing. The team finished tied for fifth in the American League, with only a 58.4 percent success rate. But with all that power, who needed base stealing?

Outscoring opponents by nearly 400 runs, leading the league in every individual offensive category except for batting average, the Bronx Bombers had five regulars who batted .300 or better. Four of the eight American Leaguers who drove in 100 or more runs were Yankees. The outfield had a composite batting average of .350; the starting eight collectively hit .327.

The Yankees had by far the most impressive pitching staff in baseball, one whose accomplishments were almost as outstanding as those of the offense. The first and only major league team to have the top four pitchers in winning percentage and top three in ERA—Moore (2.28),

Hoyt (2.63), and Shocker (2.84)—in the same season, they also had four hurlers win 18 or more games: Hoyt (22), Pennock and Moore (19 each), and Shocker (18). Dutch Ruether and George Pipgras combined for a 23–9 record. Their pitching staff ERA of 3.20 led the league and was almost a full run lower than the league average. The staff held opposing teams to a .271 batting average, lowest in the league

The pitching staff led the league in shutouts and had a 2.75 ERA at Yankee Stadium and a 3.64 ERA on the road. The Yankees led the league with 82 complete games. In the remaining 73 games, they only had to use one relief pitcher in 46 games. The Yankees were 69–13 when their starting pitcher completed games, but when relief was summoned, they were just 41–31. There were 21 different hitless appearances made by relievers.

Total home attendance for the Yankees in 1927 was 1,164, 015, an average of 15,117 per game.

All the arithmetic of the fabled season added up to strongly support claims that the mighty 1927 New York Yankees were hands down the greatest baseball team of all time. They had a magical regular season and had all kinds of confidence as they headed into the World Series.

THE WORLD SERIES

There was never a team came crashing
   through
Like Ruth and the rest of the Yankee crew.
               —John Kieran, *New York Times*

On October 1, the final day of the regular season, the Pittsburgh Pirates nipped the Cincinnati Reds, 9–6, to win the 1927 National League pennant, finishing 1½ games ahead of the defending World Series champion St. Louis Cardinals. The Bucs would be the competition for the Yankees in the 24th World Series.

As a team, Pittsburgh's batting and fielding averages were comparable to those of the Yankees. The Pirates paced the National League in runs, hits, batting average, and on-base percentage. Since they played in a huge park, their home run total was just 58, but the Bucs did smack 78 triples and had a league-leading batting average of .305. There were also some genuine stars on the team, which was essentially the same as the one that won the 1925 fall classic.

The great third baseman Pie Traynor had batted .342 in 1927; Paul Waner, in his second major league season, hit .380, won the batting title, and also led the league in RBIs. His brother Lloyd batted .355 and set a rookie record for hits with 223. First baseman Joe Harris hit .326, second baseman George Grantham .305, and left fielder Clyde Barnhart .319. Only catcher Johnny Gooch and shortstop Glenn Wright batted below .300 among the regulars.

Outfielder Kiki Cuyler, who batted .309 in the regular season, would see no action in the World Series. Benched in midseason because he refused manager Donie Bush's orders to play center field and bat second, the superstitious, independent, talented, and annoyed Cuyler would be on the scene but in the dugout throughout the World Series. In Pittsburgh, Pirate fans would taunt: "We want Cuyler! We want Cuyler."

Yankee owner Jake Ruppert was in a tremendously upbeat frame of mind as the beginning of the fall classic loomed. "The World Series always gets hold of me," he told reporters. "I get a lot of fun out of it. I am very proud of what the team has done this year and in years past. It was my hope when I became interested in the Yankees to win pennants, and since 1915 I have seen five of them come to me."

A passionate and highly interested onlooker all through the long baseball season, the beer baron was especially pleased with what his team had accomplished, the money it had made for him, and the image it had all over the sporting world. He was also especially smitten with his little manager.

"Huggins," Ruppert said, "is one of the smartest men in baseball, besides being one of the finest personally. He has gone about his work quietly and you hardly ever see him but you see the results of his planning and his keen baseball mind. He is a little marvel." The words represented quite a change in tune for the owner of the New York Yankees from the time when he first met Huggins and had recoiled at "the worker's clothes, the cap perched oddly on Huggins' head, the smallness of the man."

On the day the Yankees were scheduled to leave New York City for Pittsburgh, the Yankee Stadium bulletin board had this notice:

"The Yankees will open the Hotel Roosevelt in Pittsburgh."

In pencil, someone had written: "And how!"

As the Yankees arrived one after another at Pennsylvania Station late Sunday night, October 2, for the trip to Pittsburgh aboard the train dubbed the Yankee Special, more than a thousand loyal and excited supporters were out in full force, and so were many New York City policemen. Waite Hoyt arrived just two minutes before the train was to leave. Bob Meusel and Tony Lazzeri got there just moments before the train doors closed. Lou Gehrig had tried unsuccessfully to persuade Miller Huggins that he should not play in the Series because his mother was on the critical list in the hospital. The Iron Horse was aboard the train, too. Only Herb Pennock was absent, but he would be picked up along the way, at the North Philadelphia station. There was also a companion car, the Iron City Flyer. It was crowded with Yankee fans, all in a party mood. The train pulled out slowly, heading west toward the Appalachian Mountains.

An article in the *New York Herald Tribune* by Rud Rennie "In the Middle of the Night Aboard the Yankee Sleeping Car," captured that time:

There is usually an air of mystery about a strange sleeping car. One wonders who's behind the dark green curtains that move occasionally to the motion of the train. In this instance, however, one knows that the guttural noises up front betray the sleeping Ruth in lower 11. Those hissing sounds from lower 5 are the slumbering notes made by Bengough while lying on his back.

From the depths of lower 3 comes nothing but a vast silence, for there lies Lou Gehrig. And where Gehrig sleeps he sleeps with the quiet dignity of an Egyptian king long dead.

Huggins has the drawing room, a sound-proof place in which the mite manager might sing a paean of victory without disturbing a soul. But it is reasonable to suppose at this hour that Hug has knocked the ashes out of his bedtime pipe and is dreaming of the airtight pitching that will give him the championship of the world.

In fact, he might have since the Yankees winners of AL pennants in 1921, 1922, 1923 and 1926, and almost flag grabbers in 1920 and 1924—and aside from 1923—were always just a step away from the title.

On Monday morning, the Yankee Special arrived in Pittsburgh. The Yankees took taxis to the brand-new Roosevelt Hotel, at the corner of Pennsylvania Avenue and Sixth Street. Ruth had purchased a new brown cap for the occasion and was wearing it, but that was no disguise for the most famous baseball player in the world, even though his weight had ballooned all the way to 237½ pounds by the end of the 1927 season. Fans easily spotted him, mobbing him in the lobby of the hotel.

"Later," James Harrison wrote in the *New York Times*, "the photographers trapped him in his room, taking pictures of him in a giddy dressing gown and gay slippers. The Babe posed eating a breakfast that would have sufficed for the entire Pirate infield, with the bat boy thrown in."

The World Series would not start for two days. But what happened before the games got under way would provide a source of controversy through the ages.

The Waner brothers—Lloyd, ("Big Poison") and Paul ("Little Poison")—sent up their baseball cards to Babe Ruth, who was at ease in his room in the hotel.

"Why, they're just kids," he said. "If I was that little, I'd be afraid of getting hurt."

That was the first year the Waners played together in the Pirate outfield. "That was a great thrill for us," Paul recalled. "We even brought Mother and Dad and our sister to the World Series.

"We won before it even got started," Babe Ruth wrote later. "The first two games were scheduled for Forbes Field. Naturally, we showed up a day early and worked out in the strange park."

Forbes Field was a bit strange. Built by Pirate owner Barney Dreyfuss, who escaped from Germany at age 17 to avoid compulsory military service, it was the first ballpark made completely of poured concrete and steel, and it was in the growing, middle-class East End of Pittsburgh, two miles from downtown, northwest of Schenley Park in the southern part of the University of Pittsburgh campus. The first game played at the 35,000-seat ballpark was on June 30, 1909. Forbes Field became an immediate steel city landmark. Its outfield dimensions—left field, 365 feet; center, 457 feet; right-center, 416 feet; and right field, 300 feet, which featured an 86-foot-high roof—were far pokes for power hitters of that time period and would be for today's sluggers, too. That was one reason Babe Ruth called it a strange park and why sluggers were not that fond of playing there.

"The Pirates," Ruth recalled, "had their workout just before we went out onto the field. We came out from the clubhouse. Most of the Pirates had dressed and were sitting in the stands to watch us go through practice."

Miller Huggins, always one to seize a psychological edge, told Herb Pennock and Bob Shawkey to pitch hitting practice. "When you get it in there lay the ball right down the middle. Don't put anything on it."

Combs hit a shot into the center field stands, and Koenig hit one ball off the right-field wall and one off the left-field barrier. Then it was Babe Ruth's turn at bat.

"The first ball I hit over the roof of the right-field grandstand," the Bammer said. "I put another one into the lower tier. Then I got hold of one and laid it into the center field bleachers."

The Pirates had some players with very unusual names, such as pitcher Emil Ogden Yde, who watched the Yankees in batting practice and was especially impressed with Babe Ruth. "Holy Smoke! Does he do that often?" the Buc hurler was quoted in Joseph Wallace's *World Series: An Opinionated Chronicle*.

"We really put on a show," Ruth said. "Lou and I banged ball after ball into the right-field stands. Bob Meusel and Tony Lazzeri kept hammering balls into the left-field seats."

"Okay, sonnies," the lively Ruth, who would set nine records in the Series, said with a snarl. "If any of you want my autograph, go out there and get those balls and I'll sign them for you."

One who was able to end up with baseballs autographed by Babe

Ruth and also Lou Gehrig was batboy Joe Snyder, who was paid off with two grass-stained baseballs for working each game in Pittsburgh. Young Joe Snyder was one of those who marveled at the batting practice exhibition put on by Babe Ruth and Company. And he talked about it for years afterward.

In future days, David Maraniss, author of *Clemente*, joined the camp of those who disputed that Yankee batting practice show of force. "Part of the lore of the 1927 Yankees," he wrote, "was a boast that the Pirates, after watching the famed sluggers take batting practice before the series opener, felt so overmatched they folded and lost four straight. Harold (Pie) Traynor, Pittsburgh's Hall of Fame third baseman, had bristled at that story for decades, insisting that it was apocryphal. By Traynor's account, the Pirates were in the clubhouse looking over a scouting report as the Yankees took their pregame cuts. Whatever prodigious shots Ruth and Gehrig stroked during batting practice, apparently the Pirates saw none of them.

"But the debunking of this myth," according to Maraniss, "did not sit well with baseball's commissioner, Ford Frick, for the particular reason that it was Frick himself, as a young sportswriter for the *New York Journal*, who had spread the story in the first place."

Maraniss makes the point that the 1960 and 1927 Pirates-Yankees World Series had common themes: "audacious power, solid pitching, pinstripes, intimidation, all rendered glorious by the self-centered hyperbole of New York and its sporting press."

With all due respect to Maraniss, we give Ford Frick a chance to defend himself in comments he made in the *New York Times* of October 5, 1960.

"I was outside on the field," Frick wrote, "covering that series for the *New York Journal* and I heard Hug tell Waite Hoyt who was the batting practice pitcher that day to throw the ball right down the middle. 'Let's put on a big show for the Pirates.'

"And what a show those Yankees put on. . . . I believe it had an effect on the Pirates. I wrote it that way."

Another dissenting view about the alleged Yankee intimidation that day comes from Lloyd Waner in Donald Honig's *October Heroes*:

"Well, I don't know how that got started. If you want to know the truth, I never even saw the Yankees work out that day. We had our workouts first and I dressed and was leaving the ball park just as they were coming out on the field. I don't think Paul [his brother] stayed out there either. We never spoke of it. I know some of our players stayed, but I never heard anybody talk of what they saw. I don't know where the story came from. Somebody made it up out of thin air, that's all I can say. Every time I hear that story I tell people it's not so, but it just keeps on going."

Begging to differ, however, with Lloyd Waner are such respected writers as Arthur Daley of the *New York Times*, Leigh Montville, and Jim Reisler. They opine that the Yankees, in their batting practice slugging show before the 1927 World Series began, spooked the Bucs.

In a "Sports of the Times" column in the 1950s, Daley wrote: "The opposing Pittsburgh Pirates overwhelmed from the first batting practice when the Yankees lineup, especially Ruth, hit baseballs to strange places around and outside Forbes Field. . . .

"The Yankees won the 1927 World Series from the Pirates during batting practice before the opening game. 'Gee, they're big,' whispered Paul Waner to his brother Lloyd.

"Boom! Ruth whacked one out of the ballpark. Wham! Gehrig did the same. Then it was over the fence over against it in rapid succession as Murderers' Row teed off.

"'Gee, they can hit,' murmured the Pirate players in stark despair.

"The Buccaneers were beaten before they started."

In the highly readable and well researched *The Big Bam* Leigh Montville has this explanation: "The World Series seemed to be nothing more than a curtain call for the Yankees and Ruth after what they had done during the season, the opposing Pirates overwhelmed from the first batting practice when the Yankee lineup especially Ruth, hit baseballs to strange places around and outside Forbes Field."

Jim Reisler, in *Guys, Dolls, and Curveballs*, points out that "Ruth and Gehrig deposited home run after game run into the right field stands" in batting practice.

And finally, in an October 4, 1927, account in the *New York Times*,

Richards Vidmer, who was an eyewitness, wrote: "The Yankees final practice yesterday was a rather hilarious affair. Babe Ruth left the field in good spirits and five balls somewhere in Schenley Park. The Babe's batting spree left interested onlookers, including the Pirates, open-mouthed in wonder. Most of them had never seen his majesty the ball mauler in action before."

Jonathan Eig has the last word. In his excellent *Luckiest Man*, Eig makes this point: "In truth, the Pirates were simply overmatched."

The dope all over the place had the Pirates overmatched.

A *Sporting News* poll of 32 sportswriters who covered major league teams favored New York 17–13 to win the World Series, with two undecided. The betting line was 7–5 Yankees, even though some critics pointed out that they had lost three of their four past World Series.

The Yankees were "the most blasé team going into a World Series," James Harrison wrote in the *Times*. He pointed out that while the Yankees were enjoying their games of poker and pinochle in the hotel, the Pirates were serious and tense.

Ring Lardner, whose fame as sportswriter, humorist, and satirist transcended the sporting world, wrote in the *New York World*, "It would be clearly unfair to put these two teams versus each other on even terms. The Yankees won the pennant the day before the season opened, and the only thing they had to worry about since was the remote possibility that one of the other American League clubs would trade itself in bulk for Casey Stengel's Toledo club (winner of the American Association pennant) and thus introduce an element of competition. Whereas on the other, the Pirates are nervous. If they ain't nervous, they ain't human."

Diplomatic Miller Huggins, reflecting the views of a man who had been through many baseball wars, who had the memory of the 1926 Series that the Yankees could have, should have, won, said: "We ought to win but you can never tell. The Pirates may win four straight. We may win four straight. World Series are too uncertain."

Pirate pilot Bush proclaimed: "We are going to win. And I don't mean if, but or maybe." The Buc leader was perhaps so truly confident that he didn't even think it necessary in his pre-Series rundown of the Yankees to say anything special about Babe Ruth. At least that was the report passed down later by Pirate infielder Dick Bartell in *Rowdy Richard*:

"Donie Bush is going over the Yankee lineup. . . . 'Don't let Ruth beat you,' he says. But he doesn't offer any tips on how to avoid that fate. It's like sending somebody out in a hurricane without an umbrella and telling him, 'Don't get wet.'"

Although baseball coverage in major newspapers and magazines was firmly in place by the time of the 1903 World Series, and radio later brought the fall classic into a limited number of American living rooms by the 1920s, for many years games were "seen" by being portrayed graphically on temporary scoreboards. Mechanisms ranging from the simple to the splendid were positioned in public areas such as street corners or parks, or sometimes indoors for paying audiences at armories or theaters. In major cities, as well as throughout the American backwoods, scoreboards brought the national pastime to the fans.

A good example of how local fans "watched" the 1925 through 1927 World Series was in Waynesburg, Pennsylvania, where hundreds of spectators "witnessed" baseball action play out. A 10-foot-tall by 6-foot-wide scoreboard was constructed just before the 1925 Series by two hometown electricians to allow fans to "see" the local favorites, the Pittsburgh Pirates, play the Washington Senators. Suspended from the front balcony of the Blair Hotel, the scoreboard was about 50 miles from Forbes Field. Its baseball diamond featured movable "runners," a "ball" that could be transported around the field, and cards indicating each team's lineup. A bell was rung to celebrate home runs. The scoreboard had space for remarks such as "rain delay," "man injured," and "stolen base."

Sitting behind the whole primitive setup, one or two operators listened to game accounts broadcast over a shortwave radio, and updated the score every inning through a system of pulleys that changed the position of the figures on the diamond. The Waynesburg scoreboard re-created the action of the 1926 World Series and was all ready to do the same in 1927 when fans in the small western Pennsylvania town would anticipate every pitch, cheer every run, and grimace with every out their Pirates made.

In Seattle's Times Square each day during the 1927 World Series, 10,000 fans would gather to follow the World Series play-by-play on an automatic scoreboard. There was a hometown hero, John Miljus, on the Pirates, and the crowd rooted for him and his overmatched Pittsburgh teammates.

All of the games of the 1927 World Series were scheduled for 1:30 P.M. starts except for a 2:00 P.M. Sunday game. Prices for seats for all games were the same as in 1926: $6, $5, $3, and $1. Four umpires were assigned: Ernie Quigley and Charlie Moran of the National League and Dick Nallin and Red Ormsby of the American League.

GAME ONE

Hundreds had waited in line all night outside Forbes Field, hoping to purchase bleacher seats. Scalpers asked $25 a ticket, a price that was considered extreme gouging, which it was. The price for a World Series program that featured Miller Huggins and Pittsburgh manager Owen J. Bush on its cover sold for 25 cents.

Forbes Field opened for business at ten in the morning on Wednesday, October 5, a breezy and beautiful autumn day. Extra seats had been built out by the fence in center field. By noon, lines snaked all the way out to Sennott Street.

The early crowd was entertained, as reported in the *New York Times*, "by the customarily funny antics of Nick Altrock and Al Schacht, those indomitable comedians of the diamond . . . there was a red-coated municipal band to jazz things up." It marched out to the outfield, playing upbeat tunes. There were 41,467 fans squeezed into the park, and thousands more had been turned away. "The color scheme," the *Times* reported, "was impressive, the tans, blues, greens and crimsons, women fans supplying a contrast to the more conservative colors of the men."

In attendance were the governor of Pennsylvania, John S. Fisher; New York City mayor Jimmy Walker; baseball commissioner Kenesaw Mountain Landis; and National League president John A. Heydler.

Photographers were busy snapping away, capturing images of the hand-shaking by midget managers Donie Bush, in his first season on the job for Pittsburgh, and Miller Huggins, who appeared more nervous than he usually was.

Happily ensconced in a field box close by the Yankee dugout, Jacob Ruppert held court for about an hour. Sitting with the Yankee party was Bob Connery, president of the St. Paul Saints of the Class AAA American Association and former chief scout of the Yankees, and Al Brennan, Yankee treasurer.

Waite Hoyt made his way over to the man who signed his paychecks. "Don't be nervous, Colonel," he joked.

"Don't you be nervous," retorted Ruppert, always quick with a quip. "Never mind me. I don't have to pitch."

The pitching matchup was Yankee right-handed ace Waite Hoyt against the big horse of the all-right-handed Pirate staff, Ray Kremer, the National League's ERA leader who had won 19 of 27 decisions. Kremer had a moving fastball supplemented by a nice change of pace and a darting curveball.

The band finally stopped playing, the introductions were completed, and the game got under way. A Gehrig first-inning triple (actually a misjudged fly ball by Paul Waner, who tried to make a shoestring catch) put the Yankees on the board, 1–0, as Ruth scored. The Bucs got the run back in their half of the first as Paul Waner doubled his kid brother to third, and "Little Poison" skipped home on a sacrifice fly by Glenn Wright.

In the third inning, the Yankees scored three times on only one hit. Two Pittsburgh miscues and two walks helped the cause of the always opportunistic New Yorkers. A Kremer double and a Paul Waner single made the score 4–2 as the game moved to the fourth.

Both teams scored a run in the fifth. In the sixth, Kremer was removed. In the eighth Hoyt was taken out and replaced by Moore. The "Schoolboy" had developed a blister and had given up four runs and eight hits in 7⅓ innings. The sloppy, herky-jerky game, played in 2 hours and 4 minutes, finally ended Yankees 5, Pirates 4.

Miller Huggins, happy, was a bit unkind in his comments about Kremer. "He is the type of pitcher who is easy for my batters. I don't think we need fear him anymore."

Grantland Rice in the *New York Herald Tribune* wrote: "It was scramble and rush and hullabaloo and stampede to look upon a gaudy spectacle which turned out to be one of the dullest games of the year. If Pittsburgh couldn't beat the Yankees today, it may be a tough job later on."

Rice's commentary notwithstanding, Jake Ruppert didn't much care for the tension of the game and the close score. But he was elated and excited by the win. A fan said to him that it was not a very good game.

"Any game," the colonel replied, "is a good game if we win it."

Babe Ruth shouted: "Well, it won't be long now, boys! It won't be long now!"

And Huggins added: "We have the jump on them now. First blood always counts in a series like this, and we intend to hold this upper hand. Tomorrow I'll start Pipgras and have Bengough catching. My team showed itself the better team today and I don't look for any unfavorable change in the playing of the boys. That means I look for victory again tomorrow."

Back in New York City more than 15,000 people had jammed into City Hall Park, watching that first game play out on the scoreboard of the *World* newspaper in front of the Pulitzer Building.

Tens of thousands more listened to the call of the game on radio. It was the first World Series broadcast nationally, as 53 radio stations, 43 of them part of the NBC network, heard Graham McNamee and Phillips Carlin. On CBS, Major J. Andrew White was on 10 stations. WEAF and WJZ were the New York stations for NBC, while CBS had WOR and also the municipal station, WNYC. Radio power was on display over local station KDKA in Pittsburgh.

A onetime salesman, a onetime part-time singing baritone, Graham

McNamee had begun his climb to the top of the broadcasting world via an audition in 1923, when he took a break from a $3-a-day jury duty gig and auditioned at the WEAF studios in lower Manhattan. He got the job, and his enthusiastic voice became an echo of the times. He was "Mr. Radio" to millions of people.

During that first game a curious and also disapproving Ring Lardner sat in the press box next to McNamee, watching the game and listening to the call: "It was like attending two games," Lardner lamented later. "You saw one game and heard another."

The *New York Sun*'s review of McNamee's broadcasting was even more caustic: "He mixed players and innings and team. He made right-handed batters left-handed and announced triumphantly on occasion that the Giants were leading—all of which must have been a surprise to McGraw. He put players on bases where they weren't and left them off bases where they were."

Truth be told, Graham McNamee was a pioneer of broadcasting baseball on the radio and was groping his way around. Truth also be told, the snipings by such as Ring Lardner and the *New York Sun* and other reps of the Fourth Estate were no doubt prompted by what they viewed as an encroachment on their private turf by the new kid on the media block: radio.

"McNamee followed no rules," wrote Ted Patterson in *The Golden Voices of Baseball.* "The game and the color around it were the things and his 'wow' and 'whees' and exclamation of wonder and excitement punctuated his running descriptions.

"Accuracy wasn't McNamee's forte," Patterson wrote. "Eventually Baseball Commissioner Kenesaw Mountain Landis saw fit to remove McNamee from the Series broadcasts."

The next day, in a sidebar to the game itself, Bozeman Bulger of the *New York Evening World* passed on this bit of food trivia: "The man at Forbes Field in charge of the refreshment stand says that the favorite foods of Pittsburgh fans are small hamburger steaks stuck in a round roll and the regulation hot dog. The Pitt fan goes in rather strong for soda pop, buttermilk, and sweet milk."

GAME TWO

Miller Huggins, a gambler, a hunch player, a manager with a wealth of options all through the 1927 season when it came to his pitching staff—he had six starting pitchers available to him—tabbed George Pipgras, the big guy from Minnesota, as a surprise starter for the second game of the Series, Thursday, October 6.

"I wasn't supposed to start in that Series," Pipgras years later told Donald Honig. "As least not as far as I knew. Urban Shocker was supposed to start the second game. Well, in about the seventh or eighth inning of the first game, right out of the blue, Miller Huggins looks over at me.

"'George,' he says, 'can you pitch tomorrow?'

"'Well, sure I can.'

"'Okay,' he says, 'Get a good night's rest.'

"A good night's rest! I'll tell you what I did. I went back to the hotel and started studying the Pittsburgh lineup until my eyes started to hurt."

Miller Huggins informed Urban Shocker that he was to be first out of the bullpen.

"'Listen,' he said," Pipgras recalled. "'When you leave the game, leave the ball rough.'"

Shocker did not expect Pipgras to be around that long, and the old spitballer wanted to have a ball to work with that had some texture on it.

"But I had no intention of getting out of there," Pipgras said.

Still using an old, greasy glove that had stood him in good stead in minor league stops at Atlanta, St. Paul, Charleston, and more, Pipgras took the mound against the Pirates.

The game got under way under blue skies in summerlike conditions before 41,634 at Forbes Field. Vic Aldridge, a 15-game winner in his eighth major league season, took the mound for Pittsburgh.

The Pirates got on the board first in the first inning. Lloyd Waner tripled. Clyde Barnhart drove him in with a sacrifice fly. But the Yankees came back with three in the third as Koenig, Ruth, and Lazzeri each picked up an RBI.

Over the first seven innings, George Pipgras, his fastball blazing, scattered six hits. The game moved to the top of the eighth inning—"five o'clock lightning" time.

Bob Meusel singled over second base. Tony Lazzeri singled to right field, pushing "Long Bob" to third. With Joe Dugan at the plate, Aldridge uncorked a wild pitch. Meusel scored and Lazzeri took second. Dugan tried to sacrifice, but catcher John Beverley Gooch pounced on the ball and threw to third base, to get Lazzeri who slid past the bag and was called out. Dugan wound up on first.

Shaken, feeling the fury of five o'clock lightning, Aldridge walked Benny Bengough and Pipgras. Out went Aldridge. In came little Mike Cvengros, 5-8 and 159 pounds. The nervous southpaw plunked Combs with a pitch. Dugan was forced in. Koenig singled. Yankees 6, Pirates 1 was how the inning finally ended.

Festive Forbes Field was now boo city. Jeers and catcalls rained down on the field from unhappy Buc rooters. Others simply expressed their displeasure with the home team's ineffectiveness by exiting the ballpark.

In the eighth inning, the Bucs scored a run. But Pipgras easily closed them out in the ninth to give the Yanks a 6–2 win and a 2–0 lead in the Series.

"I was fast that day," Pipgras recalled. "I didn't throw but three curves. They kept coming up there looking for the curve but never got it."

"You pitched a great game," Huggins told Pipgras in front of a collection of reporters, "a wonderful game. And I am proud of you."

And Pipgras told the assembled scribes: "I'm the happiest guy in the world. Winning was all right, but I'm happier to have Hug say he's proud of me."

Less than gleeful, almost cranky, Damon Runyon wrote in the *New York American*: "Unless something nerve tingling transpires pretty soon, the several hundred inmates of the press section will be biting their telegraph operators in desperation. Pittsburgh was badly outclassed. The weary looking Pirates were out batted, out fielded and out pitched. They were badly out fought."

It was yawn time for many, but the Yankees were just methodically going about their business of winning baseball games. That was what they did.

It was "The World's Dullest World Series after Just Two Games!" in a *New York Herald Tribune* headline.

"Even Mr. Barney Dreyfuss, the Pirate owner was seen to yawn openly in his box and did not even go to the trouble of concealing the yawn with his cash-calloused hand," wrote the caustic W. O. McGeehan in the *Tribune* in what could have been construed as just a tinge of anti-Semitic vitriol from McGeehan aimed at the Jewish Dreyfuss, who was born in Freiburg, Germany, in 1865.

Sitting sated and satisfied in his private box close by his charges in the dugout, Jacob Ruppert was a very happy owner. He enjoyed what his Yankees were accomplishing. He savored the dullness, the no surprises.

The Yankee owner "was not one to pal around with the boys," Rud Rennie wrote in the *Herald Tribune.* "For the most part, he was aloof and brusque. He never used profanity. "By gad" was his only expletive."

It was rumored that the man they called "Master Builder in Baseball" uttered many "By gads" during the Series.

Waite Hoyt and Joe Dugan were not nearly as happy as their boss, and their language underscored their anger. Since the Roosevelt Hotel World Series lodgings for the Yankees were brand-new, guests were not even issued room keys, since there weren't any. There were also no coat hangers in the closets. So Hoyt and Dugan had simply tossed their wallet-laden trousers over a chair, and during the night someone took off with their stuffed billfolds. It was reported that Dugan lost more than $200, Hoyt more than $300.

But the Pirates had lost much more than that—the first two games of the World Series, which was headed to New York.

Tony Lazzeri was riding in a cab with a newspaperman and a couple of other Yankees.

"If you guys don't wind the Series up in the next two days, I'll shoot you," the scribe joked.

"If we don't beat these bums four in a row you can shoot me first," quipped Lazzeri.

That was how confident the Yankees were about winning and not going back to Pittsburgh.

And as Richards Vidmer wrote in the *Times*, "The teams turned toward Broadway tonight and the prediction from this point of observation is that they'll never come back to Pittsburgh. Not this year."

GAME THREE

On Friday, October 7, lines for bleacher seats were up and running at 5:00 A.M.—five hours before the gates of Yankee Stadium were scheduled to open. Samuel Ruszer of 876 East 118th Street in Manhattan told the *New York American*, "Since 1898, I've been trying to be the first in line at a World Series game, and man, if you get in ahead of me, it'll be over my dead body, Gawd forbid!"

In the pregame hype and hoopla both Babe Ruth and Lou Gehrig were presented with a floral horseshoe and floral bats. Mayor Jimmy Walker, the toast of New York, was expected to throw out the first ball, but he was late in arriving. So Admiral Charles P. Plunkett, head of the Brooklyn Navy Yard, pinch-hit for him.

There were 60,695 on hand, "the biggest money crowd in the history of the title series," in James R. Harrison's phrase in the *New York Times*. There was also the biggest gate ever to that point in time for a World Series game: $209,665. Southpaw Herb Pennock, called "the aristocrat of baseball" by writer Will Wedge, was unbeaten in four World Series decisions. But there were those who viewed his start against the team from Pittsburgh, one that had racked up an .833 winning percentage against left-handed starters from midseason on, as feeding a lamb to the lions. Oh, how wrong they would be.

The Yankees scored in the first inning off bespectacled Buc right-hander Lee Meadows. Gehrig poked the ball to the running track in left-center field, scoring Combs and Koenig both of whom had singled. But Gehrig, attempting to stretch his shot into an inside-the-park home run, was cut down at home plate.

Squire Pennock set down Pittsburgh machinelike, batter after batter. The Bucs were hitless through the seventh inning, when the

Yankees put the game away by scoring six times. Five o'clock lightning one more time! The highlight of the Yankee big inning came when Mike Cvengros—a surname, according to Grantland Rice, "that you said with a sneeze"—relieved Meadows.

Dan Parker in the *New York Mirror* described the scene: "George Herman Ruth, the big record wrecker from 72nd Street welcomed Mr. Cvengros the way an Eskimo welcomes the first rays of the springtime sun. . . . With the count two balls and two strikes, Michael shot one down Babe's alley. A blind fan would have known it was a home run the moment ash met horsehide. A baseball finding itself in the middle of Babe's gang of idolizers in the right field bleachers."

The three-run shot, Ruth's first home run of the World Series, pushed the Yankee lead to 8–0. It triggered wild cheers for the Colossus of Clout as he made his way around the bases behind Combs and Koenig.

Glenn Wright led off the top of the eighth for Pittsburgh. He grounded out. Twenty-two Pirates had batted. Twenty-two had been retired.

Next was the very dangerous Pie Traynor. He singled to left, and the crowd groaned. No perfect game. Barnhart then doubled to right-center, scoring Traynor. No shutout.

With one down in the ninth, the almost peerless Pennock gave up a third hit—a single to Lloyd Waner. But the 33-year-old Yankee then bore down, getting Hal Rhyne to fly out and Paul Waner to pop up.

The screams of one fan captured the moment: "Take off those Pirates uniforms," he bellowed, "we know you're the St. Louis Browns!" The Yankees surely manhandled the Bucs like they treated the Browns. Maybe worse.

The 8–1 romp placed the Yankees one win away from becoming the first American League team to sweep a World Series.

Herb Pennock, who Grantland Rice said pitched each game "with the ease and coolness of a practice session" that 1927 season, earned every dollar of his $17,500 salary.

In the Yankee clubhouse, screaming and dancing and jumping around the floral horseshoe and floral bats that had been presented to

Ruth and Gehrig, there was a lot of whooping it up, atypical for the usually controlled crew of Murderers' Row. But the players sensed the kill, the end of their quest. A win in one more game and they would be world champions.

"Of course," said Huggins, magnanimous in his moment of great triumph, "the Pirates are down in spirits now. But I want to dispel the idea that the Pirates are not a good ball club. They are a great ball club. We are just better, that's all.

"Pennock pitched a wonderful ball game. He had everything except for weak moments and for a time I thought he was going to have not only a shutout but a no-hit game to his credit."

"I just gave them all I had and I am glad it had effect," said Pennock. "I guess there's no explaining it beyond the fact that I had special control and when I have got control I can pretty near come making the ball do anything I want. I don't mean that as a boast. I don't believe in coming inside or outside. My idea is to mix them up and that's what I did this afternoon."

"Well friends," W. O. McGeehan wrote in the *Herald Tribune*, "I hope you don't expect too much of a story out of me in regards to yesterday's game as I was too sleepy to watch what was going on."

GAME FOUR

Saturday, October 8, was damp and cloudy, like the spirits of the Pirates. Rain in the morning would hold the announced Yankee Stadium attendance down to 57,909. "There were plenty of empty seats," James R. Harrison noted in the *Times* the next day, "even in the reserved sections, but the crowd was as vociferous as ever."

One defeat away from elimination, the National League champions gave the ball to their biggest winner, bespectacled Carmen Hill. In limited duty in six previous big league seasons, Hill never had won more than three games. In 1927, he was a 22-game-winner. Surprisingly, Huggins tabbed farmer Wilcy Moore, who had made only a dozen starts in his 50 appearances in 1927. It was a reward for all the rookie Yankee had accomplished.

The Pirates scored a run in the first inning. The Yankees knotted the score on singles by Combs, Koenig, and Ruth. The tied game moved along inning after inning. The sudden-death tension on the Pirates kept building. In the fifth inning, Ruth's second home run of the Series scored Earle Combs. The Yanks led, 3–1.

The Ruthian blast, according to James Harrison in the *Times*, "climbed uphill, while 60,000 shrieked in ecstasy and turned their eyes on the right-field bleachers. The Brothers Waner turned tail and scooted for the fence. Paul got there first—in fact he was just in time to look upward and see a badly battered baseball drop limply over the wire screen.

"On the third base coaching line Arthur Fletcher took his hat off and tossed it high into the air. Some of the fans thought it was a good idea and followed suit. And there was great clamor and tumult and a snowstorm of torn paper."

Grantland Rice's perspective was even more fanciful: "There was a sausage-shaped balloon swaying against the gray October sky. Ruth's wallop almost hit the balloon. It sailed up, far and high in a mighty arc, and when it fell it was many, many yards beyond the reach of any spectators."

Desperate, the Pirates fought back. They tied the score in the seventh: "a muff by Deacon Wilcy Moore, the Oklahoma agriculturist, and a fumble by Tony Lazzeri, the lad from Frisco's Telegraph Hill, greased the way for the Pirates. . . . Barnhart singled over second base scoring Yde and Paul Waner hit a sac fly," was how James Harrison described the scoring.

In the bottom of the seventh inning, righthander Johnny Miljus—dubbed "Big Serb," a World War I hero who, it was claimed, had sustained 15 or so wounds—and catcher Johnny Gooch composed the new Pirate battery.

"It was all even going into the ninth," Harrison wrote, "and Deacon Moore set down three Pirates in apple-pie order. For the Yankees the Kentucky schoolmaster, Earle Combs, was first at bat. He drew four straight balls from John Miljus."

Pie Traynor misplayed a Koenig bunt down the third-base line. A wild first pitch to Ruth moved both runners up. The Babe was then walked intentionally.

"Bases full and nobody out the Pirates' hopes looked as gray and bleak as the October sky above," Harrison wrote. "Gehrig was at bat—the great Gehrig, who drove more runs across the plate this season than any other batter in baseball history."

Miljus fanned Lou Gehrig.

Miljus fanned Bob Meusel.

"It looked like we'd get out of it," Paul Waner said later.

"Yankee Stadium was in a frenzy," wrote Shirley Povich in the *Washington Post*. "New York fans or not the 52,000 persons in the stands accorded the veteran a tremendous ovation. Here was being executed a baseball rarity. A veteran pitcher was matching his physical skill and his pitching acumen against three batters renowned for their slugging and on the result hung the championship and thousands of dollars in gold for the players of the teams."

Tony Lazzeri came to bat. It wasn't exactly the same situation as in the 1926 World Series against the St. Louis Cardinals, when the Yankee second baseman was struck out by Grover Cleveland Alexander with the bases loaded; nevertheless, many could not help but think back to that moment.

Lazzeri stepped up. He crouched a bit over the plate. He swung at Miljus's first pitch. A line drive to the left—foul. The second pitch came in high and wide. Catcher Gooch lunged. The ball smacked off his mitt and rolled toward the field box of Commissioner Kenesaw Mountain Landis. The speedy Combs raced in with the winning run.

The New York Yankees were world champions!

"Miljus, almost a hero, and now a goat," Damon Runyan wrote in his Universal Service column, "struggled to get through the mass of fans who had rushed out onto the playing field. The former war hero punched his glove into the air in the direction of the Yankee bench where players were trying to avoid the clutching, grabbing hand of gleeful admirers."

The last pitch could have been a failed curve or a spitball that went out of control. There was a report that it was a moist ball. Miljus and Gooch never said what the pitch was.

"If only it had ended any other way," a disconsolate Miljus would later say. "If they had knocked the ball out of the park, anything but a wild pitch. That's terrible."

The atmosphere in the Pirate locker room was somber, serious, sad. "I can't blame Miljus a mite for the wild pitch that lost the game," Buc pilot Bush said. "It was just the final break. Johnny Gooch has caught worse balls in his career, although it was a very bad pitch. We were dead on our feet from the start. Our pitching was spotty, but the Yanks did not hit us consistently. It was just a case of too many 3 to 1 and 1 to 0 victories in the final stages of the pennant race. Before I could look forward to the World Series I had to win the flag, and in doing that the team wore out, had nothing left for the Yankees."

The Yankee locker room was crazy—a circus, frenzied, and full of fun. The first two "names" to enter the inner sanctum of five o'clock lightning were baseball Commissioner Kenesaw Mountain Landis and Wally Pipp, whom Lou Gehrig had replaced as Yankee first baseman those couple of seasons past and who had completed the 1927 season as the Cincinnati Reds' first baseman.

Outside the stadium about 3,000 Babe Ruth admirers waited patiently. Many policemen kept them company, at the ready to ease the Yankee icon to his car, parked on 157th Street.

"I want to say something nice about the Pittsburgh team," Huggins said, gracious in victory to reporters. "Say something nice about the Pirates. Don't be hard on them. It was tragic to lose a ball game that way. They've had a lot of tough luck in the Series. And they were a much better ball club than they showed in the Series. I'm happy beyond words that we took this Series in four games. I've known all along that we had a great ball club. Now I guess everyone will admit we have."

"I am tickled to death that our team won," said Colonel Ruppert. "But I am happier in what I believe is a great thing for baseball."

Then ever the bottom-line businessman, the Yankee mogul

continued: "It will cost us something like $200,000, but there can be no talk now of stringing a Series out. We wanted to win in four straight games and we did, because we have a wonderful team."

Damon Runyon wrote: "Under the grandstand, Mr. Egg-Bert Barrow, the genial business manager of the Yanks, joined his tears with those of Mr. Harry M. Stevens. After the game, the former weeping for the $217,000 that he must turn back to his clients because there will be no Sunday game, and the latter brooding over the lost hot-dog traffic."

The early end to the Series allegedly cost Pirate and Yankee owners more than $200,000 each. For Ruppert, who it was estimated personally earned $50,000 weekly, the money was not a problem. Neither was the quick conclusion to the World Series. The beer baron was a man who hated unsettled accounts.

The 1927 World Series, the quickest ever played, lasted only 74 hours and 15 minutes and was just the second four-game sweep in World Series history; the Braves over Athletics in 1914 was the first.

The Pittsburgh offense was held to a .223 average. Yankee pitchers combined for an incredible earned-run average of only 2.00. Wilcy Moore's was a microscopic 0.84. The Yanks became the first team to have four different pitchers win on four straight days for the same team in a World Series.

The Yanks, who made just three errors had a team fielding average of .981. Outscoring the Pirates 23–10, the men of Murderers' Row trailed a total of only two innings during the entire Series.

Pittsburgh only once managed to score more than one run in an inning; that was in the fourth game. The Yankees used only 15 different players and just 4 pitchers. The Yankees averaged more than six runs a game. The 1–4 hitters (Combs, Koenig, Ruth, and Gehrig) batted .387, hit 2 home runs, drove in 16 runs, and scored 17. The rest of the Yankee hitters managed just a .189 average, with only 3 RBIs and 6 runs scored. Together, Ruth and Gehrig batted .357 and had a slugging average of .786. Batting .500 in the World Series, Mark Koenig led all hitters and was the only Yankee to hit safely in each game. Ruth was the leader in home runs, Gehrig in doubles, Combs in triples and base hits.

The *New York Times* declared on October 12 that it had no argument with those "who assert that these Yankees are the greatest team in more than 50 years of baseball history. George Herman Ruth once again demonstrated that he is the superman of the game. . . . As [Dodger manager] Uncle Wilbert Robinson put it, 'That guy ought to be allowed to play only every other day.'"

Uncle Robbie was right all over the place. He also had predicted: "The Pirates will get massacred because the Yankees were the best team in the history of baseball."

The Pittsburgh Pirates had their back broken by the Yankees in that 1927 World Series. Demoralized, down, decimated, the team that had won five pennants in 25 years would not win another pennant for 33 years. John Miljus would play on for a couple of more major league seasons and finish his career in the minors and forever be jeered by opponents who called him "Throw-it-away John!"

The Yankees were the toast of the town, the champions, not only the best team in baseball in 1927, but they also had strong bragging rights now to the mantle of the best baseball team of all time.

"Hats off to Combs, Koenig, Ruth, Gehrig, Meusel, Push 'em up WOP, and all the rest of the celebrated batting order" was the commentary in the *New York World*.

"If the old Baltimore Orioles are still talked about after 30 years, this team will be talked of for the next century, and hats off to Huggins, the greatest lawyer who ever sat on a bench," the *World* commentary continued.

The 1927 World Series share for each Yankee was minimal when compared to what the world champion 2006 St. Louis Cardinals received—full shares of $362,173 each. But the checks each Yank regular received—$5,592—added up to more than Mike Gazella, Joe Giard, Cedric Durst, George Pipgras, Wilcy Moore, Julie Wera, and Ray Morehart individually earned for the entire season. The big paydays awarded to substitutes, to players who had not been major parts of the Yankee machine, showcased the "all for one and one for all" motto of that team.

It was, as Waite Hoyt said, great to be young and a Yankee.

This was the actual disbursement of the total receipts ($783,217) from the 1927 World Series:

15%   Commissioner Landis's Advisory Board, $117,482.55

51%   Players' share, $399,440.67

 70%   Contending clubs, $279,608.46

  60%   Yankees, winners of the World Series, $167,765.07

  40%   Pirates, losers of the World Series, $111,843.38

30%   The other first-division teams, $119,832.20

50%   Second-place teams from each league split $59,916.10

  50%   American League's Philadelphia Athletics, $29,958.05

  50%   National League's St. Louis Cardinals, $29,958.05

33.33%   Third-place teams from each league split $39,944.06

  50%   American League's Washington Senators, $19,972.03

  50%   National League's New York Giants, $19,972.03

16.67%   Fourth-place teams from each league split $19,972.03

  50%   American League's Detroit Tigers, $9,988.01

  50%   National League's Chicago Cubs, $9,988.01

34%   Participating teams' officers, $266,293.76

  50%   Owners, $133,146.88

   50%   Colonel Jacob Ruppert, New York Yankees' owner, $66,573.44

   50%   Barney Dreyfuss, Pittsburgh Pirates' owner, $66,573.44

  50%   Submitted to League offices, $133,146.88

   50%   American League's office, $66,573.44

   50%   National League's office, $66,573.44

AFTER THE 1927 SEASON

Called the "five o'clock lightning"
taking the pennant in the fall.

—Robert L. Harrison, "1927 Yankees"

The tumult and the shouting having died down to almost a whisper," John Drebinger wrote in the *New York Times*, "the short-lived world series of 1927 was hastened into oblivion yesterday by the steady patter of rain which helped to drive thoughts further and further away from baseball. Mingling among the few actors in the drama that still remained on the scene, one scarcely could believe that only twenty-four hours had elapsed since Johnny Miljus's now famous wild pitch had rung down the curtain."

Drebinger's commentary notwithstanding, there was still a good deal of excitement among the players and their fans and the city of New

York over what Murderers' Row had accomplished. And for many weeks and months the topics of conversation centered about why Pittsburgh lost, what if Kiki Cuyler had been allowed to play, what if Gooch had been in better position to catch the wild pitch or at least knock it down so it didn't roll as far away as it did.

No matter the whys and the what ifs and the whatevers, to the victors belonged the glory and the spoils.

Each Yankee regular was scheduled to receive a full 1927 World Series full winner's share of $5,592, Miller Huggins and coaches O'Leary and Fletcher, too, as well as traveling secretary Roth. Trainer Doc Woods was voted a three-quarters share, while John Miller, billed as a recruit pitcher who joined the Yankees halfway through the season, earned a half share. Groundskeeper Phil Schenck was awarded $750, while his assistant was in line for $250. The clubhouse custodian, Fred Logan, was set for $700. The same amount was designated for Yankee batboy/mascot extraordinaire Eddie Bennett, an over-the-top sum for that era for a nonplayer.

By today's baseball standards the money was negligible. But by 1927 standards the payoff was big money and most welcome, especially for low-salaried players such as Cedric Durst, George Pipgras, Wilcy Moore, Joe Giard, Julie Wera, Ray Morehart, Lou Gehrig, Pat Collins, Ben Paschal, and Myles Thomas.

For the mighty Yankees, everything was coming up roses. Lou Gehrig's mom was off the critical list, out of the hospital, and at home. Players were set to enjoy their off-season, preparing to cash in on their world championship halo.

Still in the full blush of that World Series sweep of the Pirates, the mighty New York Yankees of 1927 seemed as strong as a block of granite. But the roster was already set to develop cracks. Ray Morehart, Bob Shawkey, Dutch Ruether, and Joe Giard, released by the Yankees, would never play in another major league game.

The members of the team began to scatter hither and yon. Bob Shawkey, Mark Koenig, and Benny Bengough headed out on a hunting trip. Herb Pennock went back to Kennett Square for a winter of breeding silver foxes. George Pipgras was off to St. Petersburg to hunt quail and small game. Pat Collins traveled home to Kansas City to manage a bowling alley. Earle Combs was set to spend time in his old Kentucky home.

Wilcy Moore headed back to his piece of land to tend to things, but before he departed, he asked Colonel Ruppert for a raise in pay for the coming season. Five hundred dollars was the figure he had in mind. The magnanimous Ruppert gave him far more than that. It truly had been a good year for the farmer from Oklahoma.

Tony Lazzeri traveled back to San Francisco. There he received a phone call from Miller Huggins, who was interested in what his second baseman intended to do with his winning World Series share.

Lazzeri said he had no idea yet, And according to the story in John Mosedale's *The Greatest of All*, the little Yankee manager cut in: "Turn the check over to me. I'll make this Series worth a lot more money to you. If there was any doubt about it, I wouldn't suggest it, but I know."

Three weeks later Huggins again contacted Lazzeri, pointing out the stock he recommended was in the mid-80s. "It will go over a hundred," the mite manager said. "That World Series will keep making money for you for a long time."

Lazzeri and other Italian American players from the New York metropolitan area engaged in a small tour right after the Series ended. Ray Morehart was the only player on that team not of Italian descent. But the Lazzeri tour was minor league compared to what Babe Ruth's business manager, ghostwriter, and agent, Christy Walsh, had organized.

Major League Baseball rules did not permit teams to barnstorm. So Walsh had "the Babe and the Buster" primed and eager to set out on an 18-state tour to promote Major League Baseball—and themselves, of course.

The hustling Walsh even created "Home Run Derby of 1927," a kind of one-more-time battle between Babe Ruth and Lou Gehrig that offered as a prize the "Copper Cup" trophy to the one who hit the most home runs by the tour's end.

Covering 8,000 miles, involving 21 games, attracting 200,000 paying customers, lasting virtually an entire month, featuring teams headed by Gehrig and Ruth, and traveling across the heartland of

America all the way to California, the mother of all barnstorming tours strutted its stuff.

In that era, the farthest west Major League Baseball franchises were in St. Louis. For many, baseball came to them only from radio accounts and news, box scores, and stories in newspapers and from magazines. If the Babe and the Buster could not be seen by these fans, Christy Walsh reasoned, he would bring Ruth and Gehrig to them. And make a profit, too. And everyone would come out ahead of the game.

With their World Series triumph behind them, as Jonathan Eig said in *Luckiest Man*, "Ruth tipped the call girls and sent them on their way. Gehrig kissed his mother goodbye."

The first games of the traveling baseball show were scheduled on the East Coast with the Yankee idols playing on the same teams or against clubs such as the Brooklyn Bushwicks and the Brooklyn Royal Giants of the Eastern Colored League.

On October 10, in Rhode Island, the initial game of the tour was set to be played in Providence, where Babe Ruth was returning for the first time since 1914, when he played for the Grays of the International League. He was called up by the Red Sox in 1915 and never played in another minor league game. But it was Lou Gehrig who thrilled the 5,000 fans in Providence, blasting the first home run of the barnstorming tour.

The next event—a doubleheader against the Lincoln Giants in the Bronx—was rained out, but for Columbia Lou, it was a sunny day. He received the good news that he had won the American League Most Valuable Player award. His 56 points beat out the 35 Harry Heilmann of Detroit received and the 34 that Ted Lyons of Chicago got. George Herman Ruth was not even considered because former winners were not eligible; however, the Bambino did get a nice consolation prize, not that he needed it. The New York baseball writers presented him with a plaque designating him Player of the Year.

The Big Bam and Buster Lou were at it again in Trenton, New Jersey, in a game that pitted a Trenton all-star team against the Brooklyn Royal Giants. Ruth hammered three home runs. After his last dinger, the game was stopped in the eighth inning because hundreds of kids mobbing the Babe would not get off the field of play. The swarming, adoring, cloying phenomenon would cause a dozen games to end early.

"There has always been a magic about that gross, ugly, coarse, gargantuan figure of a man and everything he did," Paul Gallico wrote. "It is all the more remarkable because George Herman Ruth is not sculptured after the model of the hero. . . . He was kneaded, rough-thumbed out of earth, a golem, a figurine that might have been made by a savage."

The next day, Babe Ruth's team showed up for a game against the Bushwicks, wearing for the first time black-and-white suits especially created for the tour. Ruth's team had black pants and uniform shirts with "Bustin' Babes" printed in white lettering. His players also sported white caps with a black "BB" on the front. Lou Gehrig's uniform was the same except that there was an "LL" (for Larrupin' Lous) on his cap. And across the chest of his shirt were the words "Larrupin' Lous."

More than 20,000 fans were on hand, and they were in a very rowdy and hyper mood, enjoying the sight of Lou Gehrig in right field and the Babe playing first base. Many spilled into the roped-off area in the outfield and repeatedly exited that cordoned-off space, challenging outfielders for the ball.

"It got so bad," the *New York Times* reported, "that unless an outfielder fielded a ball cleanly, the crowd gobbled up the ball. In the seventh [inning], the front line was even with the outfielders."

In the eighth inning, as perhaps a consolation prize for his fans for not having hit a homer in the game, the Babe took over and did some pitching, retiring three batters in a row. He hadn't lost his old touch on the mound. Heading into the ninth inning, Ruth's team was in the lead as the mighty showman took his warm-ups and was ready to pitch. Then, almost as if a switch had been thrown, many excited fans surged onto the field. The minimal police presence was helpless to protect the King of Swat. But he needed no protection. The fans just loved the Yankee superstar and couldn't get enough of him. The more passionate and sturdy members of the smiling horde descended on the Babe. Cheering him, they carried him off the field to the clubhouse. The game was never completed.

Premature endings of games due to inadequate crowd control was one of the problems of the tour. A frequently vanishing supply of baseballs was another problem.

Before games, the King of Swat and his powerful partner engaged in friendly batting exhibitions, bashing baseballs out of the park. Foreshadowing the home run derbies of today, it was a way of guaranteeing fans the opportunity to brag later that they had been eyewitnesses to Babe Ruth and Lou Gehrig hitting homers—even if those homers were not during the "official" exhibition games. But that was one way baseballs got used up.

Another was that fans, on the field in overflow locations, had good opportunities to get baseballs. And the ones they got, they kept. Precious souvenirs. In a game played in Asbury Park, New Jersey, the game ended in the sixth inning when Gehrig hit the last available baseball over the fence and into a lake. In that one game alone nine dozen balls disappeared, an astonishingly high number for games played in those days.

From 1920 to 1940, Babe Ruth played quite a few times in Sioux City, Iowa. The most famous of these exhibition games took place in 1927. On October 18, it was the Bustin' Babes versus the Larrupin' Lous at the Stockyards Ballpark. Thousands showed to see Ruth and Gehrig take the field and take their places as the star attractions of local teams.

It was written in the local papers for days and weeks afterward and spoken of for years afterward—the scene when Babe Ruth and Lou Gehrig came to town. The Home Run King's team won that day, 4–2, and the Master Mauler slugged a towering home run. As was becoming standard, the game was stopped several times because frenzied fans ran out on to the field to get near the legends of baseball. A young fan was almost trampled by spectators who, once on the field, became a mob. But Lou Gehrig whisked the frightened kid into his sturdy arms and saved him. The commotion, however, forced the exhibition to be canceled during the ninth inning.

In this tour of all tours postscript to the magical 1927 baseball season of the New York Yankees, newspaper headline writers along the way overreached, attempting to characterize George Herman Ruth and

Henry Louis Gehrig. Even the venerable *New York Times* got into act: "Word comes from Kansas City, Denver and points west," the "paper of record" reported on October 26, "that Babe Ruth and Lou Gehrig are 'knocking 'em dead' on their baseball exhibition tour. They have been greeted by any number of brass bands at each stopping place and have been handed the keys of all the cities they have visited thus far in their peregrinations. Mayors and Governors have turned out to extend official welcomes, and the eminent Mr. Ruth has made some sparkling replies to the toast 'Our Hero!' at sundry Rotary Club luncheons."

Although the tour didn't feature the highest caliber of competition, local sportswriters were often surprised and impressed at the "major league" effort always put forth by the Yankee superstars and their supporting cast.

Ruth and Gehrig had very limited personal time during the tour, but what they had, they graciously gave. There were many instances where they went out of their way to visit local orphanages and hospitals. There was even a game played in a prison, where the Bambino showed as much rapport with the prisoners as he had with hospital patients and orphans.

Barnstorming America, wherever they went there was always time for Ruth and Gehrig to pose for photographs, to be interviewed by newspeople, to give what would become a famous photo (and now a valuable one valued 80 years later at more than $11,000) of themselves standing and leaning on their bats, Ruth wearing a black uniform with the words Bustin' Babes" across the shirt front, and Gehrig in a white uniform that reads "Larrupin' Lous." Each player signed "Yours Truly" and his name twice.

The tour represented more than just baseball exhibition games. It underscored the magic and mystique of the New York Yankees and the aura that Lou Gehrig and Babe Ruth possessed. The 1927 postseason tour for the Yankee superstars also represented a big payday. And it was a kind of coming-out party for the 24-year-old Gehrig. Until then, he had never been farther west than St. Louis, never really been on his own. He was enjoying the tour, looser, friendlier than he had ever been. All who came into contact with him were impressed.

In Lima, Ohio, a female reporter wrote: "Well built and handsome, Gehrig . . . could make the most hard hearted Hannah melt in his arms."

Many times Gehrig was referred to as the "Iron Man," or as "Columbia Lou" for his university times. He announced—some would have called it a slip of the tongue—at one the small-town press conferences that he liked football as a sport more than baseball.

"When it comes to getting a real thrill out it, I got more kick out of playing college football than I do out of major league baseball," he said. But then he quickly added: "You can get the thrills in football, but you can't get away from the fact that the money is in baseball."

In the Midwest, Lou and Babe split up and took charge of opposing teams. The top amateurs in Lima, Ohio, Kansas City, Missouri, Omaha, Nebraska, Des Moines and Sioux City, Iowa and Denver—all came out to play the game with the icons of the New York Yankees.

From town to town, city to city, the traveling baseball road show that was the home run kings made its mark. Babe Ruth craved the spotlight; Lou Gehrig shrank from it. On the back platform of stopped trains, the Colossus of Clout, like a president or a king, came out to tarry a while, smile, smoke a cigar, tell stories, trade wisecracks. The people ate it up. The Babe had to coax Gehrig onto the platform to stand beside him. It was said that those were the times that Gehrig drew away from the Big Bam, put off by Ruth's expansive and impulsive ways, his excessively out-front and outspoken personality.

But the tour played on. Big-time celebrities, the pair was wined and dined, paid homage to, given gifts of all kinds and fashion. In Omaha, Ruth was presented with the 171st consecutive egg laid by Lady Norfolk—the "Babe Ruth" of hen layers, who had shattered a regional poultry record. A few days later, in Sioux City, a local meat packing company had a great time of it giving Ruth a ham with his name spelled out in cloves. "So Now Babe Ruth Can Have Ham and Eggs," read the newspaper caption under a photo of the happening.

In Denver, Ruth blasted two home runs at Merchants Park. One of the stunning shots was claimed to be the longest ever to that point in time, no doubt aided by the Rocky Mountain high. The Babe did a lot of stunning that day, even stealing home in the first inning, surprising the crowd of more than 5,000. The Yankee slugger was in fact an intelligent and daring base runner. He stole home 10 times in his major league career.

On the weekend of October 22–23, the Babes and the Lous, as they were being called, drew 36,000 Bay Area fans for a three-game series. On Saturday, at San Francisco, the home run twins had a time of it— swinging away with gusto, putting on a very impressive hitting exhibition at Recreation Park. The field was an ideal environment for the pounding of a baseball a country mile. Fences were not that far away, and directly behind them were houses. And far beyond center field, a church was a full city block away.

According to Dolph Camilli, a native San Franciscan and one who later played in the major leagues for a decade, "They had guys laying the ball in there real nice for them. Lou and Babe were teeing off, hitting them over those houses." Camilli said that some shots hit the church a block away.

About 10,000 watched Gehrig slash a home run and a double, leading the Larrupin' Lous to a 10–7 victory over the Bustin' Babes. Weak, blistered hands reduced Ruth's long-ball pop. He didn't hit a home run, but he did get two hits.

In the seventh inning Gehrig knocked a changeup over the center-field fence, narrowly missing a cigarette billboard on top of the clubhouse.

The Iron Horse later said: "Gee, that felt good."

"I suppose you're going to rub it in now," Ruth came back at him. "But go ahead and have your fun. I'll get ahold of one tomorrow, and when I do—"

"They'll forget that I ever hit one," Gehrig quickly quipped.

The following afternoon, Babe made good his promise, pounding out two home runs.

Leaving the Bay Area, the traveling Babe Ruth/Lou Gehrig show moved to California's Central Valley for games in Stockton, Marysville, and Sacramento, and San Jose. The battle for the "Copper Cup" trophy, to be awarded to the one with more home runs at the tour's end, was all in favor of Babe Ruth at that moment in time. He was ahead 15–7 over Gehrig, but the Yankee first baseman had hit more home runs of late.

On October 29, in Fresno, three districts closed their schools so that students, teachers, and administrators could see the games. Four Japanese Americans played on Gehrig's team and helped defeat Ruth's squad, 13–3. Their star player, Zenimura, only 5 feet tall and 100 pounds, lived in Fresno. "Pound for pound, the Nisei players were as good as the major leaguers," Al Beir, batboy for Ruth and Gehrig on the tour, told the *Fresno Bee* in 1996. "They ate, thought, and slept the game."

In Marysville, with half the tiny town present at the ballpark, Ruth and Gehrig each homered twice in the game. Bill Conlin, a former columnist for the *Sacramento Bee*, was a 14-year-old batboy at the Marysville game. "They used 'jackrabbit' baseballs that were livelier and jumped off the bat," he said.

In Santa Barbara, a batch of local bushers were on Lou Gehrig's club. Babe Ruth captained a crew of Seabees from the USS *Colorado*. Sailors were allowed in for just 50 cents. But there was a surcharge of 10 cents a ticket charged on each dollar admission ticket by the game's promoters. They called it a war tax. Since it was peacetime, it was unclear what the point of the tax was. But people paid it—anything to see the "Home Run King" and the "Prince of Pounders." The speculation was that the "war tax" existed to make up for the sailor discount.

The tour moved on. A game was played in San Diego. Final score, 3–2, no home runs, not many thrills for the fans. Then the Babe and Gehrig flew to Los Angeles for the final game of the month-long cavalcade. The largest crowd of the tour, estimated at more than 30,000, showed up at Wrigley Field, where the governor of California even threw out the first ball and other dignitaries scrambled about to get their pictures taken with Ruth and Gehrig.

A subplot of the game was a matchup between the Bambino and Chicago Cub pitcher Charlie Root, the National League's top hurler with a 26–15 record in 1927, who pitched for Gehrig's team. The matchup preceded by five years the famous moment in the third game of the 1932 World Series when Ruth "called his shot" off Root. Ruth made a gesture that many believed indicated he was pointing to center field, just before slamming the dramatic home run.

In this 1927 barnstorming game, however, the Babe did no pointing. And Root held him to a double. Gehrig, meanwhile, slugged two home runs and a double to lead his team to a 5–2 victory over the Bustin' Babes. The Los Angeles fans were more subdued than those of other locales where stormings of the field and stoppings of games were more or less the norm. In the City of Angels, fans watched and cheered and enjoyed the game but stayed off the field

After the game ended, Ruth and Gehrig signed baseballs, tossing them to kids who pushed and shoved and grappled on the field for the precious prizes.

The *Los Angeles Examiner*, a bit hyperbolic, reported: "The Thumpin' Twins threw autographed balls among the hundreds of assembled kids. There couldn't have been more excitement if the Twins had been tossing out gold pieces or passes to ride in Lindy's [Charles Lindbergh's] plane."

One more game was scheduled, in Long Beach, on Halloween. But the game was canceled because of rain.

In all, more than 21 games were played in just three weeks spread over nine states. Thirteen games came to an early end because of fan frenzy—run-outs onto the field, stopping play. Although the tour mastermind, Christy Walsh, estimated that the games drew more than 220,000 fans, the figure was closer to 175,000, judging from local newspaper accounts. No matter; the tour, grossing approximately $220,000, provided monster paydays for all involved. Ruth reportedly made $70,000 for the month's work, equaling his Yankee salary. Gehrig was paid $10,000, surpassing his Yankee salary. Walsh, according to the Babe, earned $40,000.

The Copper Cup trophy was won by Babe Ruth, who, it was said, slugged 22 home runs to Gehrig's 13. "Columbia Lou" narrowly outhit him .618 to .616.

Newspaper hype and hoopla were staples of the tour. Dubbed "Spanking Yankees," "Thumpin' Twins," "Mighty Swatsmen," "King Ruth," "Crown Prince of Swatonia," Babe Ruth and Lou Gehrig, Lou

Gehrig and Babe Ruth—the great baseball duo and their traveling road show was more popular, more ballyhooed than the lead act of Barnum & Bailey's circus.

That tour was a product of a much earlier time in America and sports history; nevertheless, it showed the potential that performers of all types and talents for decades into the future would tap into—the public's fascination with celebrities coming to them and performing.

The long grinds of the fabulous and frenetic 1927 season and the barnstorming tour were now behind them. The future would bring

Babe Ruth with Al Smith button

other barnstorming tours, including a fall 1928 "Bustin' Babes" and "Larrupin' Lou's" Orient tour.

But this first tour, coming after the season of "five o'clock lightning," with Ruth and Gehrig, the "Thumpin' Twins," in their primes, would never be able to be outdone. All the members of the 1927 New York Yankees had interesting off-seasons, with lots of memories of what had been and lots of things to do. But none had quite the time that Babe Ruth and Lou Gehrig had, spreading their image and that of New York Yankee baseball from coast to coast. Back in New York City, the home-run twins went their separate ways.

Offered a deal to play professional ball with the Philadelphia Warriors of the American Basketball League, Lou Gehrig declined. He was a talented basketball player but was content to engage in the sport against pickup teams or kids out in the street, be around his parents, take it easy.

Ruth never let up; his way was life full bore that winter. He loved his saxophone lessons and practiced diligently in his apartment in the Ansonia Hotel. "I can play two pieces now," he told his buddies from the sporting press just a bit before Christmas, "but by spring I'll be able to give you fellows a regular concert." It was reported that one scribe whispered well out of earshot of the Babe, "I can hardly wait."

Ruth's alma mater, St. Mary's Industrial School, bragged about its band. On tour to raise cash for the school, the musical aggregation appeared in Jersey City and also New York City with a special guest conductor who led with his left hand. His name was George Herman Ruth and he got a special kick out of waving his baton for the song "Batterin' Babe."

That winter there was also golf for Ruth to pursue when weather permitted, many games of bridge, duck hunting, fox hunting with Herb Pennock in Kennett Square, membership in the Elks. Action, the more the better, was the Babe's way of life.

It was all blue skies for the Big Bam. Here was a man with an irrevocable $70,000 trust fund. Here was a man with a $50,000 annuity, fully funded. Here was a man primed to play in a new baseball season and get paid another $70,000 in salary. He did, however, wind up with a cash flow issue, being $1,500 short of the funds he needed to pay his income taxes, but that was not a problem. He easily got the cash. He was Babe Ruth, and he could get whatever he wanted.

Heading into the 1928 season there were roster changes for the Yankees, but they were minimal. Gone from the 1927 team were pitchers Bob Shawkey, Dutch Ruether, and Joe Giard. But Waite Hoyt, Wilcy Moore, Herb Pennock, George Pipgras, Urban Shocker, and Myles Thomas were still there.

The catching staff included the same big three from 1927: Benny Bengough, Pat Collins and Johnny Grabowski. And there was a talented 21-year-old rookie backstop on board, too, named Bill Dickey.

The same starting infield of Lou Gehrig, Tony Lazzeri, Mark Koenig, and Joe Dugan returned, along with utility man Mike Gazella. Three new Yankee infielders were George Burns, Gene Robertson, and a scrappy guy named Leo Durocher out of West Springfield, Massachusetts. The Yankees had actually obtained Durocher, then 19, for $7,500 from Hartford in 1925. He managed one at-bat for the big club that season. "Double play" hands were what scout Paul Krichell said he had. Huggins looked upon Durocher as "a mighty fine shortstop."

There were no changes in the outfield of regulars Bob Meusel, Earle Combs, and Babe Ruth and reserves Cedric Durst and Ben Paschal.

The golden glow of the magic season of 1927 was still there. Most of the players on the Yankees were in their prime. In the main there were no thoughts of retirement, illness, loss of powers, death.

But in the years after 1927, many tragic, poignant, and strange happenings would befall some of those who had been part of the greatest baseball team of all time. Some of these happenings were part of the normal course of life. Others were cruel and unexpected, as if a curse had been set in motion.

URBAN SHOCKER

Urban Shocker, perhaps the only member of the fabled Yankees not in good health, voluntarily retired after the 1927 season. His health was failing fast. Around Christmastime of 1927, he weighed but 115 pounds.

Incredibly, Shocker managed to come back to pitch three innings in 1928 but was released by the Yankees on July 6. Too ill to run his successful radio shop in St. Louis, the man born as Urbain Jacques Shockcor moved to Colorado. He appeared on August 6 in a semipro tournament game, playing for Denver against Cheyenne. Shortly after, he contracted pneumonia. Then it seemed he was on the mend, but he suffered a relapse. On September 9, 1928, Urban Shocker passed away. His death was attributed to an overstrained "athlete's heart." He had been unable to sleep lying down for two years. Just 38 years old, he was the first of the 1927 Yankees to die.

At his funeral, at All Saints' Church in St. Louis on September 15, Lou Gehrig and Waite Hoyt acted as pallbearers. The entire Yankee team was there to pay final respects. Shocker was buried in St. Louis, in Calvary Cemetery. Later his wife was voted a full 1928 World Series share by the Yankees.

Despite an impressive record of 187–117, a .616 percentage over 13 major league seasons, including four consecutive campaigns of 20 or more victories, never having a losing season, the righthander from Cleveland never garnered more than four votes for admission to the Baseball Hall of Fame.

"Shocker's overall record," Bill Slocum wrote in the *New York Journal-American*, "in the eyes of some objective observers, is better than several pitchers who have gained admission into the Hall of Fame."

MILLER HUGGINS

Throughout the 1929 season the powerful Philadelphia Athletics kept widening their first-place lead over the Yankees. It seemed that each time Philly won, Miller Huggins anguished even more. By the middle of August the Yankees were 25 games over the .500 mark, but the Athletics were 45 games over.

Huggins had a boil on his face but refused medical treatment, saying "me, who faced the likes of John J. McGraw and tough men like that worry about a little pimple?"

On September 20, 1929, the little manager arrived late for a game at the Stadium against Boston. He was weak and pasty-looking. The boil on the side of his face close to his eye was now a very nasty red. In the dugout after the third inning, he was examined by a doctor and the decision was made to admit him to St. Vincent's Hospital. Two days later, Huggins was in "grave condition," with a temperature of 105 and receiving blood transfusions.

His sister, his constant companion for years, was at his bedside along with his brother Arthur; the superintendent of Yankee Stadium, Charles McManus; Huggins's longtime friend and business partner Bob Connery; and a visibly moved Jake Ruppert, whose relationship with Huggins was very close. Telegrams, telephone calls and cards flooded Yankee Stadium. Huggins sent for his lawyer and his pastor.

As described in *The Big Bam* by Leigh Montville, the reports were that death came from an infected boil, but Huggins had actually used a heating lamp to try to burst the growth. It was determined later that Huggins was actually suffering from a skin disease commonly known as St. Anthony's fire, according to Montville. The heat made his problem deadly, filling his body with poison.

On September 25, Miller James Huggins passed away. He was 51 years old. The Yankees were playing in Boston. News of his death came over the wires in the fifth inning. At the end of the inning, the game was stopped. Men with megaphones moved about Fenway, giving the sad news to the small crowd of 7,000 fans. The center-field flag was lowered to half mast. Bareheaded, heads bowed, both teams and the three umpires gathered around the home plate area for a minute of silence. Most players were still; a few fidgeted nervously about. In the stands, the fans rose, respectful, many deeply touched by the moment despite the fact that Miller Higgins had been the manager of the hated Yankees. The game resumed. In eleven innings the Yanks nipped the Sox, 11–10.

The entire Yankee team returned after the game to New York for the funeral. All American League games were canceled by league president Ernest Barnard; flags at ballparks were flown at half mast on the day of the funeral out of respect for Huggins, Yankee manager for a dozen seasons. Only once did his New York teams fail to finish in the first division.

The funeral for Miller Huggins was a brief service in Manhattan at the Little Church Around the Corner. His coaches and friends O'Leary and Fletcher were the pallbearers in addition to Ruth, Pennock, Gehrig, Lazzeri, Combs, and Shawkey. Afterward the body was placed on a Pennsylvania Railroad train en route to burial next to the graves of Huggins's mother and father in Spring Grove Cemetery in Cincinnati. His sister Myrtle and his brother Arthur accompanied the body.

"Next to my father and mother," a shaken Gehrig said, "he was the best friend a boy could have. He told me I was the rawest, most awkward rookie that ever came into baseball. He taught me everything I know. . . . There never was a more patient or more pleasant man to work for. I can't realize that he won't join us again."

MILLER JAMES HUGGINS

MANAGER OF NEW YORK YANKEES, 1918–1929

PENNANT WINNERS, 1921–22–23 . . .1926–27–28

WORLD CHAMPIONS, 1923, 1927 AND 1928

AS A TRIBUTE TO SPLENDID CHARACTER
WHO MADE PRICELESS CONTRIBUTION TO BASEBALL
AND ON THIS FIELD BROUGHT GLORY TO THE
NEW YORK CLUB OF THE AMERICAN LEAGUE

THIS MEMORIAL IS ERECTED BY
COL. JACOB RUPPERT
AND
BASEBALL WRITERS OF NEW YORK
MAY 30, 1932

Babe Ruth said: "It is one of the things you can't talk about much. You know what I thought of Miller Huggins, and you know what I owe him. It is one of the keenest losses I have ever felt. I, as well as the rest of the boys, cannot realize yet that we won't have him again with us on the bench."

On May 30, 1932 the first monument ever at Yankee Stadium was dedicated to "the odd little man," in Waite Hoyt's phrase, "the greatest manager who ever lived."

Admission to the Baseball Hall of Fame in Cooperstown came for Miller Huggins in 1964. He was the second of the 1927 Yankees to die.

EDDIE BENNETT

Aside from his joyous times with his beloved New York Yankees, the team that had won seven pennants and four World Series while he was with them, Eddie Bennett's life had not been a bed of roses. Born in Flatbush, Brooklyn, in 1903, he fell out of his carriage when he was an infant, injuring his spine, becoming a hunchback with stunted growth. His parents died in the 1918 influenza epidemic.

On May 19, 1932, the little Yankee hunchbacked batboy was hit by a taxicab. His leg was broken and some other bones in his body were banged up. Bennett watched the World Series on crutches.

"I'll tell you," he explained to Mark Koenig, "it was the accident that done it. The pain is giving me the willies, Mark. Sometimes, it drives me off my nut. I ain't been much of a drinker before but this son of a bitch thing is makin' me crazy. The onlyist thing that helps is to have a few good stiff ones and even then I get up at night with my back whacking me."

By midseason of 1933, Bennett had so much pain that he could no longer function as a batboy. He left the Yankees and spent most of his time in his small furnished room on West 84th Street, and began to drink a lot more than before. Jake Ruppert continued to give him financial support.

After weeks of very heavy drinking, Bennett died in his rented room of alcoholism on January 16, 1935. He was just 32 years old. His sad room had one window with a torn shade, a small bathroom without a door, a metal bed. But it was also a kind of Yankee museum, with its walls covered with autographed pictures of ballplayers, gloves, bats, scorecards, programs, clippings of stories of ball games, and drawers filled with autographed baseballs.

Bennett had no known relatives, so Colonel Ruppert paid for his funeral services in the venerable Church of St. Gregory on 19th Street and his burial at St. John's Cemetery in Queens.

Babe Ruth was out of the country on a tour. Neither he nor any other player was there to pay final respects. But the entire Yankees office staff plus Paul Krichell and Mark Roth, showed up, and a goodly sized crowd was present. A priest who had never even heard of Eddie Bennett and who knew nothing about baseball or the Yankees led the service.

Years later, legendary investor Warren Buffett strangely enough brought Eddie Bennett back into the public eye in his 2002 annual report to stockholders, commenting on why Bennett was his "managerial model." He summarized the little batboy's career and then asked:

"What does this have to do with management? It's simple—to be a winner, work with winners. In 1927, for example, Eddie received $700 for the one-eighth World Series share voted him by the legendary Yankee team of Ruth and Gehrig. This sum, which Eddie earned by working only four days (because New York swept the Series) was roughly equal to the full-year pay then earned by batboys who worked with regular associates.

"Eddie understood," Buffett continued, "that how he lugged bats was unimportant; what counted instead was hooking up with the cream of those on the playing field. I've learned from Eddie. At Berkshire [Hathaway], I regularly hand bats to many of the heaviest hitters in American business."

Eddie Bennett was the third of the 1927 Yankees to die.

JACOB RUPPERT

In April 1938, Jacob Ruppert, the man they called the "Master Builder," the man who was always the real power behind the New York Yankees, a team valued in 1939 at $7 million to $10 million, the man who was sitting on top of the beer and baseball worlds, became gravely ill.

The initial serious health problem was phlebitis (inflammation of the veins), then a liver infection. During the 1938 season the colonel was able to attend only the Opening Day game, and eight innings of another game in the middle of July.

Just how gravely ill he was became clear when Ruppert did not attend the 1938 World Series, listening to it on the radio instead. His Yankees, as they had done to the Pirates in the 1927 series, ripped the Chicago Cubs in four straight, becoming the only club to that point in time to win three consecutive World Series. Ruppert's teams had now won ten pennants and seven World Series.

On January 4, 1939, Ruppert suffered a heart attack. Friends and family started gathering at the Yankee owner's home at 1120 Fifth Avenue. On January 12, Babe Ruth, recently out of the hospital, came to visit the Yankee owner, who had been in an oxygen tent and whose first words to his nurse reportedly were: "I want to see the Babe."

"Here he is, right beside you," she said.

Too weak to speak, Ruppert reached out his hand to Ruth.

"Colonel," the Babe said, patting the Yankee owner's hand, "you are going to snap out of this and you and I are going to the opening game of this season."

Then, as the story goes, Ruth turned and started to leave the room.

The colonel called out "Babe." That was all he could say.

"It was the only time he had called me Babe to my face. I couldn't help crying when I went out," Ruth later recalled

That night the last rites of the Catholic Church were administered, and the next morning, Friday, January 13, Colonel Jacob Ruppert slipped into a coma. The 71-year-old passed away at 10:28 A.M.

On Monday, January 16, 1939, all was in place for a send-off for

Jacob Ruppert that would resemble a state funeral. The procession that carried his bronze coffin by hearse to St. Patrick's Cathedral tied some of the elements of the powerful and wealthy man's life together. It started out from the Ruppert apartment on 93rd Street where he had lived and died, a mere three blocks from where he had been born. It passed a block to the south of his gigantic beer production monolith.

The service was scheduled for 11:30 A.M., and to the minute police closed all the doors, turning away latecomers. More than 4,000 were jammed inside St. Patrick's, including brewers, public dignitaries, the bosses of the Tammany and Bronx Democratic machines, more than 500 Ruppert employees, fans, and family.

Baseball people included Lou Gehrig and Babe Ruth, both sad, both looking very much out of their element in solid dark ties and dark suits. Yankee manager Joe McCarthy, general manager Ed Barrow, farm system director George Weiss, members of the 1939 team, including Tommy Henrich and Johnny Murphy, and a score of former players mainly from the 1927 club, Yankee chief scout Paul Krichell, Boston Red Sox manager Joe Cronin and Chicago White Sox manager Jimmie Dykes, and star players such as Honus Wagner and Eddie Collins were there, too.

More than 10,000 people were out on the streets around the cathedral on that January day. The service ran for about an hour. The family was represented by one brother, two sisters, two nephews, and four nieces. They sat in the front left pew. Mayor Fiorello H. LaGuardia, U.S. senator Robert F. Wagner, and former New York State governor Alfred E. Smith sat in the front right pew.

Honorary pallbearers included Commissioner of Baseball Judge Kenesaw Mountain Landis, Yankee manager Joe McCarthy, Ed Barrow, Babe Ruth, Lou Gehrig, George Weiss, Senator Wagner, Al Smith, American League president Will Harridge, Ford Frick, who had such a time of it covering the 1927 Yankees and was now president of the National League, ex-National League president and governor of Pennsylvania John H. Tenor, and former Boston mayor and congressman "Honey Fitz" Fitzgerald.

After the service, a fifty-car cortege departed for Kensico Cemetery in Westchester County, where Colonel Jacob Ruppert's burial was in the family mausoleum.

A lifelong bachelor, but one who always seemed to have a beautiful woman around, Ruppert left an estate of $60 million, including real estate holdings valued at $30 million, just unbelievable sums for that era. The vast fortune was basically left to three women. Twenty million dollars was for two nieces.

And a third of the estate was left to a former chorus girl, Helen Winthrop Weyant, 37. Her name had never appeared in the press before. She lived in Manhattan with her mother. She was described in newspapers as a "ward," as "formerly a chorus girl," and by the *Sporting News* as "a former showgirl friend."

Claiming she had met the colonel about 14 years before his death, Weyant told reporters that that she had "no idea why he left me so much money."

Jacob Ruppert was the fourth of the 1927 Yankees to die.

Ruppert's plaque at Yankee Stadium reads:

TO THE MEMORY OF

JACOB RUPPERT

1867–1939

GENTLEMAN · AMERICAN · SPORTSMAN

THROUGH WHOSE VISION AND

COURAGE THIS IMPOSING EDIFICE,

DESTINED TO BECOME THE HOME

OF CHAMPIONS, WAS ERECTED AND

DEDICATED TO THE AMERICAN

GAME OF BASEBALL

LOU GEHRIG

The son of a janitor and a cleaning woman, Lou Gehrig, the Pride of the Yankees, played on past 1927, finishing second to Ruth in homers the next three seasons. In 1931, he hit 46, tying Ruth and stayed close in homers in 1932 and 1933. It was not until 1934, the final season of Babe Ruth as a Yankee, that Gehrig outhomered his former partner to win the home run title.

On June 3, 1932, the Yankee thumper hit four home runs in a game, becoming the first modern-day player to do so. In 1934, the handsome athlete won the American Triple Crown. He was the Iron Horse, powerful, dedicated to the game, a force that seemed to go on and on. Then, without warning near the final third of the 1938 season, Gehrig lost his verve, his zest, his force. During spring training 1939, he was weaker than he had ever been. All of his teammates, his wife, and his friends advised him to save himself, to rest.

At first base as the 1939 season started, the Iron Horse continued on. But he was a shell of himself. He swung at pitches he would have hit for home runs. Now there were only pop-ups. He bent to tie his shoelaces, but he fell down.

In one of those ironies of baseball, on May 2, 1939, Wally Pipp, whose place Gehrig had taken at first base for the Yankees years before, made the trip from his Michigan home to watch a Tigers-Yankees game. But Henry Louis Gehrig, the highest-paid player in all of base-ball, too sick to play, had removed himself from the lineup, the first time in 15 years that he was not playing baseball for the Yankees.

"I haven't been a bit of good to the team since the season started," Gehrig said. His batting average was a feeble .143—200 points below his lifetime average. His 2,130 straight games played streak was over. Positioned near home plate, he was a mere presenter of the lineup card. Pipp was stunned.

On June 19, 1939, in another bitter irony, the day of his 36th birth-day, Lou Gehrig left the Mayo Clinic with a sealed envelope. "Mr. Gehrig is suffering from amyotrophic lateral sclerosis. This type of ill-ness involves the motor pathways and cells of the central nervous sys-tem and in lay terms is known as a form of infantile paralysis. The nature of this trouble makes it such that Mr. Gehrig will be unable to continue his active participation as a baseball player."

Two days later the Yankees called a press conference. Ed Barrow told newspapermen, "Boys, I have bad news for you."

When Lou Gehrig was diagnosed with the illness, Barrow informed Lou's wife, Eleanor, that Lou "should look for another line of work," intimating that the great star's usefulness to the Yankees was over. Eleanor Gehrig never forgave Barrow, whom she called "the old bastard."

Lou Gehrig remained with the Yankees, sitting on the bench in uniform for the rest of the season, taking the lineup cards to the umpires. Barrow seemingly mellowed just a bit and reportedly came up with the idea to retire Gehrig's number 4, the number given to mark his place as the fourth hitter, the cleanup hitter, in the lineup. The Iron Horse was the first athlete in any sport to have his uniform number retired. Barrow also mandated that Lou Gehrig's locker be closed and sealed as long as Yankee Stadium stood.

"Lou Gehrig Appreciation Day" on the Fourth of July 1939, was the idea of sportswriter Paul Gallico. It was the first Old Timers' Day ever staged by a major league team. It was a doubleheader, Yankees vs. Senators. There were 61,808 fans present plus members of the 1927 Yankees who included Babe Ruth, Bob Meusel, Waite Hoyt, Herb Pennock, Benny Bengough, Bob Shawkey, Mark Koenig, and Tony Lazzeri.

The Yankees lost the opener, 3–2, but manhandled Washington, 11–1, in the second game. It was, however, the nongame moments that possessed true drama of that day in July.

The 40-minute ceremony started with a parade led by the Seventh Regiment Band, who were followed by the "old Yankees" to the centerfield flagpole, where a banner was raised saluting the 1927 Yankees. The group, dressed in street clothes, then joined current Yankees and Senators in a semicircle around microphones at home plate.

Lou Gehrig stood around uncomfortably, playing with his baseball cap as first New York City mayor LaGuardia and then U.S. postmaster general James A. Farley spoke of him in reverential terms. Yankee manager "Marse Joe" McCarthy was up next. He sobbed in front of the microphone:

"Lou, what else can I say except that it was a sad day in the life of everybody who knew you when you came to my hotel room that day in Detroit and told me you were quitting as a ballplayer because you felt yourself a hindrance to the team. My God, man, you were never that."

The big crowd screamed: "We want Lou! We want Lou!" Led out of the dugout by Ed Barrow, Gehrig, walking with a slight hitch in his gait, was overcome by the deafening ovation. Doffing his cap, he bowed his head, holding back tears.

There were tributes and gifts, including a two-foot silver trophy donated by his teammates, inscribed with the names of the players on one side and a John Kieran poem on the other. The New York Giants sent him a plaque.

"We want Lou!" The chant started again. "We want Lou!" Sid Mercer, master of ceremonies, saw the almost teary condition the Yankee icon was in. The great Yankee whispered something in Mercer's ear.

"I shall not ask Lou Gehrig to make a speech," Mercer announced from the microphone. "Gehrig has asked me to thank you for all for him. He is too moved to speak."

Half turned toward the Yankee dugout, the microphones about to be hauled away, Gehrig turned, came back, smiled a bit, wiped his eyes, blew his nose. He was there now, at the microphone, and he gave the speech that became a classic:

Fans, for the past two weeks you have been reading about the bad break I got. Yet today I consider myself the luckiest man on the face of this earth. I have been in ballparks for seventeen years and have never received anything but kindness and encouragement from you fans. Look at these grand men. Which of you wouldn't consider it the highlight of his career just to associate with them for even one day?

Sure I'm lucky. Who wouldn't consider it an honor to have known Jacob Ruppert? Also, the builder of baseball's greatest empire, Ed Barrow? To have spent six years with that wonderful little fellow, Miller Huggins? Then to have spent the next nine years with that outstanding leader, that smart student of psychology, the best manager in baseball today, Joe McCarthy?

Sure I'm lucky. When the New York Giants, a team you would give your right arm to beat, and vice versa, sends you a gift—that's something. When everybody down to the groundskeepers and those boys in white coats remember you with trophies—that's something. When you have a wonderful mother-in-law who takes sides with you in squabbles with her own daughter—that's something. When you have a father and a mother who work all their lives so you can have an education and build your body—it's a blessing. When you have a wife who has been a tower of strength and shown more courage than you dreamed existed—that's the finest I know.

So I close in saying that I may have had a tough break, but I have an awful lot to live for.

At the conclusion of his speech, believed not to be written down, Babe Ruth hugged Gehrig, whispering to him. It was their first verbal communication in about six years, ever since the Babe had taken exception to Gehrig's mother's comment about how Ruth's daughter dressed.

"After so many years, Ruth and Gehrig got together," recalled Yankee outfielder Tommy Henrich, "and it was very meaningful the way Babe—the great Babe—put his arms around Lou. You know that came from the heart. That meant a lot to me because they were on the outs for a couple of years."

"I saw strong men weep this afternoon," wrote Shirley Povich in the *Washington Post*, "expressionless umpires swallow hard and emotion pump the hearts and glaze the eyes of 60,000 baseball fans in Yankee Stadium. Yes, and hard-boiled news photographers clicked their shutters with fingers that trembled a bit."

Interestingly enough, three years after Lou Gehrig delivered that memorable speech at Yankee Stadium, Gary Cooper gave his rendition in the movie *Pride of the Yankees*, whose screenplay was written by Paul Gallico.

Baseballs signed by Babe Ruth and Lou Gehrig

Hollywood mogul Sam Goldwyn had not been that enamored of the idea of a film about a stricken baseball player. But editing of the story and the speech made things more palatable for Goldwyn.

The edited version of the speech delivered by Gary Cooper as Lou Gehrig in *Pride of the Yankees* went like this:

I have been walking onto ballfields for 16 years, and I've never received anything but kindness and encouragement from you fans. I have had the great honor to have played with these great veteran ballplayers on my left—Murderers' Row, our championship team of 1927. I have had the further honor living and playing with these men on my right—the Bronx Bombers, the Yankees of today.

I have been given fame and undeserved praise by the boys up there behind the wire, my friends the sportswriters. I have worked under the two greatest managers of all time, Miller Huggins and Joe McCarthy.

I have a mother and father who fought to give me health and a solid background in my youth. I have a wife, a companion for life, who has shown me more courage than I ever knew.

People all say that I've had a bad break. But today . . . today I consider myself the luckiest man on the face of the earth.

Nominated for 11 Academy Awards, *Pride of the Yankees* had several of Gehrig's teammates playing themselves, including Babe Ruth, Bill Dickey, Bob Meusel, and Mark Koenig.

In December 1939, the Baseball Hall of Fame waived the mandatory five-year waiting period for Lou Gehrig. On the Fourth of July 1941, a monument was erected in center field at Yankee Stadium:

HENRY LOUIS GEHRIG

JUNE 19TH 1903–JUNE 2ND 1941

A MAN, A GENTLEMAN

AND

A GREAT BALL PLAYER

WHOSE AMAZING RECORD

OF 2130 CONSECUTIVE GAMES

SHOULD STAND FOR ALL TIME.

THIS MEMORIAL IS A TRIBUTE

FROM THE

YANKEE PLAYERS

TO THEIR BELOVED CAPTAIN AND TEAM MATE

JULY THE FOURTH

1941

In 13 full seasons Gehrig averaged 147 RBIs and hit 493 homers, one every 16.2 at-bats. He had a .340 lifetime average, 1,990 RBIs, a career .632 slugging average.

His total earnings, according to estimates, were $361,500 in salary, which exceeded $400,000 with World Series shares.

On June 2, 1941, 16 years to the day after he replaced Wally Pipp at first base, Lou Gehrig passed away, 17 days before his 38th birthday. Death came to him at his home in the Fieldston section of the Bronx. At his bedside were his wife, Eleanor; his parents; his mother-in-law; and his physician.

A month before Lou Gehrig died, he had still showed up at his office at the New York City Parole Commission, where he had worked for 18 months after his retirement from baseball. He left that job, too enervated to continue. For the two weeks before he died, he was confined to his bed, unable to even hold a book or read. Eleanor read to him.

Private funeral services were held. Afterward, Lou Gehrig's body was cremated and his ashes, placed in the center of the headstone, were interred in Kensico Cemetery in Valhalla, New York. Incredibly, Gehrig's last remains are just a few hundred yards from those of Babe Ruth, buried at Gate of Heaven Cemetery. Others from Gehrig's life and times are also buried not that far away—his parents; his wife; his former Columbia University baseball coach, Andy Coakley; Paul Krichell; Jacob Ruppert; and Ed Barrow.

Lou Gehrig was the fifth of the 1927 Yankees to die.

All these long years after his death, visitors and fans continue to leave mementos at the headstone of his grave, which incorrectly lists his year of birth as 1905, even though he was born in 1903.

As Ed Barrow had mandated, Gehrig's locker remained vacant through the years. Then after Yankee Stadium was renovated in 1974–1975, the locker was relocated to the Baseball Hall of Fame Museum in Cooperstown. Eleanor Gehrig was presented with first base at that time.

CHARLEY O'LEARY

His loyalty was to Miller Huggins, who had hired him to coach for the Yankees. O'Leary did continue to coach for a while for Bob Shawkey, who took over as skipper after Huggins passed away. But when Joe McCarthy became manager, O'Leary left the Yankees, working first for the Cubs and then the Browns. On September 30, 1934, the 52-year-old O'Leary, as a pinch hitter, scored a run for the Browns—the oldest big leaguer to ever perform that feat.

Finally out of baseball, he began work for the Chicago Sanitary District as a security guard. On January 6, 1941, O'Leary passed away from blood poisoning from a chronic ulcer. He was 58 years old. O'Leary is buried in Mount Olivet Cemetery in Frederick, Maryland. He was the sixth member of the 1927 Yankees to die.

JOHNNY GRABOWSKI

John Patrick Grabowski, or "Nig," as he was called, finished his time with the Yankees in 1929. There he went on to play for the St. Paul Saints of the American Association, and in a few games for Detroit in 1931. He was a catcher from 1932–1934 with the Montreal Royals of the International League. Grabowski was later an umpire in both the Eastern and International leagues. Then he was employed as a tool-maker in Schenectady, New York.

Like several of the other '27 Yankees, Johnny Grabowski's life came to a strange and horrific ending. His house near Albany, New York, caught fire. Racing out and then rushing back into the house, as the story goes, Grabowski tried to save his automobile. But the car and the house were destroyed. The former catcher fought for his life for five days in the hospital with second- and third-degree burns, but finally succumbed on May 23, 1946. Just 46 years old, John Grabowski was buried in Parkview Cemetery, Schenectady, New York. He was the seventh member of the 1927 Yankees to die.

TONY LAZZERI

He played his entire 14-year career with epilepsy, batting .300 or better five times in his career, with 100 or more RBIs seven times. Appearing in six World Series in a dozen Yankee seasons, playing in the very first All-Star game, Tony Lazzeri left the Yankees after the 1937 season with a batting average of .292. He played briefly for the Chicago Cubs, New York Giants, and Brooklyn Dodgers. Lazzeri's final major league game was on June 7, 1939.

He managed the Toronto Maple Leafs in the International League and retired from baseball after he was released as manager of the Wilkes-Barre Barons of the Eastern League in 1943. Back home in his native San Francisco, Lazzeri became a partner in a San Francisco tavern.

On August 6, 1946, 42-year-old Tony Lazzeri was found dead in his home from an apparent massive heart attack after apparently striking his head against a banister after slipping on the stairs. His body was found by his wife, who had been away on a trip. A coroner's officer reported that Lazzeri had been dead nearly thirty-six hours when his body was discovered. There was speculation that he had had an epileptic seizure. Lazzeri was buried in Sunset View Cemetery, El Cerrito, California. He was the eighth member of the 1927 Yankees to die.

It wasn't until 45 years after his death that a petition-signing campaign instigated and orchestrated by a restaurateur in Lazzeri's hometown of San Francisco brought new attention to his accomplishments and helped get Tony Lazzeri elected to the Hall of Fame by the Veterans Committee in 1991.

HERB PENNOCK

Yankee manager Joe McCarthy allowed Herb Pennock to "pick his own spots" in his final years as his active pitching career wound down. In 1933, Herbert Jefferis Pennock finished his career as a Yankee, but he hung on for one more season, 1934, with the Red Sox.

Then it was back full time to Kennett Square and his horses and foxes and rich friends. But baseball called again. From 1936 to 1938 he was first-base and pitching coach for the Boston Red Sox, later moving up the organizational ladder to director of minor league operations.

In December 1943, Bob Carpenter bought the Phillies and hired Pennock as general manager. With Philadelphia, the former southpaw standout did a lot of good things—but not in the area of race relations.

Early in the 1947 season, Pennock attempted to block Jackie Robinson's entry into major league baseball, informing Branch Rickey, general manager of the Brooklyn Dodgers, that "you just can't bring the nigger here with the rest of your team."

Before a series that began on May 9, with Jackie Robinson there and ready to play, the Dodgers were banned from their regular Philadelphia hotel. On the field during four games, racial epithets and profanity exploded out of the Philly dugout, most of it aimed at Robinson. All of this was done within earshot and eyesight of Pennock and Carpenter. It was not the former Yankee standout southpaw's finest baseball or human rights moment.

Dodger infielder Eddie Stanky, born in Alabama, was so agitated and disgusted by the scene that he physically challenged the entire Philadelphia team.

Jackie Robinson prevailed, shattering baseball's color line. Herb Pennock continued on as Philly general manager. Then on January 30, 1948, attending a National League meeting in New York City, the man who was called the greatest lefthander in the history of the Yankees by manager Miller Huggins, the executive who was still on top of his game, collapsed in the lobby of the Waldorf-Astoria Hotel. Two hours later he died of a cerebral hemorrhage. He was 53 years old. Six days before he had signed pitcher Curt Simmons, and two days earlier had signed infielder Willie "Puddin' Head" Jones. They would be key pieces in the Phillies' "Whiz Kids" National League championship team of 1950.

Herb Pennock, the ninth member of the 1927 Yankees to die, was buried in Union Hill Cemetery, Kennett Square, Chester County, Pennsylvania. Election to the Baseball Hall of Fame was swift—that same year of 1948.

BABE RUTH

George Herman Ruth played on past 1927, an icon, an institution. "Sometimes I still can't believe what I saw," said outfielder Harry Hooper, who had been a teammate of Ruth's in Boston at the start. "This 19-year-old kid, crude, poorly educated, only lightly brushed by the social veneer we call civilization, gradually transformed into the idol of American youth and the symbol of baseball the world over—a man loved by more people and with an intensity of feeling that perhaps has never been equaled before or since. I saw a man transformed into something pretty close to a god."

The man they called the Bambino continued to lead the league in homers every year through 1931. Still a star, a draw, still a presence, but with declining skills—he managed just 22 home runs in 1934. Business was a business. The Yankees let him go.

The Big Bam always wanted a chance to manage a baseball team, especially the Yankees. But it never came to be. "Manage the Yankees?" Ruppert allegedly remarked. "You can't even manage yourself!"

Babe Ruth was offered the position as manager of the Tigers after the 1933 season. Off to Hawaii on a publicity tour, he hesitated accepting. While he was away, Detroit hired Mickey Cochrane as manager.

After he left the Yankees, Ruth moved on to the Boston Braves, the worst team in the National League, as an "assistant manager" and active player. Terribly out of shape, bloated, he nevertheless on May 25, 1935, reached back in time, slugging three homers in Pittsburgh. When he rounded third, Pirate hurler Guy Bush tipped his cap. Ruth smiled that famous smile and snapped his fancy salute. The last home run he hit that day was the last one he ever hit, number 714. No other player before had ever hit even half that many.

But a week later, with his batting average a puny .181, Ruth announced he was retiring, and the Braves announced he was being released. At that moment in time he held 56 major-league records.

On June 18, 1938, Ruth signed a contract to be a coach for the Brooklyn Dodgers and be in uniform for batting practice demonstrations.

"He was like an ex-President," Robert Creamer wrote, "famous but useless, creating a stir whenever he appeared in public, but curiously neutered, no longer a factor. He played golf, he bowled, he hunted and he waited, but the call to manage never came."

Despite the very sad ending to his career in baseball, the Sultan of Swat's achievements were incomparable.

Thirteen times he drove in more than 100 runs, with a high of 171 in 1921. He hit over .300 seventeen times, topping out at .393 in 1923. Twelve times he paced the majors in home runs, thirteen times in slugging. His .690 career slugging average remains the highest in history. When he retired, his 714 home runs, 2,174 runs, 2,211 RBIs and 2,056 walks ranked at the top of the all-time list.

Coming back to "the House That Ruth Built" for the final time on June 13, 1948, to have his uniform number 3 retired, to help celebrate the famed edifice's 25th anniversary and the 25th anniversary of the 1923 Yankees, he was a sad shadow of his once-vigorous self. Ruth wore his old uniform, which was sizes too big for him. He mingled with his teammates from the 1923 team in the clubhouse. They played a two-inning exhibition game against Yankees from other teams. The Babe looked on. The day was damp and rainy, and somehow a camel's hair coat wound up over his shoulders.

The "Voice of the Yankees," Mel Allen, introduced each of his 1923 teammates. Yankee Stadium was filled with applause and cheers. Then Allen introduced Babe Ruth. The ovation rocked the Stadium.

The camel's hair coat was doffed. Using a bat that he had borrowed from Bob Feller as a makeshift cane, he shuffled out slowly to home plate to a thunderous ovation and the sounds of the crowd of 49,647 singing "Auld Lang Syne." The Babe mentioned how proud he was to have hit the first homer in Yankee Stadium and said: "Lord knows who'll hit the last."

"Thank you very much, ladies and gentlemen," the Babe spoke in a raspy voice. "You know how bad my voice sounds. Well, it feels just as bad. You know this baseball game of ours comes up from the youth. That means the boys. And after you've been a boy, and grow up to know how to play ball, then you come to the boys you see representing themselves today in our national pastime."

Afterward in the locker room, with all the ceremonies completed, Joe Dugan poured a beer for the Babe.

"So, how are you?" his old buddy asked.

"Joe, I'm gone," the Babe said. And he started to cry.

All the years of smoking, chewing tobacco, and dipping snuff, abusing his body had finally caught up to him. Surgery and radiation treatments had done little to help him. When he had been released from the hospital on February 15, 1947, his wife, Claire, and his doctors did not reveal the fatal diagnosis of throat cancer to him.

Later that day, back in the hospital, the most famous personage in all the history of the national pastime tried to keep his sunny side up signing autographs and watching baseball on TV. Just some of the hundreds of letters that were sent to him each day were read to him by his wife. Visitors came, visitors went. At 8:01 P.M. on August 16, 1948, after a two-year battle, the Babe passed away in his sleep at age 53, the tenth member of the 1927 Yankees to die.

More than 200,000 over two days paid their final respects as he lay in state at Yankee Stadium. August 19 was one of those sweltering, humid New York City summer days. The funeral was held at St. Patrick's Cathedral, where Francis Cardinal Spellman celebrated a requiem Mass before a packed house. The Babe was always a draw. Ruth's old teammates were pallbearers. In the streets, along Fifth Avenue, and on the funeral route, tens of thousands lined up to say good-bye to the man who had been Yankee baseball.

Joe Dugan told Waite Hoyt, "I'd give a hundred dollars for a cold beer."

"So would the Babe," Hoyt said.

GEORGE HERMAN "BABE" RUTH

1895–1948

A GREAT BALL PLAYER

A GREAT MAN

A GREAT AMERICAN

ERECTED BY
THE YANKEES
AND
THE NEW YORK BASEBALL WRITERS

APRIL 19, 1949

The man many consider the greatest player in the history of baseball was laid to rest in the Gate of Heaven Cemetery in Hawthorne, New York, about half an hour from Yankee Stadium.

His tombstone reads: "May the Divine Spirit that motivated Babe Ruth to win the crucial game of life inspire the youth of America."

The Babe's gravesite is the most visited one of all baseball players and is always a place of notes and gifts and wishes from people from all over the world. Interested readers may find excerpts from the Babe's last will and testament in appendix C at the back of this book.

ART FLETCHER

When Miller Huggins had died, Art Fletcher served as acting Yankee manager for the final 11 games of the 1929 season. Although he possessed a keen baseball mind and had much experience, Fletcher rejected all offers to manage again.

When "Marse Joe" McCarthy came in to pilot the Yankees, speculation was ripe that Fletcher would be removed as a Yankee coach because there had been bad blood between the two Irishmen in 1926, when they both managed in the National League—Fletcher with the Phillies, McCarthy with the Cubs.

McCarthy, however, was much more interested in Fletcher's abilities than in old-time feuds. Fletcher stayed on and on. It was reported that the $75,000 in World Series income and other revenue from first-division checks enabled Fletcher and his wife, Irene, to live the high life. Finally, in 1945, after a long baseball career, the third-base coach retired because of heart problems. He passed away in Los Angeles on February 6, 1950, from a heart attack. He was 65 years old. Fletcher was the eleventh of the 1927 Yankees to die.

ED BARROW

On January 17, 1939, Ed Barrow was named by the executors of Jacob Ruppert as president of the Yankees.

"This was a great day for me," the man once known as "Cousin Egbert" said, beaming. "And I must say that I was proud. Mrs. Barrow and I had an extra cocktail that night before dinner." Jacob Ruppert had been dead for four days.

In 1945, Ruppert's heirs sold the Yankees to Larry MacPhail, Dan Topping, and Del Webb. Barrow was appointed chairman of the board. However, he and the new owners had many differences; his old-school ways were just one of them. Retirement for the top Yankee executive, ending a string of 24 years, came in 1947. Three years later, the Yankees honored him with an "Ed Barrow Day." Three years after that, Edward Grant Barrow was elected to the Baseball Hall of Fame. The following year a plaque in his honor was dedicated at Yankee Stadium a few months before his death at age 85. He was the twelfth of the '27 Yankees to die.

Barrow's plaque in Monument Park in Yankee Stadium reads:

EDWARD GRANT BARROW

1868–1953

MOULDER OF A TRADITION OF VICTORY
UNDER WHOSE GUIDANCE THE YANKEES WON
FOURTEEN AMERICAN LEAGUE PENNANTS AND
TEN WORLD CHAMPIONSHIPS AND BROUGHT
TO THIS FIELD SOME OF THE GREATEST
BASEBALL STARS OF ALL TIME.
THIS MEMORIAL IS A TRIBUTE FROM THOSE
WHO SEEK TO CARRY ON HIS GREAT WORKS

ERECTED APRIL 15, 1954

JOE GIARD

Joseph Oscar Giard was released by the Yankees after the 1927 season and then played in the American Association. He had been used mainly in mop-up roles and had had no decisions in 18 games in 1927.

In retirement Giard lived a quiet life in Worcester, Massachusetts. Lung cancer claimed him on July 10, 1956, at age 56, the thirteenth of the 1927 Yankees to die. Giard is buried in Mount Carmel Cemetery, Ware, Massachusetts.

PAUL KRICHELL

In 1903, Paul Bernard Krichell began his professional baseball career as a catcher with the lowly Ossining/Catskill team of the Hudson River League. Eight years later he was in the majors, with the Browns of St. Louis. One of his most inglorious moments on the diamond took place on the Fourth of July 1912. In one inning Ty Cobb stole second base, third base, and home against him.

In 1912, at age 30, Krichell's playing career—only 243 at-bats as a reserve catcher with the Browns—finally came to a long overdue end. Ed Barrow, never one to miss an opportunity, hired Krichell as a coach for the 1919 Red Sox. And by the following year "Krich" was a scout—he had found his true calling. Scouting became his life.

As chief Yankee talent picker and aided by a loyal cadre of helpers—players such as Lou Gehrig, Mark Koenig, Tony Lazzeri, Phil Rizzuto, Red Rolfe, Vic Raschi, Whitey Ford, and others became Yankees.

One of the greatest scouts in baseball history, Paul Krichell passed away in 1957 at age 74 in the Bronx, the fourteenth of the 1927 Yankees to die. He is buried in Kensico Cemetery in Valhalla, New York.

WALTER BEALL

Released in spring training of 1928 by the Yankees, Walter Beall returned to his hometown of Washington, D.C., where he hooked up with Clark Griffith's Senators, winning one decision in three relief appearances. Cut by Washington, Beall continued to ply his trade for seven more years in the minors, with Chattanooga and Montreal and in semipro baseball. Beall also was showcased along with Walter Johnson in several old-timers' games in the Washington, D.C., area. On January 28, 1959, he passed away from acute congestive heart failure at age 59. The fifteenth member of the 1927 Yankees to die, Beall is buried in Cedar Hill Cemetery in Suitland, Maryland.

PAT COLLINS

The great Bill Dickey was on the scene in his first full season as a Yankee catcher in 1929. That made Collins expendable, and Ed Barrow sold him to the Red Sox.

Lasting for only seven games with Boston, Collins made his last major league appearance was May 23, 1929, as a member of the Old Towne team. Collins went down to the minor leagues, playing for one team or another. In 1932 he finally retired from baseball.

Death came to Collins in his sleep on May 20, 1960, in Kansas City, Kansas, at age 63. He was the sixteenth member of the 1927 Yankees to die. He had been receiving treatment for a heart condition. Collins is buried in Memorial Park in Kansas City, Kansas.

WILCY MOORE

William Wilcy Moore claimed that overwork in 1927 caused the arm problems that kept him out of action in 1928. Ed Barrow decided that a season in 1929 with the St. Paul Saints might help, and it did— Moore was 22–9 with the Yankees in 1930. The next year the Oklahoman was sent to the Red Sox, and for that sixth-place team he had 10 saves, an American League high that year. He returned to the Yankees in 1932, where his relief win in the World Series closed out another four-game Yankee World Series sweep, this time of the Cubs. Just 5–5 in 1933, Moore's major league career ended, but he was not at all ready to hang up his spikes.

There were seven years spent at such stops as Kansas City, Oakland, Oklahoma City, and Borger, Texas. He finally stopped pitching at age 43. Afterward he settled down as a full-time cotton farmer, spinning stories especially about his time as a Yankee. On March 31, 1963, at age 65, Moore died from cancer in Hollis, Oklahoma, the seventeenth member of the 1927 Yankees to pass away. He was survived by his widow, Grace; three sons; and a daughter. Moore is buried in Fairmount Cemetery in Hollis.

BENNY BENGOUGH

Benny Bengough had eight seasons in New York as a backup catcher before the Yankees released him in 1930 to the Milwaukee Brewers of the American Association, who then traded him to the St. Louis Browns. He saw limited action for a couple of campaigns. It was back to Milwaukee in 1933, followed by stints as a player-manager with a couple of low minor league clubs. He returned to the majors coaching for the Browns, Senators, Braves, and Phillies.

By 1959, the lively Bengough was done with coaching, but his baseball knowledge and lively personality enabled him to begin a new career as a public relations personage for the Phillies and a TV show host. In his latter years, Bengough, whose playing weight never was above 170 pounds, had ballooned to more than 200 pounds.

With the Phillies he taught a young right-hander named Robin Roberts how to slow down his delivery and put him on the road to the Hall of Fame.

Benny Bengough had a 10-minute TV show right after Phillies' game. Smiling, he ended the program with: "And as I always say, to be a big leaguer, think big league."

On Sunday, December 22, 1968, in his public relations role with the Phillies, Bengough had just spoken before Mass at Blessed Virgin Mary Roman Catholic Church in the Bustleton section of Philadelphia. He suffered a heart attack and died. He was 70 years old, and the eighteenth member of the Yankees of 1927 to pass away.

DUTCH RUETHER

Released by the Yankees on November 28, 1927, along with Bob Shawkey, Ruether continued to ply his pitching trade for eight more years in the Pacific Coast League and for one year in the Southern League. From 1934 to 1936 he managed the Seattle Indians of the Pacific Coast League and was voted an All Star manager in his first season. Ruether had a highly successful if not profitable tenure there. Since this was during the Depression, Ruether did not get paid, but all his living expenses were taken care of. Later, Ruether scouted for the Chicago Cubs, and then the New York/San Francisco Giants for 24 years. Some of the talent he discovered included Peanuts Lowrey, Joey Amalfitano, Mike McCormick, and Eddie Bressoud. On May 16, 1970, in Phoenix, at age 76, Ruether became the nineteenth member of the 1927 Yanks to die. His body was cremated; the location of the ashes is unknown.

CEDRIC DURST

On May 6, 1930, Cedric Montgomery Durst, who had served the Yankees well, was traded to the Boston Red Sox for pitcher Red Ruffing and $50,000 in cash in one of the more controversial deals of that era, swapping a journeyman outfielder for a promising hurler. That was the lefty outfielder's last season in the majors, but he went on to have a long career in the minors as player and manager.

Durst played for the Hollywood Stars of the Pacific Coast League for three years and was voted MVP in one of those seasons. In 1936 the Stars moved to San Diego and became the Padres. Now in his 40s, Durst continued to play, batting over .300 in 1937 and 1938. Player-manager of Rochester, Omaha, and San Diego, Cedric Durst died February 16, 1971, in San Diego. He is buried in El Camino Memorial Park. He was the twentieth member of the 1927 Yankees to pass away.

BEN PASCHAL

Ben Paschal's greatest claim to fame was on April 12, 1927, the opening game of the season, when he became the last player ever to pinch-hit for Babe Ruth. The happening took place in the sixth inning of a game after Ruth had gone 0 for 3, with two strikeouts. Paschal singled. The quiet Paschal concluded his major league career on October 6,

1928, with the Yankees. Then he played in the minor leagues, in both the American Association and the Southern Association.

In retirement from baseball, he worked for the Cunningham Wholesale Company of Charlotte, North Carolina. The twenty-first member of the '27 Yankees to pass away, he died on November 10, 1974, at age 79. Paschal is buried in Sharon Memorial Park in Charlotte, North Carolina.

JULIE WERA

Missing the entire 1928 season because of a knee problem, Julie Wera played for the Yankees in 1929, his final five major league games. Then it was on to Jersey City, Hollywood, and other teams in the minors.

Out of baseball, he lived in Rochester, Minnesota, where he worked for 25 years in the meat department at Barlow Foods. He actually got together again with Lou Gehrig again when the stricken Yankee was tested at the Mayo Clinic there. Wera was described as a jovial guy who liked to talk about the old times, especially his times at Yankee Stadium.

In 1948, another strange and grotesque episode in the later life of the 1927 New York Yankees took place. A man became business manager of the Oroville Red Sox of the Far West League, claiming he was Julie Wera. He claimed his face looked different because he had plastic surgery for disfigurement caused by injuries suffered in World War II. Later that man committed suicide by taking an overdose of sleeping pills. It was then that it was discovered that Julie Wera was alive and living in Minnesota.

On December 12, 1975, the former Yankee did pass away, from a heart attack at age 73 in Rochester, Minnesota. He is buried in the St. Mary's Cemetery in Winona, Minnesota. Wera was the twenty-second member of the 1927 Yankees to die.

EARLE COMBS

One the great center fielders in Yankee history, Earle Combs just kept doing what he did best after the 1927 season ended—playing baseball.

But in 1934 the fleet Combs smashed into a wall going after a fly ball, fracturing his skull and sustaining other injuries. Doctors were concerned about his survival. However, in 1935, he was back—a miraculous recovery. After appearing in 89 games in addition to coaching, he broke his collarbone. That ended his playing career, during which he averaged almost 200 hits and 70 walks a season in his prime. Combs compiled a .325 career batting average in a dozen seasons as a Yankee.

In 1936, the Kentucky colonel became a full-time coach with the Yankees. One of his special projects was teaching a young ballplayer the ins and outs of playing center field in spacious Yankee Stadium. That young ballplayer was Joe DiMaggio.

After his Yankee coaching time concluded, Combs moved on to the Browns, Red Sox, and Phillies. In 1955 he retired to his 400-acre farm in Kentucky. In retirement Combs was active in all types of civic, political, business, and civic activities.

Inducted into the Hall of Fame in 1970 by the Veterans Committee, the modest man said, "I thought the Hall of Fame was for superstars, not just average players like me."

After a long illness Earle Bryan Combs died on July 21, 1976, in Richmond, Kentucky, at age 77, the twenty-third member of the 1927 Yankees to pass. Buried in Richmond Cemetery, he was survived by his wife, three sons, a sister, a brother and twelve grandchildren.

BOB MEUSEL

He had speed, power, and could hit for average. In seven of his first eight major league seasons, Bob Meusel batted .313 or more. Babe Ruth, from 1920 to 1929, was the only Yankee to drive in more runs than Meusel.

His Yankee time came to an end on October 16, 1929, when "Long Bob" was shipped to the Reds for cash. He played in one season for Cincinnati, and then his 11-year major league career ended. No major league team was interested in signing the moody and out-of-shape 34-year-old outfielder, so he went down to the minors—to the Minneapolis Millers in 1931 and the following year to the Hollywood Stars.

Out of baseball, Meusel was employed as a security guard for a time on Terminal Island, California, at the navy base there. Meusel had a cameo role in the 1942 film *Pride of the Yankees*, playing himself.

He was 81 years old when he died on November 28, 1977, in Downey, California, the twenty-fourth member of the 1927 team to pass. The cause of his death was not revealed. A wife and a daughter survived him. He is buried in Rose Hill Memorial Park in Whittier, California.

MIKE GAZELLA

Mike Gazella spent his entire career with the Yankees as a part of three pennant winners and two world championship teams. He was released on September 30, 1928, and went on to play in the minors for Minneapolis, Hollywood, and Newark. Gazella also managed in the minors at Ponca City, Moline, Denver, and Ventura.

One who played for Gazella remembered those days: "On the road our meal allowance was two dollars a day, and Mike would give it to us day by day so we wouldn't lose it playing poker. To get your money, you had to either get up by 7:00 A.M., when old Mike left for his daily round of golf, or leave your door open so he could put it on your bed."

In the 1940s, the man they called "Gazook" returned to work for the Yankees, as a scout.

His death was another of the sad endings that befell quite a few of the 1927 Yankees. Gazella was killed in an auto accident in Odessa, Texas, on September 11, 1978, when his pickup truck was involved in a head-on collision. The twenty-fifth member of the 1927 team to pass, he was but a month away from his 82nd birthday. At the time of his death, Gazella was the second oldest living member of the 1927 Yankees. He was buried in Holy Cross Cemetery, Culver City, California.

BOB SHAWKEY

An end to Bob Shawkey's 15-year major league playing career came after the 1927 season. "I started under Mack and finished under Huggins. Those were two wonderful breaks in my favor," he said.

But "Bob the Gob" was not finished. He stayed on with the Yankees as one of the first specialized pitching coaches in baseball history. Then, after Miller Huggins died in 1929, Shawkey took over as interim manager of the Yankees. In 1930, he was named manager and steered the Yankees to 86 wins and a third-place finish.

Replaced as Yankee manager by Joe McCarthy, Shawkey managed, coached, instructed, or scouted in the minor leagues for teams such as Pittsburgh and Detroit from 1931 to 1951. There were stops at Jersey City, Newark, Watertown, Scranton, Tallahassee, Jamestown, and many other places.

From 1953 to 1958, Shawkey was the baseball coach at Dartmouth College in Hanover, New Hampshire. He did not do that well. His teams went 44–71–1 in his five seasons there.

On April 15, 1976, 85-year-old Bob Shawkey threw out the first ball in the refurbished Yankee Stadium in front of 52,613 fans on Opening Day. The 1923 Yankees were honored, and Shawkey, winner of the 1923 Stadium opening game, was back on the mound.

The former star hurler was inducted into the Greater Syracuse Sports Hall of Fame in 1991. Shawkey had moved to the upstate New York city in 1944, and that remained his home base.

On New Year's Eve 1980, James Robert Shawkey died at age 90 after a long illness in the Veterans Administration hospital in Syracuse, the twenty-sixth member of the storied 1927 Yankee club to pass. His body was cremated, and burial was at Oakwood Cemetery in Onondaga County, New York.

JOE DUGAN

Waived by the Yankees to the Braves on December 24, 1928, Joe Dugan played in 60 games in 1929. Going from the powerful Bronx Bombers to the puny National League Bostons was a real comedown for the prideful Dugan. The following season he did not play at all. In 1931 the former star third baseman appeared in 8 games for the Tigers, for a total of 1,446 major league games. His knee was no good, and he quit the game at age 33.

Joseph Anthony Dugan, in retirement from baseball, was employed in a beer distribution business and then owned a bar and grill in New York. He also worked for a while as Red Sox scout. Although born in Pennsylvania, most of his time was spent in New England, and he lived the last five years of his life in Norwood, Massachusetts. He liked to hang out at Irish Heaven, a local drinking spot. He died from pneumonia and a stroke at age 85 on July 7, 1982, the twenty-seventh member of the '27 Yankees to pass. His burial was in Mount Calvary Cemetery, Roslindale, Massachusetts.

WAITE HOYT

A Yankee from 1921 to 1929, Waite Hoyt, the top pitcher on the powerful New York Yankee teams of the 1920s, was shipped to Detroit in 1930. He pitched for the Athletics in 1931, then moved on to his old stomping grounds in 1932, New York City where he pitched for Brooklyn and the Giants. From 1933 to 1937, he was a hurler for the Pirates. Then it was back to the Dodgers, from June 1937. His final game was on May 15, 1938. It was quite a career for the onetime Brooklyn schoolboy phenom, which began all the way back in 1918 and included stops with the Giants, Yankees, Tigers, Athletics, Pirates, and Dodgers.

It seemed that Waite Hoyt always wanted one more turn on the pitcher's mound, and he got it by finishing up where he began in his native Brooklyn, closing out the 1938 season with the semipro Bushwicks.

In his 21-year major league career, Hoyt registered 237 victories and 182 losses, with an earned-run average of 3.59. He pitched in 7 World Series, winning 6 of 10 decisions.

The highly intelligent and articulate righthander then moved into broadcasting games in New York and Cincinnati for the next 28 seasons. During his playing days Hoyt frequently was on radio, showing off his skills as a storyteller, so it was an easy transition.

In 1942, Burger Beer hired Hoyt as its principal radio broadcaster for games of the Cincinnati Reds. Later he simultaneously did radio and television. He was the "Voice of the Reds" until his retirement in 1965. Famed baseball announcer Red Barber said that Waite Hoyt was able to tell baseball stories better than any man who ever lived. During rain delays, Hoyt entertained listeners with tales of his time as a player and wowed them with anecdotes about teammates such as Babe Ruth and Lou Gehrig. Hall of Fame induction came for Hoyt in 1969.

Waite Hoyt died in Cincinnati on August 25, 1984. He had been in Jewish Hospital for weeks after a heart attack. Hoyt, one of the four remaining members of the 1927 Yankees and the twenty-eighth to pass, was 84 years old. He was laid to rest in Spring Creek Grove Cemetery in Cincinnati.

GEORGE PIPGRAS

On the scene with the New York Yankees since 1923, victorious in all three of his World Series stints in 1927, 1928, and 1932, George Pipgras seemed destined to remain a member of New York's American League franchise forever.

Forever came in May 1933; his contract was sold back to the Red Sox, the team from which the Yankees had originally received him. The star-crossed legacy of many of the 1927 Yankees got ahold of Pipgras as a member of the Red Sox.

Snapping off a curveball, performing a maneuver he had done so many times before, he broke his arm. It was a devastating moment and the beginning of the end of a terrific career. The final game for George Pipgras was on June 2, 1935.

Out of active baseball participation, pitcher Pipgras became umpire Pipgras. From 1936 to 1937 he umpired in the New York–Pennsylvania League. On August 6, 1938, he became an American League umpire and a major success. It was said that he also brooked no nonsense—during a Browns–White Sox game, he threw out 17 players. Pipgras umpired in the 1940 All-Star game and also in the 1944 World Series. From 1946 to 1949 he was the minor league supervisor of umpires.

"On the field," Pipgras said, "umpiring was great. But off the field it was a lonely life. After getting out of it, I scouted two years for the Red Sox, instructed umpires three years, then left baseball altogether."

In retirement in Florida, where he had lived since 1925, the former Yankee star fished, hunted, played golf, told the old stories, and was called on for memories of the 1927 team as each year it seemed another player passed away.

George Pipgras, one of three surviving members of the legendary "five o'clock lightning" crew, died in Gainesville, Florida, on October 19, 1986. He was 86 years old and the twenty-ninth of the 1927 Yankees to pass. His health had been in decline since 1983, when he was diagnosed with cancer. Pipgras was buried in Memorial Park Cemetery, St. Petersburg.

RAY MOREHART

When the 1927 season ended, Ed Barrow traded Ray Morehart to the St. Paul Saints of the American Association. The slight Texan was very peeved. But he played on, staying with the game he loved in the minor leagues until 1933. Then he worked for the Sun Oil Company in Dallas until retirement.

Raymond Anderson Morehart died from a heart attack at age 89 on October 13, 1989, while reading the newspaper in his favorite chair. He was the thirtieth and the next to last of the 1927 team to pass.

He was survived by his wife, two daughters, five grandsons, and two great-grandsons. Morehart was buried in Restland Memorial Park in Dallas.

MARK KOENIG

The last surviving member of the 1927 Yankees passed away from cancer on April 22, 1993, at age 88 at a convalescent hospital in Willows, California. He was the thirty-first member of that team to die. Survived by a daughter, five grandchildren, and nine great-grandchildren, he was cremated. The location of his ashes is unknown

Mark Koenig's Yankee career ended in 1930. Batting .230 in 20 games, he was traded to the Detroit Tigers on May 30 along with Waite Hoyt for Ownie Carroll, Yats Wuestling, and Harry Rice. It was said that Koenig's feuding with manager Bob Shawkey was a major reason for the trade.

After a season and a half with the Tigers, Koenig was sent to the minors in 1932. The Cubs picked him up as a replacement for their regular shortstop, Billy Jurges, who had been wounded by a Chicago showgirl, Violet Popovich Valli, whom he had been seeing but wished to see no more. According to reports, she paid a visit to Jurges in the Carlos Hotel with a .25-caliber pistol in hand, intending suicide. In the wrestling match that was said to have followed, Jurges took slugs in the rib and palm of his right hand. A third shot ended up in Valli's wrist, and she ran off. The miffed miss became a theatrical hit: Violet ("I Did It for Love") Valli—"The Most Talked-About Girl in Chicago." Jurges made a full recovery and played for another 15 years after he returned to the Cubbies in September.

And Koenig, much more than a replacement, got the old Yankee lightning back, batting .353 in 33 games, a catalyst for the Wrigley Field team as they won the pennant and matched up against the Yankees in the World Series.

Koenig was very annoyed that he had been voted only a half World Series share by his Chicago teammates, considering how much he had helped the team. He let the Cubs know how he felt. His old Yankee mates also let the Cubs know how they felt with words and also deeds, including Babe Ruth's "called shot" over the center-field flagpole.

Koenig had stops in Philadelphia and Cincinnati, as well as with the New York Giants, where he finally concluded his major league career. Ironically, Koenig's last major league appearance came against his old New York Yankee teammates in the 1936 World Series.

There was time later for "Musical" Mark Koenig as a player in the Pacific Coast League, with the Mission Reds. The lively Koenig also had parts in two movies, playing himself in the *Pride of the Yankees* and *The Babe Ruth Story*.

The enterprising former star shortstop purchased two gas stations in San Francisco and later was involved with a brewery. He spent a lot of time spinning tales about the New York Yankees of 1927 and the players of his long-ago time.

"Naturally I'd favor them," Koenig said in *Wonder Team* by Leo Trachtenberg. "I think the old timers were a lot better than these young guys now. . . . I never saw so many guys sittin' on the bench, they're injured, so many pitchers . . . they can't pitch nine innings. And the ball is livelier now. If Ruth were playing today he'd hit a hundred and two home runs."

Looking back on the time of five o'clock lightning, Mark Koenig said, "It all meshed for us, the personalities, the manager, and the luck, everything that 1927 season."

NEW YORK YANKEE SALARIES, 1927

Babe Ruth	$70,000	
Miller Huggins	$37,500	
Ed Barrow	$25,000	
Herb Pennock	$17,500	
Urban Shocker	$13,500	
Bob Meusel	$13,000	
Joe Dugan	$12,000	
Waite Hoyt	$11,000	(plus $1,000 bonus for 20 wins)
Earle Combs	$10,500	
Bob Shawkey	$10,500	
Benny Bengough	$ 8,000	
Tony Lazzeri	$ 8,000	(plus round-trip train fare for Lazzeri and wife at the start and end of season)
Lou Gehrig	$ 7,500	
Pat Collins	$ 7,000	
Ben Paschal	$ 7,000	
Myles Thomas	$ 6,500	
Mike Gazella	$ 5,000	
Joe Giard	$ 5,000	
Cedric Durst	$ 4,500	
George Pipgras	$ 4,500	
Ray Morehart	$ 4,000	
Wilcy Moore	$ 2,500	(plus $500 bonus for completing season with club)
Julie Wera	$ 2,400	

BABE RUTH'S 60 HOME RUNS, 1927

Home Run Number	Game	Date	Pitcher	Home/ Away	Inning	Men on Base
1	4	Apr. 15	Howard Ehmke (R), Phil.	H	1	0
2	11	Apr. 23	Rube Walberg (L), Phil.	A	1	0
3	12	Apr. 24	Sloppy Thurston (R), Wash.	A	6	0
4	14	Apr. 29	Slim Harriss (R), Bos.	A	5	0
5	16	May 1	Jack Quinn (R), Phil.	H	1	1
6	16	May 1	Rube Walberg (L), Phil.	H	8	0
7	24	May 10	Milt Gaston (R), St. L.	A	1	2
8	25	May 11	Ernie Nevers (R), St. L.	A	1	1
9	29	May 17	Rip H. Collins (R), Det.	A	8	0
10	33	May 22	Benn Karr (R), Cleve.	A	6	1
11	34	May 23	Sloppy Thurston (R), Wash.	A	1	0
12	37	May 28	Sloppy Thurston (R), Wash.	H	7	2
13	39	May 29	Danny MacFayden (R), Bos.	H	8	0
14	41	May 30	Rube Walberg (L), Phil.	A	1	0
15	42	May 31	Jack Quinn (R), Phil.	A	1	1
16	43	May 31	Howard Ehmke (R), Phil.	A	5	1
17	47	June 5	Earl Whitehill (L), Det.	H	6	0
18	48	June 7	Tommy Thomas (R), Chi.	H	4	0
19	52	June 11	Garland Buckeye (L), Cleve.	H	3	1
20	52	June 11	Garland Buckeye (L), Cleve.	H	5	0

Home Run Number	Game	Date	Pitcher	Home/ Away	Inning	Men on Base
21	53	June 12	Geroge Uhle (R), Cleve.	H	7	0
22	55	June 16	Tom Zachary (L), St. L.	H	1	1
23	60	June 22	Hal Wiltse (L), Bos.	A	5	0
24	60	June 22	Hal Wiltse (L), Bos.	A	7	1
25	70	June 30	Slim Harriss (R), Bos.	H	4	1
26	73	July 3	Hod Lisenbee (R), Wash.	A	1	0
27	78	July 8	Don Hankins (R), Det.	A	2	2
28	79	July 9	Ken Holloway (R), Det.	A	1	1
29	79	July 9	Ken Holloway (R), Det.	A	4	2
30	83	July 12	Joe Shaute (L), Cleve.	A	9	1
31	92	July 24	Tommy Thomas (R), Chi.	A	3	0
32	95	July 26	Milt Gaston (R), St. L.	H	1	1
33	95	July 26	Milt Gaston (R), St. L.	H	6	0
34	98	July 28	Lefty Stewart (L), St. L.	H	8	1
35	106	Aug. 5	George S. Smith (R), Det.	H	8	0
36	110	Aug. 10	Tom Zachary (L), Wash.	A	3	2
37	114	Aug. 16	Tommy Thomas (R), Chi.	A	5	0
38	115	Aug. 17	Sarge Connally (R), Chi	A	1	0
39	118	Aug. 20	Jake Miller (L), Cleve.	A	1	1
40	120	Aug. 22	Joe Shaute (L), Cleve.	A	6	0
41	124	Aug. 27	Ernie Nevers (R), St. L.	A	8	1
42	125	Aug. 28	Ernie Wingard (L), St. L.	A	1	1
43	127	Aug. 31	Tony Welzer (R), Bos.	H	8	0
44	128	Sep. 2	Rube Walberg (L), Phil.	A	1	0
45	132	Sep. 6	Tony Welzer (R), Bos.	A	6	2
46	132	Sep. 6	Tony Welzer (R), Bos.	A	7	1
47	133	Sep. 6	Jack Russell (R), Bos	A	9	0
48	134	Sep. 7	Danny MacFayden (R), Bos.	A	1	0
49	134	Sep. 7	Slim Harriss (R), Bos.	A	8	1

Home Run Number	Game	Date	Pitcher	Home/ Away	Inning	Men on Base
50	138	Sep. 11	Milt Gaston (R), St. L.	H	4	0
51	139	Sep. 13	Willis Hudlin (R), Cleve.	H	7	1
52	140	Sep. 13	Joe Shaute (L), Cleve.	H	4	0
53	143	Sep. 16	Ted Blankenship (R), Chi.	H	3	0
54	147	Sep. 18	Ted Lyons (R), Chi.	H	5	1
55	148	Sep. 21	Sam Gibson (R), Det.	H	9	0
56	149	Sep. 22	Ken Holloway (R), Det.	H	9	1
57	152	Sep. 27	Lefty Grove (L), Phil.	H	6	3
58	153	Sep. 29	Hod Lisenbee (R), Wash.	H	1	0
59	153	Sep. 29	Paul Hopkins (R), Wash.	H	5	3
60	154	Sep. 30	Tom Zachary (L), Wash.	H	8	1

The home runs of May 28, June 22, July 26, and September 6 were in the first games of doubleheaders. The home runs of May 30, September 6, September 13, and September 18 were hit during the second games of doubleheaders. The home run of May 31 was hit in an afternoon game of a split doubleheader.

EXCERPTS FROM THE LAST WILL AND TESTAMENT OF GEORGE HERMAN RUTH

I, GEORGE HERMAN RUTH, being of sound and disposing mind, memory and understanding, but mindful of the uncertainty of life, do hereby make, declare and publish this to be my Last Will and Testament, hereby revoking all other wills and codicils thereto by me at any time heretofore made.

FIRST: I direct my Executors hereinafter named to pay all my just debts and funeral expenses as soon after my death as may be practicable.

SECOND: I give and bequeath to my wife, CLARA MAE RUTH, if she shall survive me, all my household furniture, automobiles with the appurtenances thereto, paintings, works of art, books, china, glassware, silverware, linens, household furnishings and equipment of any kind, clothing, jewelry, articles of personal wear and adornment and personal effects, excepting however, souvenirs, mementoes, pictures, scrap-books, manuscripts, letters, athletic equipment and other personal property pertaining to baseball. In the event that my wife, Clara Mae Ruth shall not survive me, I direct my Executors hereinafter named to divide the said property between my daughters, DOROTHY RUTH SULLIVAN and JULIA RUTH FLANDERS, as my said daughters may agree, or in the event they are unable to agree, to divide the said property between my said daughters as my Executors hereinafter named may, in their absolute discretion determine. The determination of my Executors as to the relative values of such property for the purpose of dividing the same and in the making of such distribution shall be final, conclusive and binding upon all persons interested herein.

THIRD: I give and bequeath to my Executors hereinafter named or either of them who may qualify, all my souvenirs, mementoes, pictures, scrap-books, manuscripts, letters, athletic equipment and other personal property pertaining to baseball, and I request but do not direct my said Executors to divide the same among such persons, corporations and organizations as I may from time to time request or in such manner as they in their sole and uncontrolled discretion may deem proper and fitting.

FOURTH: I give and bequeath to my wife, CLARA MAE RUTH, if she shall survive me, to my daughter, DOROTHY RUTH SULLIVAN, if she shall survive me, and to my daughter, JULIA RUTH FLANDERS, if she shall survive me, each the sum of Five Thousand ($5,000.) Dollars.

FIFTH: I give and bequeath to my sister, MARY H. MOBERLY, now residing in Baltimore, Maryland, if she shall survive me, the sum of Ten Thousand ($10,000.) Dollars.

SIXTH: I give and bequeath to FRANK DELANEY, providing he is in my employ at the time of my death, and to MARY REITH, providing she is in my employ at the time of my death, each the sum of Five Hundred ($500.) Dollars.

SEVENTH: Under the provisions of a certain Indenture or Trust Agreement made and executed by and between me and the President and Directors of The Manhattan Company of 40 Wall Street, Borough of Manhattan, City of New York, dated the 26th day of April, 1927, I reserved the right to designate in and by my last will and testament a new beneficiary to whom the income or principal of the trust fund which is the subject of the said Trust Agreement, shall be paid after my death in the place and stead of my daughter, Dorothy Ruth Sullivan, and my next of kin. Pursuant to such reserved right and in the exercise thereof, I hereby declare and direct that the income and principal of the said trust shall be paid after my death as follows:

A. The income of the said trust fund shall be paid to my wife, CLARA MAE RUTH, during the term of said trust or the life of my said wife, CLARA MAE RUTH, whichever may be the shorter period. After the death of my wife, CLARA MAE RUTH, the income of the said trust during the remainder of the term thereof shall be divided equally between my daughters, DOROTHY RUTH SULLIVAN and JULIA RUTH FLANDERS. If JULIA RUTH FLANDERS shall be deceased, the income which she would have received had she been alive, shall be paid to her issue per stirpes and not per capita, or if there be no issue of said JULIA RUTH FLANDERS then living, all of the income of the said trust shall be paid to my daughter, DOROTHY RUTH SULLIVAN.

B. Upon the termination of the said trust during the lifetime of my wife, CLARA MAE RUTH, I direct the Trustee thereof to purchase from an insurance company authorized to do business in the State of New York, a refund annuity which will pay to my wife, CLARA MAE RUTH, during her lifetime, in equal monthly installments the annual amount of Six Thousand ($6,000.) Dollars, and I further direct the Trustee of the said trust to divide the remainder of the principal of the said trust fund, including any refund payable upon the annuity hereinbefore required to be purchased for the benefit of my wife, CLARA MAE RUTH, into two (2) equal parts; and

(1) To pay one of such equal parts to the issue then living of my daughter, DOROTHY RUTH SULLIVAN, or if she shall leave no issue then surviving, among such persons and in such manner as she may be her last will and testament direct; and

(2) To pay the other of such equal parts to my daughter, JULIA RUTH FLANDERS, if she be then living, or if she be not living, to her issue then surviving, or if she shall leave no issue then surviving, among such persons and in such manner as she may by her last will and testament direct.

EIGHTH: All the rest, residue and remainder of my property and estate, real, personal and mixed, of whatsoever kind, nature or description and wheresoever situate, of which I may die seized and/or possessed or over which I may have any power of disposition or to which I or my estate may be entitled, I give devise and bequeath to my Trustees hereinafter named IN TRUST NEVERTHELESS for the following uses and purposes:

A. To collect and receive the rents, income and profits thereof and to pay the same to my wife, CLARA MAE RUTH, as long as she shall live. B. Upon the death of my wife, CLARA MAE RUTH, or upon my death, if she shall predecease me, I direct my Trustees to pay over, transfer, convey and deliver the principal then remaining in the said trust as follows:

(1) Ten percent (10%) thereof to THE BABE RUTH FOUNDATION, INC., a corporation organized under the Membership Corporations Law of the State of New York and dedicated to the interests of the kids of America.

(2) Forty-five percent (45%) thereof to my daughter, DOROTHY RUTH SULLIVAN, if she be then alive, or if she be not then alive, to her then surviving issue per stirpes and not per capita, or if she leave no issue then surviving, to such persons and in such manner as she may by her last will and testament direct. (3) Forty-five percent (45%) thereof to my daughter, JULIA RUTH FLANDERS, if she be then alive, or if she be not then alive, to her then surviving issue per stirpes and not per capita, or if she leave no issue then surviving, to such persons and in such manner as she by her last will and testament direct. . . .

IN WITNESS WHEREOF, I have hereunto to this, my Last Will and Testament, set my hand and seal this 9th day of August, in the year One Thousand, Nine Hundred and Forty-eight.

George Herman Ruth (L.S.

In the presence of:

Dorothy Henderson Herbert P. Polk F. Van S. Parr, Jr.

SEALED, SUBSCRIBED, PUBLISHED AND DECLARED by the above named Testator, George Herman Ruth, as and for his Last Will and Testament, in the presence of us, and of each of us, who at his request and in his presence and in the presence of each other have hereunto subscribed our names as witnesses the day and year last above written; this clause having first been read to us and we having noted and hereby certifying that the matters herein stated took place in fact and in the order herein stated.

Dorothy Henderson residing at 520A -9th Street Brooklyn, N.Y.

Herbert P. Polk residing at 205 W. 89 Street New York, N.Y.

F. Van S. Parr, Jr. residing at 23 Woodland Way Manhasset, N.Y.

STATISTICS*

POSITION PLAYERS' OFFENSIVE STATISTICS

	PA	BA	OBP	SLG	POS
Earle Combs	710	.356	.414	.511	OF
Lou Gehrig	693	.373	.474	.765	1B
Babe Ruth	677	.356	.486	.772	OF
Tony Lazzeri	639	.309	.383	.482	2B, 3B, SS
Bob Meusel	561	.337	.393	.510	OF
Mark Koenig	551	.285	.320	.382	SS
Joe Dugan	414	.269	.321	.362	3B
Pat Collins	305	.275	.407	.418	C
Ray Morehart	224	.256	.353	.328	2B
Johnny Grabowski	215	.277	.350	.328	C
Mike Gazella	138	.278	.403	.417	3B, SS
Cedric Durst	135	.248	.281	.326	1B, OF
Waite Hoyt	102	.222	.245	.263	P
Benny Bengough	89	.247	.281	.353	C
Dutch Ruether	88	.262	.330	.338	P
Ben Paschal	86	.317	.349	.549	OF
Wilcy Moore	79	.080	.127	.120	P
Herb Pennock	72	.217	.250	.246	P
George Pipgras	69	.239	.261	.328	P

*http://www.baseball-almanac.com/teamstats/roster.php?y=1927&t=NYA

Urban Shocker	61	.241	.359	.259	P
Julie Wera	43	.238	.273	.381	3B
Myles Thomas	27	.333	.357	.333	P
Bob Shawkey	11	.091	.091	.091	P
Joe Giard	7	.286	.286	.286	P
Walter Beall	0	—	—	—	P

Pitching Statistics

	IP	W–L	SV	ERA	G	GS	CG
Waite Hoyt	256.1	22–7	1	2.63	36	32	23
Wilcy Moore	213.0	19–7	13	2.28	50	12	6
Herb Pennock	209.2	19–8	2	3.00	34	26	18
Urban Shocker	200.0	18–6	0	2.84	31	27	13
Dutch Ruether	184.0	13–6	0	3.38	27	26	12
George Pipgras	166.1	10–3	0	4.11	29	21	9
Myles Thomas	88.2	7–4	0	4.87	21	9	1
Bob Shawkey	43.2	2–3	4	2.89	19	2	0
Joe Giard	27.0	0–0	0	8.00	16	0	0
Walter Beall	1.0	0–0	0	9.00	1	0	0

BIBLIOGRAPHY

BOOKS

Allen, Frederick Lewis. *Only Yesterday.* New York: Harper & Lee, 1931.

Allen, Lee. *Hot Stove League: Raking the Embers of Baseball's Golden Age.* Mattituck, N.Y.: Amereon Ltd., 1955.

Bak, Richard. *Cobb Would Have Caught It.* Detroit: Wayne State University Press, 1993.

———. *Lou Gehrig: An American Classic.* Dallas: Taylor, 1995.

Barrow, Edward Grant, with James M. Kahn. *My Fifty Years in Baseball.* New York: Coward-McCann, 1951.

Bartell, Dick and Norman Macht. *Rowdy Richard: The Story of Dick Bartell.* New York: North Atlantic Books, 1993.

Brunsvold , Sara Kaden. *The Life of Lou Gehrig Told by a Fan.* Skokie, Ill.: Acta Sports, 2006.

Carmichael, John P. *My Greatest Day in Baseball.* Cranbury, N.J.: A.S. Barnes, 1945.

Creamer, Robert W. *Babe: The Legend Comes to Life.* New York: Simon & Schuster, Fireside Books, 1992.

Davis, Kenneth Sydney. *The Hero: Charles A. Lindbergh and the American Dream.* Garden City, N.Y.: Doubleday, 1959.

Durocher, Leo, and Ed Linn. *Nice Guys Finish Last.* New York: Simon & Schuster, 1975.

Eig, Jonathan. *Luckiest Man.* New York: Simon & Schuster, 2006.

Fleming, Gordon H. *Murderers' Row: The 1927 New York Yankees.* New York: William Morrow, 1985.

Frick, Ford C. *Games, Asterisks, and People.* New York: Crown, 1973.

Frommer, Harvey. *The New York Yankee Encyclopedia.* New York: Macmillan. 1997.

———. *A Yankee Century.* New York: Berkley, 2003.

Graham, Frank. *Lou Gehrig: A Quiet Hero.* Boston: Houghton Mifflin, 1969.

Graham, Frank. *The New York Yankees: An Informal History.* New York: G. P. Putnam's Sons, 1951.

Hartzell, Scott Taylor. *St. Petersburg: An Oral History.* Charleston, S.C.: Arcadia, 2003.

Heimer, Mel. *The Long Count.* New York: Atheneum, 1969.

Hollingsworth, Harry. *The Best and Worst Baseball Teams of All Time.* New York: SPI Books, 1994.

Honig, Donald. *Baseball When the Grass Was Real.* Lincoln: University of Nebraska Press, 1993.

———. *The October Heroes: Great World Series Games Remembered by the Men who Played Them.* Lincoln: Bison Books, 1996.

Lieb, Fred. *Baseball As I Have Known It.* Lincoln: University of Nebraska Press, 1977.

Light, Jonathan Fraser. *The Cultural Encyclopedia of Baseball.* Jefferson, N.C.: McFarland, 1997.

Maraniss, David. *Clemente.* New York: Simon & Schuster, 2006.

McCarthy, Kevin M. *Babe Ruth in Florida.* West Conshohocken, Penn.: Infinity Publishing, 2004.

Meany, Tom. *Ed Barrow, Master Architect.* New York: E. P. Dutton, 1960.

Montville, Leigh. *The Big Bam.* New York: Doubleday, 2006.

Mosedale, John. *The Greatest of All: The 1927 New York Yankees.* Garden City, N.Y.: Doubleday, 1983.

Mowry, George E., ed. *The Twenties: Fords, Flappers, and Fanatics.* Englewood Cliffs, N.J.: Prentice-Hall, 1963

Parrott, Harold. *The Lords of Baseball.* New York: Praeger, 1976.

Patterson, Ted. *The Golden Voices of Radio.* Champaign, Ill.: Sports Publishing, 2002.

Reisler, Jim, ed. *Guys, Dolls, and Curveballs: Damon Runyon on Baseball.* New York: Carroll & Graf, 2005.

Ritter, Lawrence S. *Glory of Their Times.* New York: William Morrow, Quill, 1984.

Russo, Frank, and Gene Racz. *Bury My Heart at Cooperstown.* Chicago: Triumph, 2006.

Ruth, George Herman. *Babe Ruth's Own Book of Baseball.* Lincoln: University of Nebraska Press, 1992.

Smelser, Marshall. *The Life That Ruth Built.* Lincoln: University of Nebraska Press, 1975.

Sobel, Ken. *Babe Ruth and the American Dream.* New York: Ballantine, 1974.

Stout, Glenn, ed. *Top of the Heap.* Boston: Houghton Mifflin, 2003.

Sullivan, Dean A., ed. *Middle Innings: A Documentary History of Baseball,*
1900–1948. Lincoln: University of Nebraska Press, 1998.

Tofel, Richard J. *A Legend in the Making: The New York Yankees in 1939.*
Chicago: Ivan R. Dee, 2002.

Trachtenberg, Leo. *Wonder Team: The True Story of the Incomparable 1927*
New York Yankees. Bowling Green, Ohio: Bowling Green Popular Press,
1995.

Voltano, Paul. *Tony Lazzerri.* Jefferson, N.C.: McFarland, 2005.

Wagenheim, Kal. *Babe Ruth: His Life and Legend.* New York: Praeger, 1974.

Wallace, Joseph. *World Series: An Opinionated Chronicle.* New York: Harry N.
Abrams, 2003.

Williams, Pete, ed. *The Joe Williams Baseball Reader.* Chapel Hill, N.C.:
Algonquin Books of Chapel Hill, 1989.

Wilson, Nick. *Voices from the Pastime.* Jefferson, N.C.: McFarland, 2000.

ARTICLES

Newhouse, Dave. "The Old Yankee." *Oakland Tribune,* September 26, 1979.

Runyon, Damon. "Ruth Clouts Homer in N.Y. 4–3 Triumph." Universal Service, October 9, 1927.

Vidmer, Richards. "Magic Numbers." *New York Herald Tribune,* July 19,
1941.

INTERNET SITES

http://www.lougehrig.com/about/speech.htm
http://www.baseball-reference.com
http://www.baseballlibrary.com/homepage
http://www.highbeam.com
http://www.paperofrecord.com (*Sporting News*)
http://www.sabr.org
http://www.violetville.org
http://www.brainyhistory.com/years/1927.html
http://www.bookrags.com/wiki/1927_World_Series

INDEX

Note: Page numbers in italics refer to illustrations.